Julius K Nyerere
**Servant of God or
Untarnished Tyrant?**

FIDELIS VERITAS

Eagle Press

Also by Ludovick Simon Mwijage
Of Magic and Mutiny

Julius K Nyerere
**Servant of God or
Untarnished Tyrant?**

Ludovick S Mwijage

Eagle Press
Brønshøj, Denmark

FIDELIS VERITAS

Eagle Press Ivs.
Bystævneparken 10
2700 Brønshøj, Denmark
Tel: + (45) 38 80 83 85 / (45) 50 29 04 27
editor.eaglepress@mail.dk
info.eaglepress@mail.dk
ISBN-10: 87-999534-4-7 (Hardback)
ISBN-13: 978-87-999534-4-8
First published: October 10, 1994
Adelphi Press, 4-6 Effie Road,
London SW6 1TD England
The Dark Side of Nyerere's Legacy
Mwijage, Ludovick Simon
ISBN-10: 1856541878 (Paperback)
ISBN: 13: 978-1856541879
1996: **Olduvai Publishers**
Skelbækgade 31, 1th,
1717 Copenhagen, Denmark
ISBN: 10: 8798587501 (Paperback)
ISBN: 13: 978-8798587507
The Dark Side of Nyerere's Legacy
May 1, 2010: **Wisdom House Publications Ltd.**
Unique House, 1 Dolly Lane,
Leeds, LS9 7NN England
ISBN-10: 1842901036 (Hardback)
ISBN-13: 978-1842901038
ISBN-10: 1842901028 (Paperback)
ISBN-13: 978-1842901021
British Library Cataloguing in Publication Data
A catalogue record for this book is available from the British Library
Julius K Nyerere: Servant of God or Untarnished Tyrant?
Mwijage, Ludovick Simon
Simultaneously published in India and USA by
Wisdom House Academic Publishers Pvt. Ltd.
126, Housing Board Colony,
Ambala Cantt.-133 001 India
9338 SAWTOOTH WAY
San Diego, CA 92129 USA
Library of Congress Cataloguing-in-Publication Data
Julius K Nyerere: Servant of God or Untarnished Tyrant?
Typeset in 11pt. Times New Roman
Printed and bound in Belgium by Coloma

CONTENTS

Is Aid the Answer?
'It won't make any difference how
money is poured into the African
continent until the corrupt are made
to stop using aid as their personal
piggy bank.'
Neil Probert, *BBC News online,*
September 13, 2010

Acknowledgement

I would like to thank the United Nations High Commissioner for Refugees (UNHCR), for affording me protection both before and after my abduction from exile in December, 1983; the Dutch refugee organisation, *Vluchtelingenwerk Nederland* (VVN) for their support, in 1986, at the height of my desperation; the Icelandic authorities for affording me legal protection following the Portuguese government's unprecedented decision in 1991 to withdraw their legal protection whilst I was on a business trip to Copenhagen; and the Danish authorities for according me residency later.

I would also like to convey my appreciation to the Kingos Church in Copenhagen, the parishioners of Kingos and friends alike for providing both material and moral support in times of dire need. In surviving such an ordeal, I developed the resilience and tenacity which today enables me to share, with the rest of the international community, my experiences as well as those of other victims who, unlike me, did not survive Julius Nyerere's detention camps.

It should be noted that the consequences stemming from the values I stand for and the views I espouse are entirely my own responsibility, and has nothing whatsoever to do with the help outlined above and in the main section of this book. That help was given to me purely on humanitarian basis.

•Ludovick S Mwijage

Illustrations Used in the Book

The illustrations used in the book were obtained from the archives where the author conducted research and from members of the victims' families. The following illustrations were reproduced courtesy of the cited publications: handcuffed political prisoners being paraded during show-trial at the Maisara Suleiman grounds (*Drum* magazine–East Africa edition, July 1971, and *Flamingo* magazine, volume 6, No 6, 1971); Mozambican political prisoners being paraded at Farm Seventeen, Nachingwea, southern Tanzania (*Daily News* of March 20, 1975, and April 23, 1975, respectively; *Wikipedia* online encyclopedia/*Tempo* № 244–1 de Junho–1975/ *Datas e Documentos da História da FRELIMO, 2ª Edição, Edição da Imprensa Nacional* 1975; Fr Mateus Gwenjere and Rev Uria Timoteo Simango being paraded before presidents Nyerere, Dr Kaunda and Samora Machel at Farm Seventeen, Nachingwea (Barnabé Lucas Ncomo/colecção noticias; A copy of a note which Nyerere's political police agent sent to Fr Mateus Gwenjere: João M Cabrita; Adelino Serras Pires: Rowland Ward Publications, Johannesburg/Fiona Claire Capstick); President Nyerere parading Abdallah Kassim Hanga at a public rally in Dar-Es-Salaam (Bettman/CORBISDATE); President Mkapa casting vote in 1995 (NORDFOTO); Nyerere handing over power to his successor, AlHaj Ali Hassan Mwinyi (Associated Press); President Jakaya Mrisho Kikwete (*This Day*, Kulikoni Image Galleries); Chief David Kidaha Makwaia, OBE, (*The Times* of London, May 11, 2007); Nyerere's handwritten note (*Jamii Forums*); Sheikh Yahya Hussein (IssaMichuzi blog spot, as published by *Jamii Forums* on January 4, 2010); and His Holiness Pope Francis (Malacañang Palace).

For the Future of Africa
Judge me harshly, if, in your ethos,
usurpation and subsequent tyranny
are acceptable.

This edition has been completly reset and page numbers do not now correspond with earlier editions. In addition, supplementary illustrations are included.

Love and thanks to Elsebeth Højgaard for her valuable support.

Preface

This new updated edition has additional information in the main section which was not widely known when the edition which preceded this was released in 2010. Indeed, an equally important item now included in this edition is the fact that, on Monday, May 12, 1975, at Farm Seventeen, Nachingwea, southern Tanzania, President Julius Nyerere took part in a show-trial at which a group of Mozambican political detainees was paraded before him (*Tempo* No 244–1 June–1975, page 36). These included, amongst others, the Reverend Uria Timoteo Simango (standing in the picture) who, at a preceding show-trial, was referred to by Samora Machel as 'Christmas Turkey' for the occasion (*Daily News*, Thursday, March 20, 1975, page 4). Strangely, this group of prisoners had been put on show-trial multiple times between March and April that same year prior to being paraded again before President Nyerere on the referral material day. Like other prisoners to whom I refer in this account, after their public humiliation at Nachingwea, they were returned to Mozambique where they were murdered without legal authorisation.

The law of international human rights outlaws show-trials. Indeed, it is difficult to discern how a declared believer in justice, and a literate person, would, on numerous occasions, sanction the use of show-trials apparently without regard for the prisoners' due process rights, regardless of whatever political crimes they were claimed to have committed.

As Nyerere's supporters vigorously pursue their campaign to have him canonised, knowledge of his active participation in what has now become known as the Nachingwea atrocious crimes, will give a new dimension to the ongoing 'investigation process'. This was started by the Catholic Church in Tanzania over ten years ago, following the Vatican's unprecedented approval that Julius Kambarage Nyerere be called 'Servant of God'.

What is more, the evidential facts adduced hereof, provide a clearer picture of how Nyerere criminally abused his power. Those of us who vehemently opposed his authoritarianism from the beginning, did so with the intention of preventing the kind of abuses outlined in this narrative from happening in Tanzania. Prevention is invariably vital to the victims than mere condemnation after such horrendous abuses have occurred.

However, there's more. The current refugee crisis (The Sea Route to Europe: The Mediterranean passage in the age of refugees, UNHCR, 1 July 2015), unseen since World War II, shows that rulers who shunned democracy on ideological and other considerations have now created a major international problem which they expect the prosperous Western societies to tackle. But the civilisation of the West and its prosperity are deeply embedded in its democratic traditions and adherence to the rule of law. Mutually agreed rules by necessity govern our world. The salient question now is: should the Western democracies simply grapple with the crisis created by the world's outlaw despots who willfully flaunt these rules, or will there be a more coherent and practical way by which the international community can effectively rein on these tyrants and stop them from inflicting unimaginable horrors on the subject they rule?

Ludovick S Mwijage
Brønshøj, Denmark
May, 2017

To all those who were incarcerated throughout Africa and remain in jail, I express my heartfelt thanks for their support for democratic freedom and human rights.

Introduction

The first edition of this book was released in London, England, in the latter part of 1994; five years before the death of its subject, Tanzania's Julius Kambarage Nyerere. Having personally sent him a copy of the book by special delivery, I had presumed that Nyerere would address some of the most structural issues I raise in the book when working on his memoirs. However, Nyerere did not write any memoirs which seems unusual for a man who translated Shakespeare's *The Merchant of Venice* into *Swahili* and who, on occasions, reportedly wrote editorials for the government-owned newspaper, the *Daily News*.

In addition, Nyerere went by the honorary title of *mwalimu*, i.e. teacher; and teachers are invariably in the habit of keeping their lesson notes. Moreover, he ruled the Tanzanian nation for twenty five years, albeit in a manner characteristic of a medieval absolute monarch.

However, following his death there have been concerted efforts from certain quarters to present Nyerere as an African leader who was, amongst other things, untainted by corruption, and who voluntarily relinquished power after admitting to making 'mistakes,' but most of all, 'brought' stability and peace to Tanzania.

In a more recent development, Tanzania's electronic *IPP Media* carried an article on July 21, 2006, by Nyerere's long-time apologist, the now late Professor Haroub Othman of the University of Dar-Es-Salaam (UDSM). In the article, Professor Othman confirmed with delight a matter which had been dominating the Catholic media in the country and abroad for some months. He stated that, 'The Catholic Church in Tanzania [had]...started the process of beatifying him (Nyerere) into a saint'.

Professor Othman's article followed an announcement which was made in January, 2005, by Polycarp Cardinal Pengo, in Nyerere's home village of Butiama near Lake Victoria.

Addressing a partisan crowd which packed the village church, Cardinal Pengo announced that the Vatican had given 'approval' that Julius Kambarage Nyerere be called '*Mtumishi wa*

Mungu' (Servant of God).[1]

According to Cardinal Pengo, the so-called approval meant that the Catholic Church in Tanzania was to commence a formal 'investigation process' and if found above reproach (as Pengo himself and supporters strongly believe), the 'Servant of God' would be beatified and public veneration allowed.

The final step towards Nyerere's sainthood would be the official canonisation of the 'Servant of God', thereby declaring Julius Kambarage Nyerere a saint.

However, presidents serve people and not God; and, since Tanzania is a secular society rather than a theocracy, Cardinal Pengo failed to elaborate fully in what sense Nyerere 'served' God during his presidency.

Instead, the Cardinal, who has a reputation for getting things done his way, mumbled incoherently that the Catholic Church in Tanzania had presented Nyerere's cause '... based on his life as a Christian and how his faith had influenced his entire political career.'

Naturally, the news shocked both the surviving victims of Nyerere's regime and the families of those victims who had perished as a result.

The traditional view of Christianity is that it tends not to be overtly, politically partisan. Indeed, from the perspective of the common man, the Church is the voice of the powerless; a spiritual refuge offering hope where there is despair; a crutch, so to speak, for the weak and vulnerable in society.

It is therefore extremely ironic that the Catholic Church should, in this case, consider a sainthood for the dictator, with no thought for the victims of his dictatorship, the majority of whom cannot speak for themselves.

In this edition I have revealed to the reader some evidential facts pertaining to Nyerere's criminal abuse of authority, and, as the process of beatifying him into sainthood gathers pace, I believe the matter merits serious, public discourse, regardless of the reader's religious affiliation.

If ultimately the Holy See proclaims Nyerere to be a saint, it will not only be sanctifying evil i.e. dictatorship, but it will also

---

1http://www.maryknollafrica.org/newsletter/2005Dec.htm

be dishonouring the memory of those who suffered and perished under his rule and would seem a wrong and dangerous precedent for posterity.

Additionally, I would like to comment on each of the other three credits attributed to Nyerere, albeit in an abridged manner. Corruption is not only confined to material corruption but also to political corruption.

Political corruption is, in my view, the worst form of corruption, particularly when it involves those who exercise the power of the state on behalf of the nation's people. It severely undermines both the concepts of the rule of law and the fundamental freedoms in any political society.

Political corruption also breeds other forms of corruption, giving rise to complacency and ultimately, criminal abuse of authority.

A renowned British historian, John Emerich Edward Dalberg Acton, who served in the House of Commons from 1859 to 1865 and was created the first Baron Acton in 1869, observed that 'Power tends to corrupt, and absolute power corrupts absolutely'. He added that 'Great men are almost always bad men'. Lord Acton certainly knew what he was talking about.

As editor of the *Rambler*, a Catholic monthly, from 1859 to 1864, he had to resign following the Church's interference with the independence of the paper. Furthermore, although arguably a strong Catholic, he opposed such measures as the Syllabus of Errors, issued by Pope Pius IX and his declaration of papal infallibility at the First Vatican Council on July 18, 1870.

Consequently, Lord Acton's aphorism on interplay between power, corruption and greatness seems to give an indication as to the two sides of Nyerere which I discuss in this account.

It shows one side of Nyerere as a national hero, who achieved independence for his nation; and the other side of him as a villain, who imprisoned scores of his countrymen, invariably without trial, and as will be read, allowed the execution of others (especially in Zanzibar) without recourse to the due process of the law. Let us consider Tanzania's international obligations with regard to these violations of human rights.

It cannot be denied, even by Nyerere's most hardened apologists, that the authors of Tanzania's post independence constitution were inspired by the United Nations Charter; in particular those aspects of the Charter concerned with civil rights and civil liberties—sometimes collectively referred to as human rights.

The interest of the United Nations in these values reflected a global concern in these subjects at the time of the founding of the United Nations.

Indeed, representatives of governments who, at the San Francisco conference on June 26, 1945, signed the United Nations Charter also appended their signatures to a document that referred to human rights in no less than seven provisions.

All subsequent members of the United Nations, which included Tanzania under Nyerere's rule, reaffirmed their belief and support for human rights.

Article 62(2) of the United Nations Charter imposes upon the Economic and Social Council, the function and power to make recommendations for the purpose of promoting respect for, and observance of, human rights. It is against that background that human rights effectively became an international onus.

It follows that, even though nation-states can theoretically prescribe their municipal law, in practice the ability to enforce it is, to a certain degree, constrained by international Treaties and Covenants governing human rights and fundamental freedoms.

What is more, fundamental freedoms include a right to democracy. Consequently, human rights and democracy are inextricably intertwined in the sense that both are enjoyed concurrently.

Naturally, there would be those who would argue that democracy is, after all, a relative term. This is because democracy does not simply imply a system of government but also a particular social organisation. Some people often speak of political democracy whilst others speak of economic democracy; so, it therefore depends on which end of the stick one is holding.

That notwithstanding, democracy *per se* cannot be quantified by a local potentate's own beliefs, be it they political, religious or cultural as some people like to argue.

Rather, true democracy that is capable of sustaining its claim to stand for the rights and sanctity of a human person is defined by precepts (discussed in detail in the main section of this narrative), which aspire to genuine democratic practice.

More tellingly, as with civil rights and civil liberties, these precepts derive their binding force from commonly accepted political principles and practice plus, of course, the whole *corpus* of international legal instruments governing human rights and fundamental freedoms.

Thus, as with human rights, democracy is not a matter of choice on the part of a national ruler but an obligatory political conduct which is capable of being enforced by the international community (read) United Nations. This is more so where its negation has negative repercussion beyond a nation-state's own borders or, if it results in widespread abuses of human rights.

This was seemingly reaffirmed when at the General Assembly in 2005, member states of the United Nations universally endorsed the principle known as 'The Responsibility to Protect'. Under this principle, should a sovereign state fail to protect those who live within its boundaries, then that onus falls to others, i.e. the international community.

Be that as it may, Tanzania's post-independence constitution utterly precluded the prospect of sovereignty being a repository of a single individual.

Instead, it defined the allocation of power between the three estates of the realm and spelt out the basis upon which political authority was to be exercised.

Additionally, it envisaged a system of government which imposed obligations on public officials who were responsible for making decisions that affected others.

Such obligations included, *inter alia*, acting fairly and in good faith; without bias or prejudice; and, with absolute impartiality and honesty.

It further envisaged a system of government under which a concerned member of the public would have the right to challenge an irrational (or unreasonable) decision made by a public official through, for example, Judicial Review, provided such an individual had a *locus standi*.

There have been some suggestions that this constitution did not, after all, contain the Bill of Rights. However, fundamental rights were recognised and guaranteed by common law, court decisions and legislation; much as were human rights recognised through received law and, of course, in the preamble of the constitution itself.

It is on the basis of this that I contend that it was a violation of the spirit of the constitution, if not an outright criminal act, for Nyerere to have usurped sovereign authority only a few years after the attainment of political independence from Britain in 1961.

Furthermore, it was a betrayal of the aspirations of the Tanzanian people to overturn the constitution under which he ascended to power; the very same constitution to which he had taken an oath to protect upon the assumption of the office of the presidency.

The system of government envisaged by the constitution he deposed, which I have described above, was replaced by the regime of personal rule under which Nyerere no longer tolerated being questioned.

The late American president, Theodore Roosevelt, once said that 'To announce that there must be no criticism of the president, or that we are to stand by the president right or wrong, is not unpatriotic and servile, but morally treasonable to the...public'.

That may not be true, of course, if one would be thinking along the lines of Niccolò Machiavelli, who thought that success can be achieved by flattering the powerful. However, this can sometimes transcend the frontiers of flattery, resulting in the destruction of the flatterer's intellectual capacity, ultimately turning him into a sycophant of terrifying proportions.

It is not surprising therefore, that some of the apologists of a regime of personal power, under which Nyerere ruled Tanzania, fail to recognise the lasting effects of opportunism on society created by this system. They also fail to recognise the impact of the patronage that followed Nyerere's indiscriminate seizure of private property in the supposed name of 'nationalisation', and the resulting unbridled nepotism, which political patronage encourages.

Instead, they passionately refer to the powers of the office of the American president to justify their argument that a 'strong president' was needed by Tanzania, in the supposed name of 'nation-building'. This would appear to imply that in the countries where national leaders did not usurp sovereignty, there was no 'nation-building' there at all.

Whatever the argument, comparing the office of the United

States president to that of his Tanzanian counterpart is totally misleading and based on false assumptions.

America has always been a democracy with discernable separation of powers between the Judiciary, the Senate and Congress. These institutions enjoy the kind of independence which is unknown to Tanzania, even during this time of multi-partyism.

Indeed, had, God forbid, a sitting American president overturned the constitution and subsequently instituted a regime of personal power similar to the one Nyerere imposed upon Tanzania, he would probably have faced criminal prosecution. It would be unheard of for the Catholic Church in America to contemplate proposing such a president for sainthood.

Unless such attitudes in Tanzania change, we risk other societies considering us inferior.

Still more concerning is the fact that an illegal constitution, which was introduced following Nyerere's also illegal imposition of personal rule, is now what operates under the new era of multi-partyism, despite its monopolistic nature.

Karen Blixen, also known as Isak Dinesen, a prominent Danish Africa pioneer, must be spinning in her grave. It was Blixen who famously stated that, 'In order to make up a unity, particularly a creative unity, the individual components must be of a different nature, they should be, in a sense, contrasts'.

However, such perceptive opinion has no room in the ruling *Chama cha Mapinduzi* i.e. Party of the Revolution (May Benediction be Bestowed Upon it). For it, *mshikamano* i.e. unity, rests in its absolute monopoly on political and state power by whatever means; means which include frequent amendments to the constitution and, indeed, employing all effective instruments of state power at its disposal with the view to achieving that objective.

As you will see in this account, there are far-reaching effects stemming from nearly thirty years of Nyerere's abuse of political power and the psycho-social impact this has had on Tanzanian society.

With that in mind, the reasons why Nyerere had no qualms about handing over power to his chosen successor, and at a time of his own choosing, should be apparent.

It should also not be difficult to estimate how much of Tanzania's meagre resources were expended to create a political empire which Nyerere believed would outlive him. Whether such a misguided political venture will ever endure, and if so for how long, remains to be seen.

Some commentators on Tanzania history enjoy praising Nyerere for his supposed honesty in admitting to having made 'mistakes' during the twenty five years of his uninterrupted reign. Apparently, Nyerere made such admissions as he was about to retire.

However, I must emphasise that if Nyerere had been a democrat, most of his 'mistakes' could have been avoided. He could have listened to the views of others; the opposition would not have been gagged and the media shackled.

On the other hand, I reject the notion that it would take three decades for a man of Nyerere's celebrated intellectual prowess to realise that he was actually toying with the lives of millions of his countrymen, with his seemingly unworkable political experiments.

Indeed, if it took Nyerere so long to realise his 'mistakes', his intelligence has been misjudged. Moreover, anyone of average intelligence could have foreseen his 'mistakes'.

For instance, when Nyerere moved people into collectives, he claimed he was doing this to provide them with clean water, dispensaries, schools, recreational facilities and other similar desirables. However, one does not necessarily have to take such extraordinary measures in order to achieve such objectives.

Considering Tanzania is roughly four times the size of the United Kingdom, it must be apparent that the cost of relocating the entire population into new collectives would greatly surpass the cost of providing such services to the people in their own districts.

Nevertheless, it is the often inflated claims that Nyerere 'brought' stability and peace to Tanzania that equally demand appraisal. Presumably, it is obvious that the stability and peace under discussion does not equate with the regime under which Nyerere ruled Tanzania.

Nonetheless, it should be pointed out that in the case of the Tanzanian mainland i.e. Tanganyika, that her former Victorian colonisers, the Germans, succeeded in demolishing the tribal structures which have often spawned tribalism in the majority of African countries. This explains why tribalism today is less pronounced in Tanzania than in neighbouring countries.

Obviously, upon independence, Nyerere nurtured this situation for the sake of holding the nation together.

That notwithstanding, there is a perception that peace is not simply the absence of war but the existence of justice.

Moreover, African countries which were, or remain mired in turmoil, were once perceived to be as stable and peaceful as Tanzania is today. It is not many years ago that countries such as imperial Ethiopia, Côte d'Ivoire under the post-independence regime, Sierra Leone, Liberia and most recently neighbouring Kenya were respectively, amongst other countries in the region, considered to be models of stability and progress, until everything suddenly started to unravel.

A seasoned observer of Tanzania's political scene ought to have realised that conditions which precipitated conflicts elsewhere are prevalent in Tanzania today.

For example, corruption is so endemic in Tanzania today, that it must be considered whether this will not create alternative sources of power, with severe consequences to the country's future stability.

On the other hand, factors such as political cronyism, improper use of public governmental power, population explosion coupled with growing poverty, are not known to be conducive to enduring peace and stability.

Poverty, to be sure, has already spawned conflict in some other African countries. It is also linked to international crime, such as terrorism.

In a letter to *The Times* of London dated May 18, 2005, Dr Gerald Danaher states that in 1950, Tanzania had a population of about eight million. In 1975, he says, the population of Tanzania had risen to sixteen million, and, by 2000, to about thirty two million people. By 2050, Dr Danaher estimates Tanzania's demographic change would be about sixty four million people. This rate of population growth, some now fear, will not make 'poverty a history' but a reality.

Leaders of Western democracies, led by Britain's former Prime Minister Tony Blair, have made, and continue to make, positive efforts to reduce the level of poverty in Africa: reducing tariffs and subsidies, doubling aid and cancelling debt and so on and so forth.

Despite these efforts by Western leaders, there are those who argue that cancelling debt is actually rewarding both bad economic behaviour and individuals within state institutions who stole aid money.

Others believe that debt relief, more aid and fairer trade are not in themselves a panacea to Africa's intractable economic problems.

In an article which appeared in the British newspaper *The Independent*, of December 27, 2005, Richard Dowden, the director of African Royal Society, argues that '...while more aid, debt relief and better trade deals could speed up African development, they have been grossly oversold as the answer to Africa's problems.'

These factors, he says, were 'marginal' in precipitating Africa's economic failure. This means they will remain equally 'marginal' in improving the economic welfare of African countries.

From Dowden's viewpoint, African development can only happen if '...African governments want it to happen.' But do African governments really want it to happen?

In May, 2007, the world was stunned when African nations, who were the majority block on the 53-member organisation, put forward Francis Nheme, the Zimbabwean Environment Minister, to become the chairman of the United Nation's Commission on Sustainable Development (CSD); the body which monitors the environment and development.

However, at this point Zimbabwe was running one of the world's most disastrous economies with inflation steadily sky-rocketing virtually every single day.

This was taking place amid Robert Gabriel Mugabe's increasing tyranny which, incomprehensively, other African leaders refused to condemn.

If African rulers hankered for sustainable development and social growth for their countries, how then could they choose Zimbabwe, which had a totally failed economy, to head such an influential United Nations body?

Was it not obvious that a move like that would have a negative impact on Africa's much desired sustainable development; the rule of law that goes in tandem with it; and, perhaps could even have had impact upon the work of the Commission itself?

So, in view of this (and other factors which I outline later in this narrative), Africa's intractable problems will likely linger as long as some basic domestic factors in most African countries, Tanzania included, remain unchanged.

One of Britain's great statesmen, Sir Winston Churchill, once lamented that never in the history of African nation-building has it taken so long, cost so much, to achieve so little.

Today, Sir Winston might have again lamented at the prospect of foreign aid still being handled by institutions and managers of yesterday who either squandered or grossly misappropriated public funds.

Let us take a look at a few recent examples involving misappropriation of funds in Tanzania.

In January, 2008, the Norwegian government decided to withdraw 250 million Kroner which it gave to Tanzania in support of a nature regeneration project.

The decision followed an investigation by Arthur Andreasen, a Danish accountant who, for twenty years, worked in Tanzania.

In his report, which seemingly caused a stir in Norway, Andreasen showed that between a third and half of Norwegian aid to Tanzania vanished before it reached its recipients.[2] However, it was not only Norwegian aid that was misappropriated.

According to the weekly Danish newspaper, *The Copenhagen Post*, of April 25 to May 1, 2008, Danish aid to Tanzania was similarly stolen, much to the frustration of the benign Danes who have been giving aid to Tanzania since the 1960s.

Danish aid to Tanzania amounts to 500 million Kroner annually, making it the seventh largest donor to the country.

According to Andreasen though, as quoted by the same paper, up to half of that money was stolen by the politicians and officials to whom it was entrusted.

He added that the money was stolen by way of allocating it to non-existent projects or people; or simply by writing fictitious or excessively high bills and receipts.

Andreasen's report was not dissimilar to that of *Ernst & Young*, an independent, international accounting firm, which was published about the same time.

According to this report, in 2005, 133,015,186.220.74

---

2 http://www.dr.dk/Nyheder/Penge/2008/04/15/080713

billion Shillings (133 million US Dollars), was improperly paid by the Central Bank to twenty two local companies, many of them apparently fictitious.

The companies involved included Money Planners and Consultants, Maltan Mining Company Limited, Bora Hotels, Apartments Limited, Venus Hotel Limited, VB & Associates Company Limited, Bina Resorts Limited, Njake Hotel and Tours and Bencon International Limited.

Others were Kagoda Agriculture Limited, B.V. Holdings Limited, Mibale Farm Liquidity Services Limited, Excellent Services Limited, G & T International Limited, Navy Cut Tobacco (T) Limited, Ndovu Soap Limited, KERNEL Limited, Malegesi Law Chambers (Advocates), Clayton Marketing Limited, Changanyikeni Residential Complex Limited, M/S Rashtas (T) and Kiloloma & Brothers[3].

Apparently, the bank was making payments to these companies through its External Payment Arrears (EPA) account.[4] The similarity between the two reports was compelling.

For example, 90,359,078,804.00 billion Shillings was paid to thirteen companies on the basis of fake or forged documentation.

The other nine firms were paid 42,656,107,417.00 billion Shillings ostensibly without any documentation at all to justify the payments.

In January 2008, shortly after the report had been released, President Jakaya Mrisho Kikwete sacked the governor of Tanzania's Central Bank (also known as Bank of Tanzania—BoT), Dr Daudi Timoth Said Ballali.[5]

He then appointed Dr Ballali's own locum, Professor Benno

---

3 http://bit.ly/93Zr4Z
4 The EPA account was originally set-up by the government to help service balance of payment, whereby local importers would pay into the account in local currency, after which foreign service providers would then be paid back by BoT (Bank of Tanzania) in foreign currency. However, due to poor foreign currency reserves in the 1980s and 1990s, the debt within the account ballooned to $677 million by the year 1999. Efforts under a scheme known as 'Debt Buyback'- which involved some debt cancellations – was then negotiated under Paris Club. This helped to reduce the debt level to $233 million in 2004. Despite these efforts, unscrupulous officials and businesses were able to take advantage of one of the plans devised to reduce the account debt, under which a creditor could endorse debt repayment to a third party (Daily News, November 23, 2008).
5 http://news.bbc.co.uk/2/hi/africa/7181065.stm

Ndulu, to the post.

Apparently, Dr Ballali was dismissed whilst in the United States of America for medical treatment, where he later died in mid-May 2008.

Following his death, there were conflicting reports as to the actual cause of his death, with those close to him contending that he was 'poisoned'.[6]

Also, the government seemed to compound the situation by being economical with the truth, with regards to his whereabouts in the first instance. It also took almost a week before the government could confirm his death.

Even so, what was not in dispute was that prior to going abroad for medical treatment, Dr Ballali had provided a handwritten statement, in which he reportedly explained candidly what had actually happened to the EPA payments, to the *Taasisi ya Kuzuia na Kupambana na Rushwa (TAKUKURU)*; a government body which is supposed to fight and prevent graft.

At this point, some Tanzanians wondered why Dr Ballali was allowed to leave the country before the public heard his own version; or, why the authorities had not questioned him further or charged him, given that he was the head of the bank at the centre of the EPA scandal.

Consequently, this led to the speculation that, had he been charged, he would have disclosed information which would have implicated the government itself, something the latter was allegedly trying to avoid.

Therefore, it seemed to some people that the government let him go, knowing he would die there and that EPA (as the scandal became commonly known) would be buried with him.

However, Dr Ballali was a banker of international standing, having worked for the International Monetary Fund (IMF), before joining the Central Bank as its governor on July 14, 1998.

So, it would seem implausible that a banker of such calibre would not retain a copy of his statement to *TAKUKURU,* or even record an extra statement, leaving it with someone or an institution he trusted prior to his death.

---

6 http://www.raiamwema.co.tz/news.php?d=827

However, it was *TAKUKURU*'s apparent failure to take action following Dr Ballali's statement, which led to the suspicion of a government cover-up.

Those who suspected a government cover-up did so for other reasons.

This was not, after all, the first time that a similar scandal involving the same bank, had taken place, as will be read in the subsequent chapters of this narrative.

In addition, the culture of *kulindana* (protecting each other), which was one of the salient attributes of a regime of personal rule still prevails in Tanzania today, despite the institution of a multi-party system which replaced it.

Finally, almost all twenty-two companies were formed and/ or headed by government officials, albeit mostly by virtue of their official positions.

In some cases, however, some of the companies were set up with the direct involvement of people in the highest authority.

Kagoda Agriculture Limited (hereinafter *Kagoda*), one of the fictitious companies, serves as a good example in this regard.

This company was registered on September 29, 2005, following the direct order of former President, Benjamin William Mkapa.[7]

Then, within a brief period of eight weeks, his government through *Kagoda* and using forged documentation, acquired a total of 30,732,658.82 million US Dollars (more than 40 billion Shillings) under the pretext of 'national security,' from the bank's EPA account.

At this juncture, the Central Bank's external auditor, Samuel Sithole, from the international *Deloitte & Touche,* of South Africa, alerted the Tanzanian authorities to *Kagoda's* criminal activities.

Zakia Meghji, the then Minister for Finance, wrote to Sithole reaffirming that the money *Kagoda* withdrew from the bank was used on matters of 'national security.'

This, however, did not quite offer an explanation regarding the use of forged documents by *Kagoda* in procuring the funds from the Central Bank; documents all of which were signed by a single attorney named Bhyidinka Michael Sanze of *Malegesi Law*

---

7 Ibid.,

Chambers (Advocate) of Dar-Es-Salaam.

Four days after writing to Sithole, Meghji retracted this, claiming to have been 'misled' by the governor, Dr Ballali.

However, in his statement to *TAKUKURU*, which I have discussed above, Dr Ballali reportedly stated that he steadfastly refused to authorise payments based on forged documentation, but that he was 'pressured' by an influential, senior politician together with another 'powerful' government official to do so, in the interests of 'national security'—which is what he told Meghji.

Even so, it was still unclear as to why a person of Dr Ballali's reputation would go ahead and authorise payments based on forged documents rather than resign his post altogether.

What was clear though was that, apart from *Deloitte & Touche*, other Tanzanian-based, foreign, financial institutions also alerted the Central Bank authorities of possible illegal dealings in EPA's payments.

For instance, on November 2, 2005, Barclays Bank wrote to Tanzania's Central Bank seeking clarification of a large sum of money totalling 3,868,805,737.13 billion Shillings that had been paid into the account of Barclay's new client, *Mibale Farm Liquidity Services Limited.*

The Central Bank ostensibly cleared the payments; however, Barclays Bank decided to return the money to the Central Bank and closed the account of the company.

Prior to this, Nina Pendael Eshum, of the Standard Chartered Bank, raised a similar alarm after the Central Bank paid a staggering 14,383,416,515,00 billion Shillings into the accounts of *VB Associates Company Limited* and *Bencon International Limited* respectively.

Also, Kenya Commercial Bank (T), expressed the same concern to the Central Bank after the latter had paid the sum of 1,720,498,412.70 billion Shillings into a new account of *Malegesi Law Chambers (Advocates)* which it had opened with Kenya Commercial Bank (T).

As with the Barclays Bank incident, in all these latter cases the Central Bank replied promptly by clearing the payments— mostly carried out by two of its senior officials namely, Iman David Mwakyosa and Esther Mary Komu of the Central Bank's Debt Management Department.

In addition to this, the internal auditors of the bank's own Supervision Unit did not react following letters expressing concern from the four banks mentioned above.

All told, it seemed *Kagoda* was able to siphon off so much money from the EPA account, and in such a short time, because it had simultaneously opened accounts through the six branches of CRDB Bank in the commercial capital, Dar-Es-Salaam.

These included account numbers (in sequence) 01J1021795700 Holland Branch; account number 01J1021795701 Azikiwe Branch; account number 01J1021795702 Tower (PPF Tower) Branch; account number 01J1021795703 Kijitonyama Branch; account number 01J1021795704 Lumumba Branch and account number 01J1021795705 Vijana Branch.

Also, money siphoned off from the EPA account was paid out through other banks. These included, Kenya Commercial Bank (TShs 18,188,468,486); United Bank of Africa (UBA) (TShs 8,207,088,464); Eurafrica (TShs 6,300,402,225); Bank of Baroda (TShs 5,912,901,644); NBC (TShs 3,931,766,300); Diamond Trust (TShs 2,381,529,339) and Exim (TShs 2,225,035,393).

All in all, the Kikwete government implemented most of the recommendations which the 24-page report, with over 100 supporting documents, proposed (including the dismissal of the Central Bank's governor, Dr Ballali, now deceased, among other bank officials implicated in the affair, which the report recommended should be sacked).

However, the government did not implement section four of the report which calls upon it to institute criminal investigation in relation to the thirteen companies that had used fake or forged documentation (discussed *supra*) to obtain money from the bank.

Instead, the government decided to form a presidential investigation team (also known as task force), headed by the Attorney-General, Johnson Mwanyika, assisted by the Inspector General of Police, Said Mwema, and the Director of Preventing and Fighting Corruption Bureau *(TAKUKURU)*, Dr Edward Hosea.

One of the team's main tasks was to 'recover' the money from individuals involved in the scandal, before October, 31, 2008.

Although the government did not state as to how it would 'recover' the money from them; it did stress that those who failed to return the money before the end of the deadline, would face criminal prosecution.

Indeed, by November 12, 2008, the government had arraigned twenty suspects in the courts who failed to return the money before the end of the deadline.

Not surprisingly, apart from Jayant Kumar Chandubahi Patel (also known as Jeetu Patel), whose nine companies allegedly fetched TShs 10.3 billion (US $ 10 million) from the bank, the rest of the accused seemed to be *'vidagaa'* (small fish) whose role in the affair was comparatively negligible.

Consequently, the Kikwete government was under renewed pressure, to institute similar criminal proceedings against all those that had returned the money before the end of the deadline.

Inevitably, people were seething with anger at the prospect of theft, as a crime, being negated by the thief giving back what had originally been stolen.

Not only that, but the government's brazen attempts to treat swindlers of its own Central Bank with kid gloves; whatever their social status; seemed contrary to President Kikwete's own declared devotion to the concept of the rule of law under which, *inter alia*, all people are equal before the law.

Also, it seemed such attempts were actuated by political expediency to the detriment of the due process of the law.

That political expediency seemed to arise from the revelation that not only did the Mkapa government misappropriate public funds, but that it also deliberately lied to all concerned over the activities on which the money was spent.

According to newspaper reports, the money was actually expended by the government to finance favoured parliamentary candidates of its own *Chama cha Mapinduzi* nationwide during the 2005 general election campaigns (see also the chapter on the first multi-party election of October 1995 in the concluding part of this book).

Notwithstanding, not all the money was directly put into those election campaigns.

According to *East African Business*, of April 7, 2008, only about TShs 20 billion (US $20 million), was put into election campaigns. The rest, according to the paper, was 'deducted' from the overall amount (that *Kagoda* withdrew from the bank i.e. US $ 30,732,658.82), by an unnamed financial backer of the ruling party who supposedly financed its 1995 and 2000 general election campaigns.

It would seem that whoever had the power to do this also had strong institutional authority, and seemed to control all the monies that had been illegally siphoned off the Central Bank's EPA account.

Also, according to *Raia Mwema* (Good Citizen), of January 23, 2008, some TShs 600 million in cash, disappeared in the commercial capital, Dar-Es-Salaam, but for obvious reasons, the theft was not reported to the law enforcement agencies.

In another incident, the paper further reported, out of the 200 million Shillings that was to be handed to a contact person who was later to disburse the money to the *Chama cha Mapinduzi* candidates in the Lake (Victoria) zone, only 80 million was handed to that contact person.

And, the contact person, upon realising that he too, after all, had the opportunity, only disbursed TShs 20 million out of the TShs 80 million he was given.

Needless to add, the fact that EPA money enabled the ruling party to win a landslide victory during the 2005 general elections may partly explain why President Mkapa was so keen on legalising *takrima* (referred to later).

This is supposedly the traditional African hospitality (in my view criminality), whereby candidates with pots of cash (*Kagoda* cash, shall we say?) influenced voters with all the varied 'gifts' imaginable.

But, *takrima* seemed more of a *'Bongo'* thing than 'African.' Apparently, *Bongo* is a slang term by which Tanzania is known. It denotes the unorthodox application of one's faculties in dealing with a difficult social life (especially one involving making a living).

The slang was spawned by the severe economic hardships of the late seventies and eighties following Nyerere's policy which compelled Tanzanians *'kujitolea mhanga'* i.e. making hard sacrifices in support of various liberation movements in Africa. This policy was equally polemical.

This is because, practical wisdom dictates that people should take care of family and people close to them before they worry about others. Put it this way: 'charity begins at home'.

However, for reasons I describe in this narrative, Nyerere had come to conclude that the Tanzanian 'family' encompassed the entire African continent and beyond, where imperialism was still attempting to rear its ugly head.

After all, the creed of his political party (and Tanzania's sole one) *Chama cha Mapinduzi*, stated in very simple and unequivocal terms how all human beings were '*ndugu*' (relatives) of the Tanzanian 'family' and that Africa was one.

Therefore, it was on the basis of this expressed belief that Nyerere came to a definitive conclusion that Tanzania's own independence was actually 'meaningless' unless the entire African continent was free: freedom that is, within the context of his own belief in 'mono-party democracy'.

Of course, for that to be achievable, Nyerere had to expend the nation's meagre resources in support of this noble cause: forget for the moment the fact that this policy was of no national interest whatsoever, to Tanzania itself.

Indeed, in the seventies, prior to the collapse of the East African Community (EAC), which is now being revived, East Africans remember how one of the Community's airline was implicated in a bungled bid to ferry a band of armed men to a neighbouring sister state, where they were to launch an attack against a sitting dictator. Approval for use of this carrier is known to have emanated from Nyerere himself.

Others still have a vivid recollection of how the *MV Mapinduzi*, a Tanzanian government commercial vessel, was used to ferry guerrillas ('freedom fighters' in their view) from port to port, in furtherance of Nyerere's noble liberation cause.

Had the 'freedom fighters' themselves or their financial backers been paying for the cost of operating these services, then surely there would not have been much debate about the issue.

However, in line with Nyerere's referral policy, neither the guerrillas nor their financial backers had to bother paying for services rendered to them by the Tanzanian state.

Instead, it was overburdened, poor Tanzanian taxpayers who had to meet the operational expenses for these services, which, given what was involved in actually rendering them, mostly required payment in hard currency.

Yet Tanzania under Nyerere had a chronic shortage of

foreign reserves; and, so, to keep things going, money had to be scrounged from sympathetic donor nations or foreign financial institutions. At a price!

Of course, Nyerere had forewarned Tanzanians what to expect: the liberation of Africa, he would argue, was not a *lele-mama* (local dance) affair but a state of war; so Tanzanians, he emphasised, must henceforth be prepared to '*kujitolea mhanga*' (making hard sacrifices) in support of liberation efforts in foreign lands.

Crucially, this was *agizo la chama* (a party directive) which was not optional or amenable to public discourse. This was because, since the imposition of a single party rule in Tanzania, the distinction between the party and state was completely blurred and party directives almost had similar legal effect as statutory law.

With members of Nyerere's six political police organisations, commonly known as *Usalama wa Taifa* (*UwT*), untiringly scouting for dissenters, many Tanzanians obligingly heeded the '*kujitolea mhanga*' directive to the brink of starvation.

However, whilst these Tanzanians faced the unbearable hardship of his policies, Nyerere and his coterie were curled up at his Msasani residence in Dar-Es-Salaam, sipping Earl Grey.

The situation as outlined above was made worse by Nyerere's earlier-mentioned indiscriminate seizure of private property, in the name of nationalisation, which precipitated the flight of capital from the country *en masse*.

To rub salt into the wound (and for clearly discernable factors), most of the now nationalised major productive economic units i.e. banks, transport system, farms *et cetera*, could no longer produce enough to support the bulging services sector.

All these, together with other factors, resulted in the economic crisis which left corruption alone as the only functioning activity of nationalised economy. But the mandarins whom Nyerere relied on to rule the country benefited the most from corruption (and by stealing aid money) whilst Nyerere, for obvious reasons, simply looked away.

To ascertain if he was fully informed of this structural matter, I personally wrote him an open letter in the early part of 1983 in which I stated, amongst other things, that whilst Tanzanians were daily going without basic commodities, some senior officials in his government had quietly salted away a lot of money in their foreign accounts.[8]

As I show in this introduction corruption in Tanzania today has definitely spiralled out of control. Fortunately, people are now able to know about it because of the free media and the existence of legal opposition, both of which were taboo under Nyerere.

Be that as it may, *takrima* became a *Bongo* thing, in the sense that, despite comparatively corrupt practices and economic mismanagement in most parts of Africa, no other country had ever gone so far as legalising the use of (illegally obtained) funds, for politicians to buy (or bribe) their way to public office as shown by the Mkapa government.

In other African countries too, the people there are hospitable and they have Central Banks as well.

Whatever the case, prior to the institution of the presidential investigating team, and contrary to the recommendation of the *Ernst & Young* report, the current political leadership must have explained to the public, in the spirit of responsible governance, as to what they knew about the scandal and when. They should also have explained the usefulness of the presidential investigating team as opposed to taking legal action which the report recommended. Similarly, the public should have been told whether or not individuals within the hierarchy, including the president himself, benefited from the EPA money in one way or another.

I have applied the phrase 'responsible governance' on purpose because, you see, as one of Britain's Prime Minister, Stanley Baldwin once said, 'Power without responsibility has been the prerogative of the harlot throughout ages.'

Moreover, addressing those concerning aspects of the matter was particularly salient in view of the fact that the current political leadership is mostly comprised of senior officials, who were serving in the previous government of President Mkapa.

Additionally, the media was asserting that the senior political leadership was, indeed, involved in the EPA scandal.

According to *East African Business,* of April 7, 2008, a source close to the presidential investigating team was quoted as saying: 'The written statements have worried the team. The

---

8 See page 33, *New African*, October 1983

suspects have severally mentioned the ruling party and its top leadership and sometimes giving evidence of letters and related correspondences'.

At times, the source added, some senior government officials had been implicated.

Then she added almost lamentably '*CCM* is unreachable...' This left the question of 'who is going to freeze *CCM*'s accounts?' unanswered.

Therefore, addressing those key points from the start would have given the presidential investigating team more credibility. Also, it would have allayed fears of the government wishing to use the investigating team to white-wash itself.

This is more so, in the face of the suspicion that the government could not possibly investigate itself, especially in a case in which it is so deeply implicated.

True, the institutions of the state are interdependent because of their being part of the same governmental machinery. However, the independence of such institutions from undue interference by the Administration is an essential part of democracy as well as natural justice.

But, when members of the president's own investigating team begin to express 'worry' (actually fear) because senior political leaders, the ruling party and senior public officials are identified as being implicated in the case, then it is not difficult to prove that the independence of such institutions is non-existent.

Similarly, if the Police, *TAKUKURU* and the Financial Intelligence Unit (FIU), which was established by an Act of Parliament in 2007 to deal with money laundering and other similar illegal financial activities, were able to function independently, then they could have certainly detected an organised fraud of such immense proportions on their own, before outsiders did it for them.

Perhaps, in view of the nature of corruption revealed in this narrative, some might wonder how such agencies would be corruption-free, so as to be able to investigate others who are accused of corruption elsewhere.

However, had Tanzania striven to strengthen institutions from the start, instead of strengthening a regime of personal rule, corruption might have been minimal or reasonably containable.

This is because politicians and public officials, regardless of their designation, would have been discouraged from stealing from their own government, out of knowledge that, if discovered by (independent) law enforcement agencies, they would be handed to (independent) judgement mechanisms that would punish those responsible for wrong-doing, just like anybody else.

Additionally, this might have discouraged politicians from enacting *ad personam* laws, behind which they hide when using their positions to enrich themselves at the expense of the poor tax-payer.

But, since the current constitutional order encourages and condones political cronyism and patronage; and makes the president the god of everything under the Tanzanian sky; it is hard to envisage the opposite happening.

Nonetheless, prevalence of justice and for it to be seen as being done is, as I contended earlier, the most effective way of sustaining social cohesion in a political society.

However, when kleptocracy rules and the culture of *kulindana* (protecting each other) subverts the due process of the law, then the scales of justice will only tilt in the favour of those being protected, more so at the expense of those protecting them.

For a society with feeble institutions such as Tanzania, such a situation, politically speaking, is not entirely divorced from the imminent consequences of corruption which I have highlighted at the start of this introduction.

All in all, *Kagoda* seemed to trace its roots from another seemingly dubious company called *Afritainer (T) Limited.*

In August, 2000, *Afritainer* obtained 13 billion Shillings (13 million US Dollars), from the Central Bank's External Payment Arrears (EPA) account.

More significantly, it acquired this money shortly before the second multi-party elections were held; elections that returned President Mkapa to office for the second term.[9]

What is more, *Afritainer* used exactly the same telephone numbers i.e. 2861371 and 2861372 respectively, that five years later were to be used by *Kagoda* on its supposed official stationery. This seemed to indicate a link between these two companies.

All told, *Kagoda*, as it were, was not the only company to

---

9 http://www.raiamwema.co.tz/news.php?d=86

37

be set up with the active involvement of former President Mkapa.

Meremeta Gold Ltd (hereinafter *Meremeta*) was another company which was formed by order of the former president.

In a letter to the London-based *Deutsch Bank AG, London*, Marten Lumbanga, a senior Mkapa *aide,* asserted that the decision to form *Meremeta* was taken in the year 2000 by President Mkapa himself, 'through cabinet'.[10] This meant that *Meremeta* was a state-owned company.

Indeed, in a very comprehensive research paper by Thomas R. Yager which appears on the US Geological Survey Minerals Yearbook-2005 website, *Meremeta* is listed as such.

Then, like a vampire sucking blood from an entranced victim, his government—under his personal order—proceeded to suck the Central Bank's money to the tune of TShs 155 billion (US $155 million).

Apparently, *Meremeta* was not on the *Ernst & Young* list of shame. But as can be discerned from the figures, it siphoned from the bank a lot more money than all the companies in the *Ernst & Young* report combined.

From the start, the Mkapa government stated that, apart from mining activities, *Meremeta* was also to buy gold from small gold miners.

It further stated that the mining of gold which was to take place around the areas of Tembo and Buhemba respectively in Mara region, northern Tanzania, would benefit the nation and government through the Ministry of Defence (the *Nyumbu* battalion in particular) and National Service.

Consequently, on October 1, 1997, the Mkapa government directed the Treasury Registrar to issue a Certificate of Compliance in what clearly seemed to confirm *Meremeta* as being a state-owned company.

Therefore, in order for the *Meremeta* project to lift off the ground, the Mkapa government claimed to have approached *Nedcor Trading Services Limited,* of South Africa for a loan.

It is not clear why the government favoured the services of this particular company ahead of numerous others.

What was clear, however, was that *Nedcor Trading Services*

---

10 http://www.raiamwema.co.tz/news.php?d=619

Limited had links with *NedBank,* also of South Africa.

According to *Raia Mwema* (Good Citizen), of April 9, 2008, *NedBank* received US $ 118,396,460.36, part of the money that the Mkapa government ordered transferred from the bank on December 20, 2005; just a day before the swearing-in of President Kikwete.

This followed the selling of Treasury Bonds by the Central Bank. Apparently, it was the Treasury Bonds which the government was using to procure funds from the bank, using *Meremeta* and the above amount was part of the Treasury Bonds that were converted into US Dollars.

Also, apart from the aforesaid transaction involving *NedBank,* some employees of the same bank were routinely being mentioned as directors of yet another controversial company, *Deep Green Finance Services Limited* (hereinafter *Deep Green*).

Ostensibly, *Deep Green* had duly been registered in Tanzania. However, for inexplicable reasons the government allowed it to operate without being registered with the Central Bank as required by law.

Then, within a period of four months, between August 1, and, December 10, 2005, *Deep Green* had obtained TShs 10.4 billion (US $ 10 million) from the Central Bank's External Payment Arrears (EPA), before it quickly filed for bankruptcy.

Significantly, this also happened during the period leading up to the 2005 general elections; elections that brought President Kikwete to power, with 'overwhelming' majority.

The government never quite explained why *Deep Green* came into existence around this period; nor, for that matter, could it explain the circumstances under which it so quickly turned from *Green* to red i.e. bankrupt. Indeed, neither could the government explain the circumstances under which vital records pertaining to *Deep Green* mysteriously vanished from the office of Registrar of Business Registrations and Licensing Agency (BRELA).

What the government did emphasise though was that the money which was paid to *NedBank* was in relation to *Meremeta's* debts. This being more so, since *Meremeta* was a 'state company'.

It was only in January, 2006, when *Meremeta* was declared bankrupt in the United Kingdom, that its real owners became known.

39

It was now revealed that *Meremeta* was actually owned by *Triennex (Pty) Ltd,* of South Africa and that Tanzania's Treasury Registrar had only a fifty percent share. Other shareholders were said to be *London Law Services Ltd,* of Temple Avenue, who had a one percent share and *London Law Secretarial Services Ltd,* of the same address, who also held a one percent share.

Significantly, even so the Mkapa government had all along maintained that *Meremeta* was a 'state company' under the aegis of the Ministry of Defence and National Service, the Certificate of Compliance (number 32755) which was issued two days after the government ordered this, seemed to allow *Meremeta* to open a branch in Tanzania as a 'foreign firm'.

Furthermore, although *Triennex (Pty) Ltd* was South African, *Meremeta* was actually registered (on August 19, 1997), in the Isle of Man (registration number 34 24 504), in the United Kingdom, which is why it had to file for bankruptcy there.

Despite this, in July, 2007, the government astounded everyone when it published statistics indicating that *Meremeta* was still operational, having produced 2.27 tons of gold. Not everyone was convinced, because the year before having been declared bankrupt, the activities and assets of *Meremeta* were transferred to another company called *Tangold.*

Apparently *Tangold* was registered in Mauritius on April 5, 2005, and issued with certificate number 553334. On April 8, 2005, the company obtained the Global Business Licence (C2/GBL); and, on February 20, 2006, it was issued with a Certificate of Compliance to operate in Tanzania.

However, *Tangold* had previously been entangled in the narrated web of mendacity and fraud, involving the Central Bank's money.

Following the earlier-mentioned transfer of funds to *NedBank on* the 20th of December, 2005, some US $ 13,736,628.73 was paid into the *Tangold* bank account (number 011103024840) at NBC Corporate Branch, in the commercial capital Dar-Es-Salaam. (Following the sale of Treasury Bonds, the total amount that had been converted to US currency that day was US $ 131,736,628.73).

The third part of the money had, of course, been paid to *Meremeta's* own account.

However, as the *Swahili* saying goes '*Njia ya muongo ni*

fupi' (The route of a liar is short i.e. truth will out). For, on January 1, 2003, when the above bank account was supposedly opened, it was a public holiday in Tanzania.

Not only that, but the fact that the *Tangold* bank account was opened in 2003 means that the company was operational in Tanzania (at least, fictitiously) long before it was formally registered in Mauritius in the year 2005.

Nonetheless, it was the activities of Andrew John Chenge, a key member of the *Tangold* board (other board members included Central Bank's governor Dr Ballali, now deceased, former Permanent Secretary in the Prime Minister's Office Vincent Mrisho, former Ministry of Energy and Minerals Permanent Secretary Patrick Lutabanzibwa and former Treasury Principal Permanent Secretary Gray Mgonja) which were as controversial as *Tangold* itself.

For a decade, Chenge was the Attorney-General under President Mkapa, whose government conceived the whole idea of bringing into existence the companies that were to defraud the state of billions of Shillings.

A very proud and wealthy man (he became wealthy after being appointed Attorney-General), Chenge was blamed by some in Tanzania for some of the bad mining contracts into which the Mkapa government had allegedly entered with some foreign mining companies.

Indeed, so bad were some of these mining contracts that Mkapa's successor, President Kikwete, had to form a presidential committee headed by Mr Justice Mark Bomani, to review the contracts in the mining sector.

That was not enough though, to dissuade President Kikwete from naming Chenge, to whom he was fairly well acquainted, to be his Infrastructure Minister.

Apparently, Chenge's appointment into Kikwete's cabinet followed the resignation, in February 2008, of Prime Minister, Edward Lowassa; Minister for Minerals and Energy, Nazir Karamagi (who was also embroiled in a Buzwagi gold mine scandal) and East African Co-operation Minister, Dr Ibrahim Msabaha.

It seems that the three men had been compelled to resign from President Kikwete's government following yet another scandal, also involving another non-existent company known as *Richmond Development Company LLC* (hereinafter *Richmond*) of the United States of America.[11]

What happened was that on June 23, 2006, the government of President Kikwete, through *Tanzania Electricity Supply Company Limited* (TANESCO), awarded TShs 172.9 billion (US \$172 million) to *Richmond*, to supply 105.6 megawatts of turbine-charged power to TANESCO.

However, six months later *Richmond* had not kept its delivery promise despite stating (falsely, of course) in the contract that it was 'a company limited by shares, duly organised, validly existing and in good standing under the laws of Tanzania'.

Consequently, TANESCO's board of directors decided to hire the services of an international law firm, *Hunton & Williams LLP*, of Richmond, Virginia in the United States of America, to do the background check on *Richmond*.

Ordinarily, a background check on the company invariably precedes the award of a contract, rather than the other way round.

Following a background check, *Hunton & Williams LLP* discovered that *Richmond* had misrepresented its corporate status in both Tanzania and Texas—the latter being the state where *Richmond* had (again) falsely stated in the contract to be 'incorporated', despite being a 'briefcase' company (interestingly, *Richmond* spawned yet another controversial company known as *Dowans*. Although its services were also terminated due to public pressure, some senior management in TANESCO, for reasons widely seen as their own, were threatening in March 2009, that Tanzania would experience severe power shortages within months unless the government allowed TANESCO to purchase old machines left behind by *Dowans* for generating emergency electricity supply).

All told, Change's tenure as President Kikwete's Infrastructure Minister was short-lived.

For, on April 20, 2008, he too was forced to resign his post after the British newspaper, the *Guardian,* revealed on April 12, 2008, that Chenge retained an off-shore bank account on the island of Jersey, containing over one million US Dollars.

---

11 http://news.bbc.co.uk/2/hi/africa/7232141.stm

Apparently, it was suspected that the money had been corruptly obtained following the purchase, in 2001, of a £28 million air defence radar system (hereinafter radar) by the Mkapa government from the British arms manufacturing company *BAE Systems*[12].

Precisely, the purchase of the radar known as Plessey Commander Fighter Control System was allegedly made following Chenge's legal advice, as the Attorney-General.

However, like the other deals outlined in this account, this one was also controversial.

This is because its purchase was vehemently opposed by a large section of Tanzanians, the World Bank and the International Civil Aviation Organisation, amongst others.

Those who opposed its purchase believed the radar to be 'useless' to Tanzania (a Highly Indebted Poor Country—HIPC) and 'overpriced.'

Not surprisingly, Britain's Serious Fraud Office (SFO) was conducting an investigation into the deal; which investigation it seems, led to the discovery of Chenge's US $ 1.5 million (Tsh 2.1 billion) bank account in Jersey.

It also appeared to have led to another discovery that in May 1998, US $ 600.000 was paid to Dr Idris Rashid, the Managing Director of TANESCO; the company that was later implicated in the *Richmond* affair; from Chenge's Jersey ('conduit') bank account (before being appointed TANESCO's Managing Director, Dr Rashid was Central Bank governor).

Consequently, in April 2008, officers from the Serious Fraud Office (SFO) flew to Tanzania where they conducted a search at both Chenge's offices and his residence in Dar-Es-Salaam.

In his usual style, Chenge did not deny retaining a bank account in Jersey (or elsewhere abroad, as some well-informed sources suggest), nor dispute the cash it allegedly contained.

Instead, he characteristically shrugged off the one and half million US Dollars in that bank account as mere *'vijisenti'* i.e. pennies, over which people need not make an issue. He was probably right in the light of the following.

On January 19, 2007, before details of Chenge's *'vijisenti'*

---

12 http://news.bbc.co.uk/2/hi/africa/7357976.stm

43

(pennies) were revealed, the *IPP Media,* quoted Sailesh Pradji Vithlani ('Mr Fat'), a Tanzanian middleman with long-established connections with senior members of the army and government, as admitting that 12 million US Dollars was paid into a 'secret' foreign bank account.

Vithlani, who, according to news reports was apprehended by the British authorities in July, 2009, further claimed that it was that 'commission' which had resulted in the Mkapa government entering into a business deal with the British arms manufacturing company, *BAE Systems.*

In April, 2010, *BAE Systems* agreed to repay the Tanzanian government £28 million (after pertinent legal aspects have been resolved) but denied any wrong-doing[13]. However, the Tanzanian government remained tight-lipped over Vithlani's claim.

What is more, according to *The Times* of London, of December 16, 2006, the deal was financed by a £40 million Barclays Bank loan which, according to the newspaper, was financed from aid given to Tanzania to assist sustainable development, including primary education.

From the evidential facts adduced thereof, it would seem apparent that the purchase of the radar was pushed by personal interests rather than national interests.

One may not necessarily need more proof to concur with the view that the development of Africa is within the grasp of its political leadership, only if they want it to occur.

All told, former President Mkapa is to this day dogged by questions pertaining to the wealth that he and his former Prime Minister, Frederick Sumaye are alleged to have amassed during the ten years they held their respective offices. However, it is the manner in which this alleged wealth was acquired which left much to be desired.

For example, in 2004, President Mkapa and his Minister for Minerals and Energy, Daniel Aggrey Ndhira Yona, formed a company known as *Tanpower Resources Company Ltd* (hereinafter *Tanpower*). In 2005, *Tanpower* acquired *Kiwira Coal and Mines Limited*; a state company; for 700 million Shillings whereas the actual price was estimated at TShs 4 billion. (Towards the end of

---

13 http://www.tzaffairs.org/2010/05/corruption-good-news/

November 2008, Yona, and Basil Pesambili Mramba, the former Minister of Finance in President Mkapa's government, were both charged with abusing public trust. Both men were implicated, amongst other things, in the illegal tax exemptions involving *Alex Steward (Assayers) Government Business Corporation* of Washington DC; exemptions that allegedly caused the Tanzania Revenue Authority (TRA) to loose TShs 11,752,350,148.00 billion (US $11 million[14]).

Additionally, a few months prior to President Mkapa's retirement in 2005, his government, through *Tanzania Electricity Supply Company* (TANESCO), also awarded TSh 380 billion (about US $ 271 million) to the state company which *Tanpower* had just acquired. Apparently, the company itself which had since been re-named *Kiwira Coal and Power Limited* (hereinafter *Kiwira*) was awarded the contract to supply 200 megawatts of coal-fired electricity to the national power grid.

At this point though, President Mkapa, his wife Anna, his son Nicholas Mkapa, Nicholas Mkapa's father-in-law, the now late Joseph Mbuna and a certain Evans Mapundi, had since acquired many more shares in *Kiwira* than most.

Furthermore, on July 10, 2007, the state-owned National Social Security Fund (NSSF) provided a short-term loan of US $7 million (about Tsh 10 billion) to *Kiwira* seemingly without any collateral offered as security. Moreover, although the loan was supposed to be paid back in six months with interest, at the time of writing this introduction, the loan had not been paid at all. Nonetheless, it is the so-called 'capacity charges' which TANESCO daily paid to *Tanpower* (and other companies; some of whose ownership remains a carefully-guarded secret[15]) which provided more ammunition to those who accuse the former president of '*majwaguism*' (a *Bantu* word denoting the highest form of unbridled greed).

To be sure, on April 22, 2008, Aloyce Kimario, a Member of Parliament for Vunjo constituency (*CCM*) stated in Parliament that the total sum of Tsh 146 million which TANESCO daily paid to *Tanpower* as 'capacity charges' caused TANESCO's operational

---

14 http://www.dailynews.co.tz/home/?n=11635
15 These included, *inter alia*, Independent Power Tanzania Limited (Tsh 144 million); Songas (Tsh 243 million); Aggreko (Tsh 57.6 million) and Dowans (Tsh 152 million).

costs to rise and was tantamount to 'sabotaging' TANESCO on the part of the former president[16]. However, some Tanzanians felt this was more than merely 'sabotaging' TANESCO.

Regrettably, they believed this to be the most expeditious way under which Tanzanians were to pay the maintenance of the Mkapa family for generations to come for use of electricity, and other bills accruing from 'dubious' privatisation schemes carried out under Mkapa's rule.

Strangely, despite all the political and financial clout which the people behind *Tanpower* and *Kiwira* had respectively, these companies still seemed incapable of meeting TANESCO's immediate energy demands—this being more so especially in the wake of the above-mentioned *Richmond* scandal.

Indeed, on Thursday, July 23, 2009, the Kikwete government announced in Parliament that it intended to pay *Tanpower* some Tsh 50 billion (about US $ 49.5 million) so that *Tanpower* could relinquish its shares in *Kiwira* as the government intended to re-possess the company. The decision clearly seemed designed to get the former president and his confederates off the hook, in so far as *Kiwira* was concerned.

However, even so the payments were designed to defray 'all the costs they (*Tanpower*) incurred after taking over the mine (*Kiwira Coal and Mines Limited*)' they seemed incredibly generous in comparison to what *Tanpower* had supposedly invested in machinery after the acquisition of the company, not to mention what it had paid to acquire it.

On the other hand, the government gave no indication as to whether or not *Tanpower* would continue to receive its guaranteed (and also truly generous) daily remuneration of Tsh 146 million from TANESCO which was in the form of 'capacity charges'; now that the 'capacity' of *Tanpower* to perform adequately appeared to have openly been brought into question.

In addition, there was a general feeling that if this was the way the Kikwete government intended to proceed in order to tackle institutional corruption in Tanzania, then it would encourage rather than discourage it. Nonetheless, there remained much to be desired.

According to news reports, in May 2002, President Mkapa's

---

16 http://allafrica.com/stories/200804230732.html

46

government gave a South African engineering firm called *NET Group Solutions* a lucrative contract to run TANESCO for two years under a 'Management Support Services' scheme. Initially, there seemed to be nothing wrong with this move as most Tanzanians felt TANESCO was in critical need of re-organisation in order to improve its efficacy.

However, it soon turned out that *NET Group Solutions*, which was established in 1987, was actually 'a very small firm' with inadequate capacity to handle Tanzania's national grid. Additionally, it was further revealed that the firm's Tanzanian partner was a company owned by President Mkapa's brother-in-law.[17]

Following this revelation, it would seem apparent that other companies which were better equipped were by-passed because President Mkapa wanted his brother-in-law also to be given the 'opportunity' to hop on Tanzania's gravy train.

The process of privatisation in Tanzania carries a condition of including local investors at a minimum of at least twenty percent.

However, from what I have described above (and continue to describe *infra*) this condition is what members of the ruling elite exploit, allowing them (and/or immediate members of their families) to form companies (albeit mostly with intent to siphon funds from the state treasury) through which they enter into partnership with foreign investors as the above-cited case attests. However, there are other good examples in support of this argument.

For instance, companies such as *Dev Consult International Limited* which at the time of writing this introduction was owned by the now disgraced President Mkapa's former cabinet minister Daniel Aggrey Ndhira Yona and his son Danny; *Choice Industries Limited* which was owned by the father-in-law of Nicholas, President Mkapa's son, and *Forsnik Enterprises Limited*, which was owned by the latter and his wife, Foster Mbuna Mkapa, amongst other companies. All these companies, it must be emphasised, acquired shares in *Tanpower* almost at the time *Tanpower* was about to takeover *Kiwira Coal and Mines Limited* in 2005.[18]

---

17 http://www.afrol.com/News2002/tan006_dawasa_private.htm
18 http://www.thisday.co.tz/

Nonetheless, it was the 10-year lease contract, with an exclusivity clause, which the Mkapa government granted to Tanzania International Container Terminal Services (TICTS) in 2000, which similarly caused yet another controversy. Apparently, this was extended for a further 15 years in 2005—meaning that the exclusivity clause was to remain in force till the year 2025.

Ostensibly, the clause seemed designed to give virtual monopoly to TICTS over all container handling at the Dar-Es-Salaam port; this perhaps in recognition of TICTS's extraordinary revitalisation efforts of the container operations at the port.

Indeed, those remarkable efforts by the company known to be backed by the Hong Kong-based *Hutchison Whampoa Limited*, was hailed by the majority of Tanzanians as the country's biggest success stories of privatisation.

However, as the congestion at the port became routine, some Tanzanians started to blame the monopoly which guaranteed TICTS exclusivity as the primary cause of the congestion.

In reality however, it seemed the debate over the affair was kindled by the Mkapa government's own previous involvement in fictitious companies (discussed earlier) and other questionable investment deals than the clause itself: sort of an after shock after such a plethora of scandals. It was like people were blaming themselves for not opening their eyes earlier enough before all this happened.

Significantly, the hullabaloo generated by this specific matter, and its lingering impact, seemed to indicate that corrupt African leaders, although seemingly doing what might 'please' foreign investors and donors alike, their corrupt practices could, in the long-term, prove detrimental to the interests of the latter and by implication, Tanzania's own.

I mention damage to Tanzania's interests here in the sense that, as things stand, Tanzania's viability in both social and economic context remain, at least for the foreseeable future, inextricably linked to continued Western economic prosperity.

You see, when politicians and public officials milk the coffers of their own state dry, it means that money will have to be found elsewhere—in this case Western donors—in order to support the infrastructure and pay for vital social services. Evidence of this is clear to the reader and does not require restating.

I am not in any way suggesting this to be the panacea to the clearly nauseating situation that I have so far carefully documented. Rather, I am intent on stating the fact.

That fact is, that if for some reason Western economic interests were, God forbid, to be affected to the point of ceasing to dispense economic aid to Tanzania (and to other African countries), then in all frankness, it would be Tanzania's own social and economic interests that would be adversely affected; more so than those of the West.

In view of this factor, the continued well-being of Western economic interests is Africa's concern much as it is to the West itself; and this must be clear.

That notwithstanding, the so-called donor fatigue when combined with the referral corruption at high levels of the Tanzanian government may ultimately result in diminished foreign aid, not to mention foreign investments.

In a famous speech made in July 2004 to the British Business Association of Kenya, the former High Commissioner to Kenya, Sir Edward Clay, stated that rapacious African rulers '…are eating like gluttons before vomiting on the shoes of donors'.

Without intending to repeat myself, you have so far seen the nature and scope of the *majwagu* (gluttony) culture in Tanzania.

It is understandable for most diplomats and donors alike to refrain from locking horns with Dar-Es-Salaam over this nascent albeit abominable culture.

However, in the course of time, the same people may come to conclude that perpetual 'vomit' on their shoes is equally unacceptable. Only then, perhaps, shall we see the beginning of the end of the *majwagu* culture in Tanzania; culture which, as it is, appears to be rapidly transforming itself into some real form of Frankenstein monster.

Be that as it may, as the exclusivity clause remained a matter of protracted public debate, the Kikwete government felt compelled to intervene and extinguish the embers of discontent which the debate had seemingly raked.

Consequently, following protracted negotiations between TICTS and the Kikwete government, the contentious clause was finally removed after the Memorandum of Understanding (MoU) was signed by relevant parties on July 27, 2009. This effectively paved the way to competition and gave shipping lines the freedom to choose an operator of their choice. The move was widely seen as one which would lead to lower tariffs and that the Inland Container Terminals (ICTs) would be used more effectively. More importantly, TICTS agreed to present a five-year investment plan for scrutiny by the Tanzanian authorities before the end of the year 2009. This was thought to be the first time that TICTS would have done this since it entered into contract with the Tanzanian government in the year 2000.[19] Whether all these measures were to resolve factors which precipitated the debate in the first instance remained to be seen.

All told, the above-mentioned cases were not dissimilar to another fiasco under which the Mkapa government had privatised (some say hastily and without proper evaluation) the *Dar-Es-Salaam Water and Sewerage Authority* (DAWASA) in 2003.

Indeed, unlike in the other cases, the DAWASA case marked the beginning of a legal action (which was decided in favour of Tanzania) that proved controversial in aid and development circles.

Equally controversial though, was the Tanzanian government's drastic decision which it took on June 1, 2005. This decision saw the brief detention, followed by the deportation, of three British expatriates namely, Cliff Stone, Michael Livermore and Roger Harrington who were the senior managers at *City Water*, a consortium which was responsible for managing Dar-Es-Salaam's water supply.[20]

Apparently, the controversy centred mainly on the treatment meted out to the three officials. It was prompt and arguably drastic.

Yet, the government could not quite explain why it had never taken similar drastic measures against the catalogue of senior government officials that I have named above (and in the main section of this narrative) who committed (or continue to commit) far more serious economic crimes against the Tanzanian state; and whose actions are sure to have a severe and lingering impact on the entire society than the case of the three *City Water* officials. Were the Tanzanian authorities trying to make an example of the three officials?

---

19 http://www.dailynews.co.tz/home/?n=3110&cat=home
20 http://www.guardian.co.uk/business/2007/aug/16/imf.internationalaidanddevelopment

If so, did it not occur to the Tanzanian authorities that corruption of the nature I have outlined above created a very complicated environment that might frustrate even the efforts of those genuinely attempting to assist Tanzania realise her development objectives?

Whatever the answer to that question may be, DAWASA as it were will remain a study case in aid and development circles; and, even possibly beyond.

For one thing, the United Nations set out the Millennium Development Goals (MDGs) with the principal aim to free men, women, and children from the 'dehumanising conditions of extreme poverty'. It would seem apparent that high level corruption in Tanzania as well as other domestic factors which I describe in this account, contribute more to these 'dehumanising conditions' more so than the DAWASA case.

All told, it was the issue of *Mwananchi Gold Company Ltd*, (hereinafter *Mwananchi*) which made the majority of Tanzanians feel as though they were being repeatedly stabbed in the back by their own government. This multi-billion Shilling investment was inaugurated by Benjamin Mkapa on December 1, 2005, for the purpose of '...processing of gold' in Tanzania.

Indeed, Tanzania had no mineral processing facility since the closure of the diamond-cutting firm *TANCUT* in the late 1980s. Thus, for many Tanzanians, the desire to introduce additional wealth by inaugurating *Mwananchi* seemed not only appropriate but an imperative economic venture.

However, in common with other controversial companies mentioned in this account, *Mwananchi*, very quickly, and once more under suspicious circumstances, was declared insolvent in December 2008. This was despite the share holdings of the *National Development Company*, NDC, (15 percent), foreign investors under the *Chimera Company Limited*, (20 percent), and *Mwananchi Trust* (29 percent). The Central Bank had held a 36 percent share, but in May 2008 submitted an ownership withdrawal notice to the company's board of directors.

Nor did it help matters when it was revealed that, as in other preceding and dubious deals, the Central Bank had made a considerable loan to *Mwananchi* prior to the latter filing for bankruptcy, without giving acceptable reasons as to why and how

Mwananchi was suddenly going into receivership.

To add insult to injury, former president Mkapa and his wife, Anna; who a section of the Tanzanian media routinely refer to as 'Mama' Anna Mkapa; are alleged to have formed a company known as *ANBEM Limited* (hereinafter *ANBEM*), only four years after President Mkapa came to power in the year 1995.

Indeed, documents related to the registration of *ANBEM* describe the former First Couple as '*wafanyabiashara*' (entrepreneurs), and the sole directors of the company.

Similarly, the same documents show that the company's offices were at Plot 15, Luthuli Road, which is the government building within the compound of *Ikulu* (State House) and it is used by each incumbent First Lady as her office.[21]

Indeed, it is from the same building whence the current First Lady, Salma Kikwete, conducts her business pertaining to her non-governmental organisation (NGO) *Wanawake na Maendeleo* (Women and Development) Foundation.

All told, former president Mkapa, and his wife, Anna, conducted their business activities from the building paid for by the poor tax payer. The business official records show this to include, *inter alia* 'Carrying on business and to act as merchants, general traders, warehouse, stockists, shopkeepers and operators of supermarkets, commission agents and carriers' and, much more business activities that seemed to take much of 'His Excellency's' time away from the functions and demands of the presidency.

It is on the basis of these facts, amongst others, that some people felt that being engaged in business whilst president-cum-head of state, presented a serious conflict of interests, let alone considering the acquisition of *Kiwira Coal and Mines Limited*.

Nonetheless, *Kiwira Coal Mines Limited* was not the only state company to be acquired for a *bei poa* (cool price) during the Mkapa presidency.

Many parastatal organisations and government buildings were routinely sold for an equally *bei poa* (cool price) particularly amongst members of the ruling elite and their immediate family members.

Equally, the properties of the former president which he

---

21 http://www.thisday.co.tz/?l=10863

reportedly owns in Lushoto district, Dar-Es-Salaam and allegedly in South Africa have of late generated a heated debate regarding the integrity of the leaders that Nyerere chose for Tanzanians.

It must be emphasised that, although less discussed, in his lifetime, Nyerere never quite trusted his own people to identify and choose their own leaders. Instead, in what amounted to an insult to his own people's intelligence, he chose rulers for them.

Additionally, although much blame is placed on the rulers he chose for Tanzanians, few seem to blame those who chose rulers for them who also turned out to be self-serving.

Not only that, but the former president arrogantly refuses to answer charges levelled against him in the belief that he has *'kinga ya katiba'* i.e. sovereign immunity, even in such matters involving serious fraud and theft, such as the EPA case, for example.

And, his successor, President Kikwete, feels that despite all that, *'mzee wa watu'* (poor old chap), should be 'left alone' to enjoy his retirement 'peacefully'.

In reality, however, it seems unlikely that the former president will be 'left alone' until such structural issues are properly addressed—and in accordance with the law.

Unless, of course, if Tanzania is intent on creating 'oligarchs,' similar to those who sprang up in Russia following the demise of communism.

The only snag however is that; and this should be of great concern to all stake holders and the ruling elite itself; if the situation continues unchecked, as it seems it will, it could have the potential of misrepresenting the market economy system in Tanzania.

Such misrepresentation could inevitably result in the resentment of the very same system that the people had enthusiastically embraced in the belief that it would help them better their lives.

Already, the inability to tackle high level corruption within itself has fostered a mistaken belief among some Tanzanians that their leaders are 'selling' the country to 'foreigners' i.e. investors, for their own material gain.

It has become common these days in Tanzania to hear some people refer to the entrenched ruling elite as *wenyenchi* (owners of the country) but at the same time referring to ordinary citizens as *wananchi,* with no say in whatever the former does with regard to the country.

Tanzanians have a reputation for coining phrases and dissident slang out of serious situations, albeit mostly with an element of banter rather than opposition to the *status quo*.

However, the coining of *wenyenchi/wananchi* slang vividly reflects the ruling elite's failure to take into account the unequal power relationship between the state and its citizens. In the long term, neither does this bode well in a twenty first century civil society.

It is, in my opinion, a constitutional deficiency accruing from the manner in which the current constitutional order evolved.[22]

So, as Tanzania's population balloons, so does the ruling elite itself. In the end, the scramble for the meagre resources between the vast majority of the poor and the ruling elite who, as it happens, have better access to these resources than the former, could equally cause unwanted cracks in the country's social cohesion.

The above described EPA scandal and the described manner in which members of the ruling elite have been acquiring public property, vividly demonstrates how easily the ruling elite can have access to these resources than the former.

Nonetheless, it is the manner in which the government has been dividing up existing provinces and districts, a move seen by some as designed to create posts for members of the ruling elite, which further supports that point.

On May 9, 2002, for example, the Mkapa government declared that a new region called Manyara, had been curved up from the existing Arusha region. Ostensibly, this was done without proper consultation with the people of the region concerned.

Additionally, the government created new districts from the existing districts of Iringa, Songea, Shinyanga, Mwanza, Tabora, Morogoro, and Handeni, again without first listening to the views of the people in the districts involved. The new districts (shown after colon) were created thus as follows:

Iringa: Kilolo; Songea: Nantumbo; Shinyanga: Kishapu; Mwanza: Nyamagana; Tabora: Iyui; Morogoro: Nvomero and Handeni: Kilindi.

On July 29, 2005, just a few months before leaving office, President Mkapa again told Parliament he was ordering seven

---

22 Also see http://allafrica.com/stories/200004170118.html

more districts to be split up into two.

This decision as well was seen by some as an attempt to appoint 'his loyalists' to head the divided up districts prior to handing over power to his successor.

The split up districts and the new ones (in parentheses) include: Bukoba (Bukoba Rural, Missenyi); Biharamulo (Biharamulo, Chato); Dodoma Rural (Bahi, Chamwino); Hai (Hai, Siha); Masasi (Masasi, Nanyumbu); Monduli (Monduli, Longido) and Muheza (Muheza, Mkinga).

Needless to add, Tanzania's ruling elite started ballooning following Nyerere's imposition of personal rule. Also, its expansion was further exacerbated by Nyerere's political scheming of wanting his ruling elite to comprise a considerable element of the military.

Since colonial rule, Tanzania's military contained a significant *Kuria* element, the tribe hailing from the same part of the country as Nyerere himself.

Consequently, Nyerere came to regard this element as one he could use to consolidate his power.

Indeed, by having the ruling elite composing a military element, Nyerere sought to forestall the prospect of the military having to resort to the gun in order to take part in politics (although elsewhere on the continent where the military had had to intervene, the principal reason was broader economic and social issues rather than mere political representation).

However, Nyerere was so infatuated with this idea such that he had to accord the army, then universally known as *wembe wa chama* (blade of the party), the status of a province with complete representation in Parliament.

More significantly, from this point on, the army's officer corps started being plucked from the ranks of his sole political party (President Kikwete, who holds the military rank of colonel was, for instance, inducted into the army in this way). Equally, the rank and file was now also being required to belong to his sole political party.

As the army bloated following the introduction of this scheme, Nyerere started appointing the most senior officers into his own cabinet whilst appointing others to become 'national' Members of Parliament. Alternatively, he would send others abroad as ambassadors or diplomatic staff while others would be appointed to head districts and provinces; others would be appointed to head the nationalised sectors of the economy—thanks once again, to the power of patronage that resulted from his imposition of personal rule and which enabled him to accomplish this scheme with complete ease.

These entire manoeuvres, it must be emphasised, enabled Nyerere to elevate junior army officers to senior positions in order to avoid frustrating them to the detriment of his regime. Also, it sent an encouraging message to them that personal loyalty to him would be well rewarded.

And there were more 'rewards' (more appropriately sops). Nyerere could still post some of his officers to foreign countries where Tanzanian troops had remained stationed, for decades (referred to later).

Thus, Tanzania under Nyerere appeared to have two large armies: one which remained home, and another that was stationed overseas, in various countries.

Apart from factors which I further discuss in the main section of this account, Nyerere had come to view the troops he had stationed abroad as some kind of Rapid Deployment Force (RDF); which force he could deploy at will where he to face an insurrection back in Tanzania. It was a manipulative exploitation surpassing even that of Niccolò Machiavelli, if one were to set its economic consequences to Tanzania aside.

All in all, the situation today is not exactly the same as it was under Nyerere's regime of personal power.

Nationalisation, for example, is something of the past. This implies *inter alia* that members of the ruling elite can no longer count on being appointed to head the now privatised sectors of the economy as indeed had been the practise under the centralised economy.

On the other hand, almost all Tanzanian troops who were stationed abroad have returned home albeit regrettably with some permanently maimed and others in body bags. In one recent example, on August 23, 2004, a total of 101 Tanzanian soldiers were buried at Naliendele cemetery, in Mtwara region, south of Tanzania.

These were part of the Tanzanian troops that were stationed in Mozambique for several years to assist the *Frente de Libertação de Moçambique* (*Frelimo*), i.e. Front for the Liberation of Mozambique, in its second phase of the so-called '*a luta continua*' i.e. the struggle continues.

Apparently, this commenced a few years after Mozambique's independence from Portugal on June 25, 1975; and, was necessitated by armed opposition to *Frelimo* which I also discuss later in this account.

Precisely, the return of Tanzanian troops from foreign lands; with the officer corps swelling the ranks of the already bulging ruling elite; prompted the government to start looking for new ways of dealing with the multiplication of its own members: hence the dividing up provinces and districts, and other moves reminiscent to this as witnessed recently.

It is perfectly possible that the government's intention in dividing up these districts and provinces is to bring services close to the people as it likes to contend.

However, as long as the people themselves in those districts and provinces have no political right to directly elect their own leaders, who can directly be answerable to them rather than the government that appoints them, this view will inevitably prevail.

And, whatever argument the government has over this issue, it can hardly be sustained since it fails to adequately address the problem of lack of proper representation which is created by the government's appointment of district and provincial commissioners.

Additionally, it does not address the potential conflict that could possibly arise following the scramble for the meagre resources between the vast majority of the poor and the ruling elite.

On the other hand, it does not tackle the issue of nepotism which, like corruption, has permeated throughout the segments of the Tanzanian society.

On January 21, 2008, newly appointed Central Bank's governor Professor Ndulu, told a press conference in the commercial capital, Dar-Es-Salaam, that the siblings of some political heavyweights (*vigogo*), formed part of the bank's work force.

Apparently, Professor Ndulu was responding to allegations that the majority of these were employed without following laid down procedures and, that some of them were under qualified.

Professor Ndulu's revelation was merely a tip of an iceberg.

It has become common these days in Tanzania to hear relatives and siblings of some politicians heading this department or that government ministry; or, sitting on Central Committee and, or, the National Executive Committee (NEC) of the ruling *Chama cha Mapinduzi.*

I am not in any way suggesting that the siblings and relatives of Tanzanian politicians have no right to participate in the country's political process.

Rather, what I am saying is that in a democratic society, which Tanzania is professing to be, nepotism is incompatible with the ideals of political representation.

Indeed, if such ideals are to be upheld, then political participation should be done in an open, transparent manner as opposed to fraudulent practices that currently characterise Tanzania's electoral process.

It is imperative for this to be so, to avoid marginalising citizens who have the ability to serve their country, but who are without *Kagoda* cash and 'name recognition' as members (and siblings) of the ruling elite.

It is through the realisation of this, and other aspects that I have discussed earlier, that can seemingly dispel the prevalent notion whereby Tanzania's ruling elite is widely seen as treating the country as if it was its own private fief.

All told, the issue of the self-serving ruling elite has the potential of further alienating Tanzania's young who comprise the majority of the population. This could culminate in the sense of despair and hopelessness.

Moreover, a situation such as that, when coupled with the government's misguided desire to keep the legal opposition securely tamed, could create and prolong a vacuum (*ombwe*) which could be easily exploited by some forces with a radically different agenda to society.

Either, a vacuum such as that could radicalise the otherwise moderate, political and social forces. This factor as well, is equally incompatible with the principle of 'evolution' rather than 'revolution'. The latter has invariably shown to be messier than the former.

However, if conditions which precipitated conflicts elsewhere begin to wane rather than increase, more investors could, with more confidence, extend their markets, which in turn would provide more jobs for the local population and, significantly, a vision for the young. This would be one long-term approach, amongst others, to deal with Tanzania's growing poverty, which in turn could produce further remedies.

Nevertheless, there is also the problem of the Union with Zanzibar which, incredibly, has shown the capacity to perpetuate itself *sine die*.

On January 12, 1964, 'Field Marshal' John Gidion Okello, a Ugandan labourer, resident on the island at the time, organised and led an armed band of 'indigenous' Zanzibaris which overthrew the country's Sultan (Okello remained in control of Zanzibar for two consecutive months before being thrown out of the country, and without a penny, by his 'indigenous' rival, Sheikh Karume, who, according to Okello, never really took part in the revolution). The revolution was arguably bloody.

According to *BBC News online* of May 8, 2010, as many as seventeen thousand people were killed in the revolution.[23] Since then political killings have continued apace largely because of the way the regime itself evolved and, also because previous killings have not been addressed by the authorities. As George Santayana said, 'Those who can't remember the past are condemned to repeat it.'

Significantly however, the proliferation of these killings and enforced disappearances continued long after Nyerere had moved in (some say with the tacit approval of the West) to organise an *Anschluss*, shortly after the revolution.

Nonetheless, the hastily forged political Union (there is contention that the Union lacks a proper legal basis) between Tanganyika and Zanzibar from whence the country's current name Tanzania derives, has caused more friction between the two countries than anything else; and, history has shown that when tensions begin to mount they very seldom abate; rather they evolve.

The Union between Tanganyika and Zanzibar is no different to other Unions around the world. So, the mainland authorities i.e. Tanganyikans, should be encouraged by its peers not to overreact whenever the issue of the Union is mentioned.

When the people of Quebec talk of seceding from the rest

---

23 http://news.bbc.co.uk/2/hi/africa/country_profiles/3850393.stm

of Canada, the Canadian government does not send armed troops into the province. Rather, the matter is often resolved amicably and in a civilised manner, through a political dialogue or, if need be a referendum.

Similarly, when Alex Salmond of the Scottish National Party (SNP), keeps toying with the idea of Scotland becoming independent from the rest of the United Kingdom, Her Majesty's government does not put him in prison, or charge him with 'treason' as the Tanzanian government did in mid-May, 2008.[24]

In this incident, some people from the island of Pemba (which forms part of Zanzibar) were arrested in the middle of the night, by the Tanganyika security services and then flown to Dar-Es-Salaam where they were charged with 'treason'.

Prior to these arrests, some twelve people from Pemba island had gone to the United Nations representative in Dar-Es-Salaam, to deliver a letter in which they argued for the secession of Pemba from the rest of Zanzibar (and, by implication withdraw from the Union with Tanganyika).

Consequently, the mainland authorities which consider Zanzibar (which is semi autonomous) in the context of a province rather than a nation, hurriedly despatched its security services to apprehend those perceived to empathise with the idea of Pemba's independence. All were held incommunicado.

They included, amongst others, Salim Mohamed Abeid, the resident of Mtambile, Mohamed Mussa Ali of Kiwani and Hidaya Khamis Haji of Mkoani.

Others were, Ahmed Marshed, Khamis Machomane, Mariam Hamad Bakar all of whom were residents of Kichangani, Wawi in the region of Pemba South as well as Gharib Omar Ali, a resident of Wete and Jirani Ali Ahmed of Micheweni, Pemba North.

It seems strange, that since the sixties there has never been an actual resolution to the issue of the Union; considering Tanzania's rulers pride themselves on resolving the conflicts of neighbouring states.

Towards the end of his life, Nyerere was mediating in the

---

24 http://allafrica.com/stories/200805130433.html

conflict of Burundi. Consequently, it seems ironical that such skilled mediators were, and still are, incapable of finding a durable solution to the issue of the Union with Zanzibar. Is it perhaps that the mainland authorities wish to leave this matter unresolved for as long as it takes, because it is a convenient distraction from their own woes?

In this narrative, I set out to expose the hidden suppression which existed whilst European tourists were enjoying their *safari* holidays. Additionally, I intend to give voice to the victims who perished during Nyerere's rule and who can't therefore speak for themselves. Not least, I also feel I have something to say which is of public interest.

I hope and trust that this exposé will help widen the 'investigation process' mentioned earlier, which I nonetheless believe lacks credibility, as it is conducted by the same institution and the people that initiated the idea of Nyerere's sainthood in the first place; hence the need for a wider investigation process.

Widening the scope of the investigation is imperative, in my view, if only for the fact that Nyerere was not a president of some Catholic organisation but a head of state, whose decisions and actions affected many people in Tanzania and beyond, and in a variety of ways.

Also, in this edition I have included new facts and information which do not appear in the preceding two editions. This is because, at the time the two editions were released, I had not completed my own investigations into these incidents due to practical problems.

Conversely, I have not included other information which I would have liked to include because of lack of information due to the very same practical problems.

In some cases however, some of the facts had not been available to me until very recently, or where they were available to me, I had not finished having them cross-checked. Otherwise, much of the new information involves recent developments that have taken place since Nyerere expired in 1999.

In my introduction above, I quote some international legal instruments, which make human rights (and democracy) an international onus, over which no local potentate should be allowed to ride roughshod with apparent impunity.

Indeed, in recent times the whole issue of human rights has had an encouraging new dimension in so far as sub-Saharan Africa is concerned: the establishment of the United Nations High Commission for Human Rights and the International Criminal Court (ICC); a permanent court which was set up in 2002 to deal with war crimes and genocide around the world. It has no retrospective jurisdiction however, but it can deal with crimes committed after July 1, 2002, when the 1998 Rome Statute came into force.

Then there is the trial in Arusha, Tanzania, of those accused of involvement in the Rwandan genocide; the ongoing trial in Sierra Leone of those accused of crimes against humanity; the investigations of Uganda in relation to its military involvement in the Democratic Republic of Congo (DRC) which were carried out in 2004; and the indictment of the top leadership of the rebel movement in Uganda known as the Lord's Resistance Army (LRA) on multiple counts of crimes against humanity and war crimes.[25]

However, it is the apprehension of Charles 'Ghanky' Taylor, Liberia's former, notorious warlord, who is currently standing trial in The Hague that may mark the end of the culture of impunity in Africa.[26]

It also conveys a message to African rulers that none of them is above the law as some of them tend to believe.

Taylor was a friend of Foday Sankoh, leader of the Revolutionary United Front (RUF), a rebel movement that is responsible for numerous atrocious acts against the civilian populace in Sierra Leone during its ten years of brutal campaign against the government. The two men are said in the indictments to have met at a training camp in Libya in the 1970s.

Apparently, Taylor allegedly sold diamonds for the rebels and used the proceeds to procure weapons for them.

The charges he faces include terrorising the civilian population and collective punishment (acts of terrorism which is a War Crime-WC); unlawful killing: murder, which is a Crime Against Humanity (CAH); violence to life, health and physical or mental well-being of a person, in particular murder (WC): sexual violence involving rape (CAH), sexual slavery and any other form

25 http://news.bbc.co.uk/2/hi/4320124.stm
26 http://www.charlestaylortrial.org/trial-background/who-is-charles-taylor/

of sexual violence (CAH); outrages upon personal dignity (WC): physical violence involving violence to life, health and physical or mental well-being of persons, in particular cruel treatment (WC); other inhuman acts (CAH): use of child soldiers involving conscripting or enlisting children under the age of 15 years into armed forces or groups or using them to participate actively in hostilities which is a Violation of International Humanitarian Law (VIHL): abductions and forced labour; enslavement (CAH) and pillage (WC).

Altogether Taylor, who at the height of his power-drunken stupor, likened himself to Jesus Christ, is facing 11 charges over his support for the rebels in Sierra Leone; although some people might have liked to see him stand trial on similar charges for the equally brutal war he pursued in his own country.

On May 26, 2008, Ethiopia's Supreme Court sentenced Colonel Mengistu Haile Mariam, the country's former brutal despot, nicknamed Africa's Pol Pot, to death in absentia.[27]

It overturned, on appeal, the ruling by the High Court of December 12, 2006, sentencing Mengistu and eighteen of his most senior *aides*, including former Vice-President Fissiha Desta and Selassie Wogderesse, the former prime minister, to life in prison.

Mengistu, who at the time of writing this introduction was living in Zimbabwe, conducted a 'Red Terror' campaign in Ethiopia in which hundreds of thousands were killed or fled into exile.

According to *The Times,* of London, December 13, 2006, 'It was not uncommon in the mid-1980s to see students, suspected government critics or rebel sympathisers hanging from lamp posts each morning'.

Other victims were simply executed (without trial) in the notorious state prison on the outskirts of the capital, Addis Ababa.

Mengistu himself was reported to have regularly participated in the garrotting and shooting dead of opponents in order to 'lead by example'.

However, Ethiopia's Supreme Court passed the death sentence noting that the defendants' crimes amounted to genocide.

According to *The Times*, 1,018 people were known to have been convicted towards the end of 2006, for their role in the 'Red

---

27 http://news.bbc.co.uk/2/hi/africa/7420212.stm

63

Terror' campaign.

In February, 2007, the International Criminal Court (ICC) issued arrest warrants for Ahmed Harun and Ali Mohamed Ali Abdel-Rahman, also known as Ali Kushayb, for war crimes and crimes against humanity.

At the time the warrants were issued, the former was a Sudanese government minister and the latter a *Janjaweed* militia leader.[28]

Additionally, on July 14, 2008, International Criminal Court (ICC) Prosecutor, Luis Moreno-Ocampo, submitted to the judges, an application for the issuance of an arrest warrant (under Article 58) against Sudanese President, Omar Hassan Ahmad Al Bashir, for genocide, crimes against humanity and war crimes in Darfur.

The prosecution contends that Al Bashir masterminded and implemented a plan to destroy in substantial part the *Fur, Masalit* and *Zaghawa* groups on account of their ethnicity.

Apparently, the arrest warrant was issued on March 4, 2009, by a panel of judges in The Hague, on the charges presented by the prosecutor of the International Criminal Court (ICC) but stopped short of charging Bashir with the crime of genocide.

However, according to Laurence Blairon, the court's spokeswoman, Bashir was criminally responsible for 'intentionally directing attacks against an important part of the civilian population of Darfur, Sudan, murdering, exterminating, raping, torturing and forcibly transferring large numbers of civilians and pillaging their property'.

On July 12, 2010, the International Criminal Court (ICC) issued a second warrant for President Bashir for charges of genocide. This followed a ruling by appeals judges at the International Criminal Court (ICC), on February 3, 2010, that the court's pre-trial chamber should review its earlier decision not to include the charge of genocide in the arrest warrant against Bashir.[29]

In addition to the charges he already faces President Bashir is now charged with 'genocide by killing, genocide by causing serious bodily or mental harm and genocide by deliberately inflicting on each target group conditions of life calculated to bring

---

28 http://www.guardian.co.uk/world/2007/may/02/sudan
29 http://www.bbc.co.uk/news/10603559

about the group's physical destruction.' Bashir, is the first sitting president to be issued with an arrest warrant by the International Criminal Court (ICC).

Earlier, on May 24, 2008, Jean-Pierre Bemba Gombo, the former vice president of the Democratic Republic of Congo (DRC), was apprehended in the Belgian capital, Brussels, on charges of war crimes and crimes against humanity.

This followed an arrest warrant which was issued by the International Criminal Court over atrocities that were allegedly committed by Bemba's forces in 2002, in the Central Africa Republic (CAR).

Apparently, Bemba, leader of the *Mouvement pour la Liberation du Congo*, i.e. Movement for the Liberation of Congo, which later transformed itself into a political party, had been asked by Ange Felix-Patasse, the former president of the Central Africa Republic (CAR), to help put down a coup attempt.

Whilst in the Central Africa Republic, Bemba's forces allegedly committed widespread abuses of human rights including massive sexual crimes.

Eventually, President Felix-Patasse was overthrown the following year and his successor, President François Bozizé, pressed charges for murder and rape against Bemba. These were referred to The Hague where Bemba is now awaiting trial following his arrest in Belgium.[30]

Towards the end of the previous year, the International Criminal Court (ICC) was considering opening new cases in Darfur region over attacks on peacekeepers and humanitarian workers. In September, 2007, rebels in the Darfur town of Haskanita killed twelve Africa Union peacekeepers. Indeed, on June 17, 2010, two rebel leaders namely, Abdallah Banda Abakaer Nourain and Saleh Mohamed Jerbo Jamus, appeared at the International Criminal Court (ICC), to face war crimes charges over these attacks.[31]

Also, according to the *International Herald Tribune* of June 14, 2006, ministers of an Eastern Africa group agreed to draw up a list of Somali warlords suspected of committing crimes against humanity, so that they could be presented to the International

---

30 http://news.bbc.co.uk/2/hi/africa/7418932.stm
31 http://www.bbc.co.uk/news/10338072

Criminal Court (ICC) for prosecution.

There is also the case of Thomas Lubanga Dyilo, who led the ethnic *Hema Union des Patriotes Congolais* (i.e. Union of Congolese Patriots) militia group based in the Ituri region of eastern Democratic Republic Congo (DRC). Lubanga, who was transferred to The Hague on March 17, 2006, became the first war crimes suspect to be charged at the International Criminal Court (ICC). He is charged *inter alia* with 'enlisting children under the age of fifteen into armed groups; conscripting children under the age of fifteen into armed groups and using children under the age of fifteen to participate actively in hostilities'.

According to *BBC News online* of August 28, 2006, other charges against Lubanga who, for six years had been fighting '... partly for the control of Ituri's large deposits of gold', may follow, once sufficient evidence has been compiled.[32] These may include murder, torture, rape and mutilations apparently carried out by rebels under Lubanga's command. Some credible human rights groups say, in one massacre, Lubanga's savage militiamen killed civilians using a sledgehammer.

On October 17, 2007, Germain Katanga, also known as Simba, who led the ethnic *Lendu Force de Résistance Patriotique en Ituri* (*FRPI*), i.e. Forces for Patriotic Resistance, also based in Ituri region, became the second warlord to be sent to the International Criminal Court (ICC) to face charges of war crimes and crimes against humanity.

The *FRPI* militia group are accused of carrying out the massacres of *Hema* people, in the bitter inter-ethnic war involving various militia groups (some of whom are yet to be brought to book) in the Ituri region, where by the end of 2003, an estimated 50.000 people had been killed and hundreds of thousands left homeless.[33]

Also, on February 6, 2008, Mathieu Ngudjolo Chui (also known as Cui Cui Ngudjolo) was arrested and transferred to the International Criminal Court in The Hague to face charges of war crimes and crimes against humanity.

As the highest commander of the *Front des Nationalistes et Intégrationnistes* (*FNI*), i.e. Allied Forces of the Nationalist and

---

32 http://news.bbc.co.uk/2/hi/africa/5293094.stm
33 http://news.bbc.co.uk/2/hi/africa/7050506.stm

Integrationist Front, Ngudjolo is alleged, amongst other crimes, to have played an essential role in the planning and implementation of an indiscriminate attack against the village of Bogoro in Ituri, in February, 2003.

Other Congolese warlords being sought by the International Criminal Court include Bosco Ntaganda ('the terminator'), the alleged chief of staff of *Congrès National Pour la Défence du People* (*CNDP*), i.e. Congress for the Defence of the People, and General Laurent Nkunda (alias Laurent Nkunda Mahoro Bwatare) who was reportedly arrested by the Rwandese authorities on January 22, 2009.[34]

On January 9, 2009, the son of former Liberian President Charles Taylor was sentenced by a United States court to 97 years in prison for torture.

Apparently, Charles McArthur Emmanuel, also known as Chuckie Taylor, was the head of the notorious Anti-Terrorist Unit (ATU) whilst his father ruled Liberia.

Imposing the sentence, United States District Judge Cecilia M Altonaga stated that 'It is hard to conceive of any more serious offences against the dignity and the lives of human beings'. She added that 'the international community condemns torture'.[35] A month later, a similar view was unequivocally stated in Kenya.

On February, 12, 2009, Kenya's Parliament voted against a bill that would have established a special tribunal to try those implicated in the 2008 post-election violence which claimed 1,500 lives.

By rejecting the Bill, the Members of Parliament (MPs) openly expressed lack of faith in Kenya's justice system. For that reason, they wanted those involved in the violence (a sealed list of which had been handed to former United Nations Secretary-General Kofi Annan, by Mr Justice Phillip Waki who chaired the commission of inquiry into the violence) should be tried by the International Criminal Court (ICC) in The Hague.

According to *BBC News online,* of February 12, 2009, some Kenyan MPs felt that creating a special local tribunal would entrench the culture of impunity.[36]

Still more encouraging, towards the latter part of 2006, following

---

34 http://www.timesonline.co.uk/tol/news/world/africa/article5576706.ece
35 http://news.bbc.co.uk/2/hi/americas/7820069.stm
36 http://news.bbc.co.uk/2/hi/africa/7886395.stm

concerted pressure from the international community, Senegal did finally agree to put Hissene Habre on trial.

Habre, who led Chad from 1982 to 1990, is charged over the activities of his Intelligence Service, which is accused of arbitrary arrests, mass murder and systematic torture.[37] Looking back, examples of state-sanctioned political killings were also commonplace in the Uganda of Idi Amin; the Guinea of Ahmed Sékou Touré; the Central Africa Republic (CAR) of Jean Bédel Bokassa; the Equatorial Guinea of Francisco Marcias Ngwema; the Liberia of Master-Sergeant Samwel Kenyon Doe and the Rwanda of Grégoire Kayibanda; especially against members of the minority *Tutsi* community whom he routinely referred to as '*inyenzi*' i.e. cockroaches. In December 1963, for example, some 14.000 *Tutsis* were systematically killed in the southern province of Gikongoro. It seems that this was a prelude to the horror of genocide that was sparked, but planned earlier, by the assassination of President Habyarimana Juvénal, a *Hutu*, on the evening of April 6, 1994. The genocide claimed an estimated 800.000 lives, mostly *Tutsis;* in the Nigeria of General Sani Abacha; the Togo of Gnassingbé Eyadéma; the Malawi of *Ngwazi* (chief-of-chiefs) Dr Hastings Kamuzu Banda, just to name a few countries.

The tyrannical rule of these despots, together with those whose atrocious crimes I have outlined above (and in the main section of this book), killed greater numbers of their own people than at any other time in the continent's political history.

With that in mind, it would be no exaggeration to say that a black African today may enjoy far more legal protection under a white man than under the rule of his own kind.

When in 1974, the people of the Indian Ocean Island of Mayotte chose to remain under French control, very few Africans understood why they did this. Of course, the other three islands namely, Grande Comoro (Ngazidja), Mohéli and Anjoun voted for independence which they proclaimed on July 6, 1975. However, as discussed later in this narrative, within weeks of declaring independence, things started to go terribly wrong. First, there was a Nyerere-sponsored *coup d'état* which brought Ali Soilih, a declared socialist to power.

Soilih's regime adopted highly controversial policies; policies

---

37 http://news.bbc.co.uk/2/hi/africa/5140818.stm

68

which included *inter alia*, discouraging the study of history on the basis that it was recorded by the reviled colonists.

To be sure, the president ordered vital public records incinerated, claiming that they were also written by the same colonial authorities. Although since independence the islands' economy had deteriorated, President Soilih still found time to legalise the use of cannabis throughout the Comoros. It is unclear why the Comorian president considered these measures to be more important than Comoro's long-term stability and economic growth.

What was clear, however, was that even after President Soilih was toppled and killed (1978), the chaos in the Comoros continued unabated. At this point, some Comorians lost their lives on the high seas as they attempted to reach French administered Mayotte. Others, who were able, fled the islands to France (or, elsewhere in the West) in order to escape repression and to seek legal protection there. Not only that, but according to *French Press Agency* (*AFP*) about a third of 200.000 residents of Mayotte did arrive there illegally from the Comoros. It has to be emphasised that the Mahorans were not reversing route i.e. fleeing Mayotte to the Comoros.

On the contrary, Mayotte remained comparatively stable and prosperous, with a Gross Domestic Product (GDP) of about ten times higher than that of the Comoros.

On March 29, 2009, the residents of Mayotte voted overwhelmingly to become a full part of France.[38] At this juncture, chaos in the Comoros had reached its nadir having, since declaring itself independent, experienced twenty *coups d'état*.

Whether the Mahorans originally declined independence to avoid a similar mess that was later witnessed in the Comoros; or whether there were other factors, is irrelevant at this point. What is relevant is that by casting a 'yes' vote, the Mahorans made it abundantly clear to the rest of the world that they prefer complete legal protection of their former colonial power rather than protection under the rule of their own kind. The same could be said of Sierra Leone: if the British authorities had not intervened there to end the orgy of mutilations, how long would that have continued? What of those African refugees

---

38 http://news.bbc.co.uk/2/hi/europe/7970450.stm

whose bodies are regularly washed up in the Canaries, Malta, Italy or elsewhere in Europe, when their makeshift rafts capsize on the high seas as they attempt to reach a white man's land to seek legal protection there? What does the loss of such young African lives tell the world in terms of social stability and human rights back in their own homelands?

The institution of the International Criminal Court (ICC), will not only act as deterrent to potential murderous African rulers but will also invariably give dignity to the memory of those who suffered and perished, wherever a local potentate or warlord is made to account for his actions before the International Criminal Court.

In other words, the establishment of the International Criminal Court (ICC) has completely redefined the dynamism of political power and the rule of law, emphasising that criminal abuse of public governmental power will no longer go unchallenged or unpunished in this modern era. It is, as I noted earlier, a refreshing, new dawn in sub-Saharan Africa with regard to fundamental freedoms and human rights.

Notwithstanding, there is need on the part of black Africans themselves, to assume a totally uncompromising attitude wherever a local potentate tries to take away their basic rights. They should always ensure that there is transposed within a system of government, in-built checks and balances against any possible assumption of sovereign authority by a single individual.

Furthermore, they should ensure, as a matter of right and principle, the institution of investigative (or, controlling) commissions, with the view to examining past and present abuses in their own countries. Should they fail to do this, they will invalidate their right to deprecate the implied actions of foreign forces who have been accused of transgression against black people.

In the following narrative, I take the reader to the brutal world of Tanzania's own Intelligence Service against its own kind. Please read on.

Ludovick Simon Mwijage
Copenhagen, Denmark
September 30, 2010

Mbabane, Swaziland

It was Tuesday, December 6, 1983. A friend and I had just finished a frugal lunch in a shed next to a butchery in Mbabane, Swaziland, opposite the *Swazi Observer* newspaper premises. We had bought beef from the butcher, roasted it, and then eaten it with hard porridge. It was a popular place where people would meet for a midday meal and chat.

I had just lunched with a Kenyan friend, John Cartridge, who had been stranded in Swaziland for several days. His version of how he came to be in this predicament was not entirely coherent, though it sounded circumstantial. He said he had been working in Lesotho, another southern African kingdom, as a motor mechanic and a businessman. Cartridge even boasted of having repaired the official car of King Moshoeshoe II, the Lesotho monarch who died in 1996. He said he was stranded because his passport had been impounded by a local hotel where he and a Malawian business associate had failed to pay their bills from a previous visit.

Rumour had it that Cartridge's passport had indeed been impounded by the hotel, but only after a business deal with the hotel turned sour. Cartridge and his partner had apparently tried to sell petrol economisers to the hotel's manager. As it turned out, the economisers proved quite useless to the manager and, according to some sources, he then decided to keep Cartridge's passport in the hope of recovering his money. Cartridge strenuously denied this claim.

Whatever the truth, it was because Cartridge's passport had been impounded that he was unable to proceed home. It was at this time that I first got to know him, through another Kenyan expatriate called Okienya who was then working with Posts and Telecommunications as an accountant in Mbabane.

I had come to Swaziland from Nairobi in April 1983 to seek refuge after a spate of arrests in Tanzania, my home country, in January. Julius Nyerere's government was arresting people it accused of dissention. I considered myself unsafe in Nairobi because of the proximity of Tanzania and because of threats I had received before the Kenyan authorities transferred me to Thika Refugee Reception Centre.

A benign German Catholic church minister at Thika

THE NAIROBI TIMES

PRICE 2/-

MONDAY, JANUARY 31, 1983

No. 378

Dar teacher flees to Kenya

By NOEL OKOTH

A TANZANIAN schoolteacher has fled his country into Kenya over what he terms as indiscriminate arrest by President Julius Nyerere's regime of people suspected to be sympathisers of the recent coup plot.

Mr. Ludovick Mwijage, a Bukoba town resident, told *The Nairobi Times* yesterday th he defected only this r... h after a wave of arrests in the lake-shore region in the past few days. He arrived in Kenya through the border town of Busia on Saturday

member of the Tanzania's Chama cha Mapinduzi (CCM), said the arrests have so far netted at least 400 civilians in Bukoba and Mwanza, among them a handful of his colleagues. Said he, "We are unfairly considered dissidents. My colleagues who subscribe to the same views

over the current economic and political issue in the country were arrested".

According to Mwijage, the arrests have intensified in the

two lakeshore towns because the "government thinks there is stiff opposition" in these areas. He said there was growing discontent against political and economic policies of the Tanzanian regime. Of the recent party elections, the schoolteacher said, "It was like putting old wine in new bottles.".

Saudis open oil pipeline

JEDDAH, Sunday, *(Reuter)* King Fahd of Saudi Arabia today inaugurated a giant oil pipeline across the kingdom to a new industrial city created in the desert on the Red Sea coast.

The king, accompanied by members of the royal family, normally opened the 11.5 billion "petroline" that will fuel huge refining and petrochemicals plants being built at Yanbu and supply a crude oil marine export terminal.

The 1,200-km pipeline, which began pumping crude on trial in July 1981, will allow some of the kingdom's oil exports to by-pass the vulnerable straits of Hormuz at the mouth of the gulf.

The $1.85 million barrels of

Turn to back page

Beirut artillery

town had given me 4200 Kenya shillings, enough to cover the price of a one-way air ticket out of Kenya to Khartoum, Sudan. But two of my fellow countrymen in a similar situation to mine were still traversing Uganda, short of cash and hoping to reach Juba, southern Sudan. Uganda was unsafe; there were still many Tanzanian security officials in the country after their invasion in 1979.

I decided to divide the money between my two colleagues and sent it through a courier, to ensure they left Uganda at once. I then contacted friends in Europe to enable me to leave Kenya, where I had arrived on January 28, 1983.

I had now decided against going to Khartoum but had settled for Swaziland. Friends in the Nienburg Teachers' Union in the then Federal Republic of Germany (West Germany), arranged to have my ticket paid and advised me where to collect it. After picking up the ticket at *Lufthansa*'s offices in Nairobi, I returned to Thika Refugee Reception Centre to bid farewell to friends, all of them fellow African refugees. I also felt inclined to thank the authorities at the Centre for the great kindness and courage they displayed in working with refugees.

I then went to Nairobi to thank the Tanzanian women's community who had hidden me from the day I crossed into the capital until I was transferred to the Thika Centre. In those early days in Kenya, the Tanzanian women paid for my room at a guest house they believed was safe; they also gave me money for small items. I was deeply moved by the love, care and concern they showed for me, and felt proud of this wonderful part of the African cultural heritage. Out of concern for my own security, I bade farewell without saying when I was leaving Kenya and where I was going. I thought of the old African saying, 'Never spill millet in the midst of hens,' and believed my hostesses understood my behaviour and would forgive me.

I have always wondered how I managed to fly from Jomo Kenyatta International Airport without arousing suspicion. I had no baggage; all I had was a paper bag containing a telex from Germany, several letters from Tanzanian friends, a toothbrush and a tube of toothpaste, and a singlet and a change of underwear.

* * * * * *

Having no baggage to claim, I proceded through Customs at Matsapha Airport, Swaziland, without delay, thanks largely to holding a Commonwealth passport. I did not require a visa and had no cause to explain my situation to Swazi officials. I proceeded to Mbabane, the capital, taking a ride with an Eritrean UN official who had collected a relative from the same flight.

By the time I arrived in Mbabane it was late afternoon, and I noted that the following day was a public holiday. Finding accommodation was my main concern as I wandered aimlessly along Allister Miller Street, Mbabane's main road. As I passed *Jabula Inn*, a main road hotel, a lean man who looked to be in his late fifties or early sixties emerged. Apparently he had detached himself from a group of people he was conferring with in the hotel foyer. He wore a fez hat and was far too dark to be Swazi (most Swazis are light in complexion).

His right hand held a set of joined beads which he counted quickly and repeatedly, as if he was meditating or praying, although he continued to talk with people as he did this. He gesticulated and looked at me as if he recognised me. I returned the look, thinking I recognised him from somewhere. We exchanged glances and it occurred to me that I knew the man, but I couldn't recall from where.

He made the first move, greeting me in *Swahili*. I returned his greeting, surging forward to shake his hand. There was no doubt the man I had just greeted was the renowned Nairobi-based Tanzanian astrologer, Sheikh Yahya Hussein. Now I remembered seeing his picture in newspapers almost every day, advertising his trade, although I could never work out how he recognised someone like me he had never seen before.

Hussein invited me into his room, cutting through a long queue of people who had come to consult him. He was, as he frequently told the Swazi press, a prophet, faith-healer, palm reader and a fortune teller, not merely an astrologer who could determine the influence of the planets on human affairs. He even told the local media that King Hussein of Jordan was one of his clients, and he provided them with a photograph of him shaking hands with the late Hashemite monarch. This, of course, generated more business for him.

Hussein led me into his room with quick, short strides,

nodding at people in the queue. He was booked in Room 1 at *Jubula Inn* and had a room-within-a-room inside his quarters. This provided him with the space he needed: one room for 'consultancy', the other for his private sleeping quarters.

He invited me into his private room; it seemed there was someone else in the 'consulting' room. A beautiful woman, about half Hussein's age, sat on the unkempt bed, seemingly vegetating. She held a can of Castle Beer which seemed empty. Hussein talked briefly to the man in the other room, then joined us.

Africans generally respect elders as sages of infinite wisdom. Hussein's professional standing and the trust others confided in him encouraged me to tell all. Moreover, he had the title of sheikh, which, with its spiritual overtones, projected a sense of moral purity and authority. To my surprise, he knew quite a bit about my situation.

Before I had finished my story Hussein telephoned the receptionist and asked her to come to his room. A tall, well-built and big-eyed woman called Thembi Simelane, arrived and Hussein instructed her to give me a room for several nights at his expense. She agreed, but said the vacant room had to be tidied up. As we waited Hussein asked me to place my paper bag, which I still nursed on my lap, under his bed. He wanted me to go and buy some articles for him. On my return I retrieved my paper bag and, being very tired, proceeded to the room Hussein had hired for me. It was there that I realised that some items in my paper bag were missing: the telex from Germany, the letter I had received from my friend Amos Ole Chiwele, a refugee recognised by the United Nations (UN), and the cover of my air ticket.

I hastily returned to Hussein's room hoping to recover these items, which I nevertheless doubted could have fallen out of the packet. A thorough check under Hussein's bed revealed no trace of the missing items. Hussein supervised as I searched the bed, claiming that nobody had touched my bag during my absence. I did not, at any time, imply this might have occurred. The items had unfortunately disappeared, rather mysteriously.

Swaziland granted me political asylum within weeks. But due to other factors which I had overlooked in Kenya (Tanzanian troops were stationed next door in Mozambique), the United Nations High Commissioner for Refugees (UNHCR) in Mbabane was working hard to find a country in which I could be permanently settled. Indeed, on the day Cartridge and I lunched together I had only one and a half months in which to leave for resettlement in Canada.

* * * * * *

Having completed our lunch, Cartridge glanced at his watch like someone about to miss an important appointment. I wondered aloud if he was pushed for time. He said he wasn't and suggested we go for a cold beer at the *Mediterranean Restaurant*. I considered it a reasonable idea.

The *Mediterranean Restaurant* is situated on Allister Miller Street, in uptown Mbabane, and was owned by people of Asian origin from what was then the People's Republic of Mozambique. The restaurant offered well-grilled Mozambique prawns and generally had a superb menu. In a country like Tanzania, with its rampant poverty, the *Mediterranean* would have ranked as a restaurant unfit for second-class citizens. In Swaziland, where abject poverty is minimal, it was a place for everyone.

It was hot and sunny, typical of Mbabane at that time of year. We felt instantly relieved as we arranged ourselves on the raised bar seats. Cartridge ordered the first drinks; we sipped, then switched to East African politics. I forget who initiated the discussion, but recall that it continued for some time and attracted a lot of listeners.

We dwelt on Nyerere's popular thesis that black Africans are born socialists. Cartridge insisted that Nyerere, by introducing 'Ujamaa', was trying to enhance our traditional roots and values. I replied that if Africans were naturally socialists, there was no point in trying to convert them to what they were already supposed to be. Cartridge listed what he thought were Nyerere's achievements: unity, improved literacy, the provision of rudimentary health services, water for rural areas, and so on. I replied that these were not necessarily achievements that could be attributed to 'Ujamaa' or a political system which prohibited other parties. I cited countries such as Botswana, Mauritius, Senegal, and even Egypt as having achieved much the same, without declaring themselves socialists, and under democratic systems that allowed political parties to operate.

My contention was that no achievement could justify the existence of a dictatorial system of government: dictatorships deprive people of their liberty. I argued that Tanzania's achievements under Nyerere were in danger of being eroded because the system lacked permanent democratic institutions. No machinery existed for the smooth transfer of power from one group to another; nor was there any means for citizens to point out their leaders' mistakes before those mistakes assumed disastrous proportions.

I pointed out to Cartridge that the absence of democratic values in Tanzania and Africa generally would give the impression of a dangerous continent, perpetually unpredictable. Such an environment was not conducive to economic growth and social progress and would frighten investors and donors alike. A stable and relatively predictable Africa would be attractive to investors, who would then be more willing to invest in industry. Africa would prosper, where now it suffers political and economic deprivation.

To drive my point even further, I told Cartridge that 'Ujamaa' was Nyerere's single-minded ideology; Tanzanians would soon start wondering what the experiment was all about.

Cartridge and I then turned to the debt crisis facing Africa. I argued against always blaming external factors: donor nations; the poor international economic order being unfavourable to Africa; the breakdown of commodity prices; inflation, and even colonialism, although some of these arguments are valid. The fact is that when the colonialists left about forty years ago, Africans were left with the resources to develop themselves into nations at least as resilient as before colonialism. Unfortunately, this did not happen.

Moreover, the management of internal policies is just as important as how sub-Saharan governments handle their external debt. It is not too late to develop sub-Saharan countries into viable, mature nations. The primary task of governments is to create viable economies. Yet, with endless infighting and dependence on foreign subsidies, the assertions of African leaders that they control their countries and their futures is greatly diminished. Failed African economies do much to bolster the claim to credibility of South Africa's largely white-managed economy, which outshines any other on the continent.

As I expounded my ideas to Cartridge, I became quite oblivious to my surroundings. Suddenly I realised that a short, brown woman was standing in front of us, her eyes firmly set on us as if she was preparing to make a point.

* * * * * *

The woman in a white tight-fitting skirt introduced herself as Lindiwe (years later, my efforts to find her proved futile). I was uncertain whether she had been there throughout our conversation; nor could I work out whether she had been serving us all along or if she had come to replace another member of staff.

We exchanged greetings with Lindiwe, who promptly proposed to accompany us after she finished work at 4pm. Cartridge and I were caught off-guard by her proposal, and Lindiwe seemed reluctant to be turned down. Such behaviour is rare from African woman, and is provocative and challenging. Cartridge and I probed each other's faces trying to establish who Lindiwe had her eye on; her frequent smiles and flirty manner suggested I was the target.

After 4 pm we proceeded with Lindiwe to Msunduza Township, where I had secured accommodation at a Youth Centre paid for by United Nations High Commissioner for Refugees (UNHCR). My room was tiny but neat, with a wooden bunk bed, a small table and chair and a reading light.

We had some beers which we concealed in paper bags— the Youth Centre, run by a church organisation, did not allow the consumption of alcohol on its premises. Lindiwe did not drink at all that day. I obtained some cups from the matron, who later joined us with two seamstresses from the Youth Centre. As we talked and joked, I heard a knock on the door. I opened the door and there was Jo.

I had known Jo briefly and he was something of an enigma to me. I had met him two days earlier in Manzini, Swaziland's second largest town. The events preceding that meeting with Jo, with the knowledge of hindsight, need repeating.

A friend of mine (at least I thought so then), Colonel Ahmed Mkindi, Tanzania's Military Attaché in Zimbabwe who has since retired, had persuaded me to move to Manzini, claiming that my security was threatened if I remained at one place for too long. I told him I would confer with UNHCR officials; he objected, saying UNHCR lacked the resources to afford the comfortable abode he had in mind and was prepared to pay for. That day, Mkindi really looked concerned about my safety.

During his visits to Swaziland, Mkindi would put forward various proposals to me, for example, obtaining assistance from Libya to set up a clandestine radio station. This would be a radio station similar to the one Zanzibar dissidents had set up in the early seventies, but funded by different sources. Alternatively, he suggested reactivating the group of young Tanzanians who were clamouring for political and economic change. My replies were always that he should sell his ideas to people in Tanzania. I also made clear that I disapproved of seeking assistance from an idiosyncratic regime such as Libya.

Colonel Mkindi and I never felt free with each other. We did not talk like compatriots holding similar political opinions, let alone like comrades-in-arms. He contradicted himself constantly, and he had that perpetual worried look of a person of questionable character. He would introduce sensitive political topics about Tanzania, and then be unable to hold eye contact during the discussion. His eyes would rotate sideways, like someone in possession of stolen goods.

I remember one day when Mkindi jetted in from Harare and came directly to the Youth Centre to find out what progress had been made regarding my departure to Canada. He proposed that, because I received only a small allowance from UNHCR, we should go to the Swazi Plaza in Mbabane to buy some food and he would pay. Mkindi bought me so much food and other items that it looked almost as if I was going to open a retail store at the Youth Centre. Far from being happy, I was shocked. He had even offered to buy me a bottle of whisky; I talked him out of it, saying such luxuries were best forgotten in exile.

While we were loading the goods into his car, a Ugandan expatriate and friend of mine, David Magumba Gwaita, suddenly appeared. I introduced Mkindi to my friend, but to my amazement Mkindi appeared to panic. Even Magumba noticed that Mkindi had suddenly become disorientated, but we could not work out why. Magumba thanked Mkindi for his care and concern and offered to accompany us to the Youth Centre to help unload the items. As my

Ugandan friend followed us, Mkindi explained his sudden change of mood: he said he did not wish to be seen in my company, as this could result in terrible consequences if it was reported to Tanzania.

I was not convinced. He had come to see me many times and had acted as 'courier' between me and some people in Tanzania. Many Tanzanians in Swaziland, including some he might have had reason to fear, had seen us together. Mkindi was, for example, a friend of Ahmed Kombe, who at that time worked as a teacher at the Institute of Health Sciences in Mbabane. On one occasion Mkindi extended an invitation to me from Kombe to have dinner. For several hours after dinner at Kombe's home we discussed the political situation in Tanzania, critically analysing the appalling economic conditions and growing poverty.

A week after that dinner a junior Tanzanian army officer stationed in Mozambique had brought a personal message from one of our compatriots in Maputo. This young officer was himself sympathetic to our cause. His message basically implied that Ahmed Kombe was the brother of the then Director of Intelligence (DI) in Tanzania. On the day Mkindi purchased groceries for me, I asked him if this was true. He reacted without astonishment. Ahmed Kombe's brother, Imran Hussein Kombe, who was later shot dead by the police after supposedly mistaking him for a notorious 'car thief', then held the rank of brigadier. Since Mkindi himself held a high military rank, I would have expected he would know Imran Kombe well, even if he did not know or approve of his past activities. I also found it surprising that Mkindi was unaware that Ahmed Kombe was his colleague's brother.

'You don't seem surprised to know that Ahmed Kombe is Brigadier Kombe's brother', I asked him as we silently headed towards the Youth Centre in Msunduza Township.

'Err... what? No, sure I am,' he replied rather absent-mindedly. When I asked him how much he knew about Brigadier Kombe, Mkindi replied that he knew him only in a 'professional context'. I made a note of that phrase.

'Professional context? Does it mean that you too work for the secret service', I inquired. He seemed distressed and failed to maintain eye contact; his face had a guilt-ridden appearance. Finally, he attempted to ingratiate me by saying I was an 'intelligent, perceptive young man,' I cut him short before he could finish, as I thought he had resorted to this tactic to evade an important matter. His avoidance of the question prompted me to dwell on it.

Mkindi now said that by 'professional context' he had meant that both he and Brigadier Kombe were in the army.

'Imran and I are soldiers,' he said, mopping his sweating face with his right palm. But he referred to the Director of Intelligence informally, by his first name, rather than by his rank or surname. To me, this suggested that Mkindi knew Brigadier Kombe better than he cared to admit. The alarm went off and, for the first time, I started to become worried.

The previous month, the then Attorney-General of Swaziland, Patrick Makanza, himself a Tanzanian, held a christening ceremony for his young son. Among those present were Mkindi, who sat next to me, and Ahmed Kombe, who was busy taking photographs. I soon realised that Kombe had taken more pictures of me and Mkindi than of anyone else. Yet this never seemed to bother Mkindi, in spite of his later claim, in front of my Ugandan friend, that he did not want to be seen with me. After all, my Ugandan friend had nothing to do with Tanzanian politics, and I told Mkindi he had no reason to worry.

But it was the day Mkindi bought me the groceries that he finally persuaded me to move to Manzini. His argument was that he feared for my safety at the Youth Centre.

The next morning Mkindi arrived at the Youth Centre with a man he introduced as his friend, a former white Rhodesian (now Zimbabwe) who had since moved to South Africa. We loaded most of my belongings into the Rhodesian man's truck. I was not sure I was doing the right thing since being fed the security scare by Mkindi. For this reason I even refrained from informing the UNHCR of my move, since I wasn't sure I would stay very long in Manzini.

We stopped at many places on our way to Manzini. At each stop Mkindi would demand to eat something; he would also drink tea with a lot of sugar. He seemed unconcerned about controlling his eating, given that he was a fat man.

We pulled up at a boarding house in Manzini owned by a woman of mixed ancestry (coloured) known as Mrs Smith. It was situated on the left corner on the way to William Pitcher Teachers' College. It was a large room with two wide windows and good ventilation. Mkindi paid the full board for the month, and then demanded a receipt which he kept in his pocket. He had seemed particularly keen to retain the receipt; when I suggested that I should keep the receipt, he refused. 'No,' he said, he wanted to keep it as a 'souvenir.' He might have thought he was making a joke, but I failed to buy his 'souvenir' talk. My suspicion about his real intentions intensified. For instance, when I asked him how he had got to know of the guest house he wanted me to put up at, he answered that he had once spent a night there.

But that did not offer a direct answer to my question. The guest house was an isolated, quiet place with hardly any boarders—three at most. Moreover, I was not convinced that a senior diplomat, in normal circumstances, would have spent a night at a guest house on the outskirts of town, rather than in a hotel in the town centre. Even if Mkindi's story was believable, it did not explain why he had spent so much money buying food and other items for me. After all, he should have known that the place he wanted me to book into offered full boarding facilities.

The next morning I decided to go to Mbabane to collect my mail, which came through the offices of UNHCR. I still thought it was premature to inform them I had moved to Manzini. As I waited for a bus in front of *Uncle Charlie's Motel*, a white Volkswagen Golf car stopped in front of me. The lone driver lowered his window and invited me in. He was short and wore an unruly beard, like a student of Marxism-Leninism. Noticing that I was hesitant, he introduced himself as he talked through the lowered window. He said that he had seen me several times at the Youth Centre, where he claimed he went to visit a friend. He mentioned the name of a person I knew George Starita, a refugee from South Africa, who has since returned following the dismantling of apartheid.

By mentioning the name of someone (George) in the same boat as me, he established his credentials. I got into the car.

'My name is Joshua. People call me Jo. It saves time.' I told him my name. He said he recognised me, and that was why he had stopped. He said he never stopped for people he did not know; I said that with crime on the increase he could lose his car at gunpoint.

'This is it!' he said, and started driving aimlessly towards a local hospital which I knew was not the way to Mbabane.

He asked me if I was in a hurry, and I replied that I was. He excused himself, saying he wanted to talk to a friend 'for a few minutes' before heading to Mbabane. As it turned out, it was not to be a few minutes. Jo kept driving aimlessly around the area know as Two Sticks, stopping at several houses before he finally decided to drive to Mbabane. He had offered to give me a ride in the afternoon and had told me he would be going back to Manzini. Later I decided to take a bus back to Manzini; I had forgotten about him altogether. But he did not seem to have forgotten me.

That night I did not sleep, wondering why I had come to Manzini. Suspicion centred not only on Colonel Mkindi, but also on Manzini's proximity to Mozambique. Manzini is closer to Maputo than Mbabane is. During the night I decided that the reasons Mkindi had given as to why I ought to move were flimsy. I decided this would be my last night in Manzini. Early next morning I called a taxi, packed my items, and headed for the bus rank. An hour later I was back in Mbabane, at the Youth Centre.

Now here was Jo standing at my door, barely twenty-four hours since I had left Manzini. I told Mrs Smith, the landlady in Manzini that I had decided to leave, but did not tell her where I was going. I did not even ask for a refund of the money Mkindi had paid for the accommodation.

The big question was, how did Jo know I had gone back to the Youth Centre? Unless, of course, if he had gone to where I had briefly put up in Manzini and been told I had checked out. Possibly he had come to see if I had come back to the Youth Centre. But the questions persisted. How did he know where I had lived in Manzini? I had never mentioned it to him. Besides, we were not friends, and I did not know where he lived, nor did I wish to know. If he had gone to Manzini to look for me, what were his reasons? We were not friends and had nothing in common.

These thoughts raced through my mind when I opened the door and found myself facing Jo. I tried to dismiss my suspicions lest I should become paranoid. I invited him in and gave him my seat and a cup of beer I had in my hand. He greeted the others in the room and then blamed me for having left Manzini without telling him. He inquired, 'My friend, why didn't you tell me you were leaving Manzini?'

'Did I have to', I replied sharply. Suddenly the room fell

silent as everyone seemed to want to listen to the conversation. All eyes shifted to me; I immediately realised that the others in my room had not followed the exchange between Jo and myself. They had heard my question and it sounded impolite. I tried to correct their impression by saying that I did not mean to be rude to Jo; I had left Manzini for reasons of my own.

It was hot in Manzini, more so than in Mbabane, I told Jo. Lindiwe agreed. Jo said he had thought he would look me up to see how I was doing, and replied that it was very kind of him. My attention then shifted to the three women who had been in my room; they stood up and made for the door.

* * * * * *

Everybody was leaving. The two seamstresses and the matron said they had finished their work and were going to tend to family matters. Jo claimed he was going back into town to collect photographs for George Starita who was at the University of Swaziland (UNISWA). I could not understand why he had not collected the photographs on his way to the Youth Centre; after all, George often passed through the Youth Centre. Jo then suggested that he would check the Youth Centre again before going back to Manzini. I declined to say he should not, since I had not asked him in the first instance to come and see me.

John Cartridge now excused himself, saying he needed to meet someone at *Jabula Inn*. I thought his departure was intended to be tactful, in order to give Lindiwe and myself a chance to speak freely and privately. I had persuaded him to stay until we could see Lindiwe off, but he refused. I also asked Cartridge to phone my girlfriend, Imelda Khumalo, who was due to finish work shortly and expected me to meet her in town. I had provided him with her telephone number and instructions that I would be meeting her in about one and a half hours. Imelda was pregnant at the time and it was imperative that I should spend some time with her. I was worried that if I was late in meeting her she would show up at the Youth Centre and wonder what Lindiwe was doing in my room. On the other hand, I did not want to hurt Lindiwe's feelings by asking her to leave before she wished to.

Jo returned just as I prepared to see Lindiwe off. He offered to take us into town; on the way Lindiwe asked if I would buy her some *Kentucky Fried Chicken*. At *Kentucky*, after I had bought the chicken, I found to my surprise that Jo had paid for it before I could. I did not know whether Jo and Lindiwe knew each other, but a shrewd observer would have concluded they were at least familiar to each other. Why had Jo decided to entertain my visitor? Without unduly worrying further, I concluded that Jo was perhaps trying to catch her eye.

We dropped Lindiwe at her workplace. 'Take care you guys,' she said as she got out of the car waving to us.

By now Jo knew my timetable. With more than an hour left before my intended meeting with Imelda, he suggested I accompany him to the *Swazi Spa* in Ezulwini Valley, a fifteen minute drive from Mbabane. He said he was going to meet an uncle who had been attending a business meeting. He had established his credibility as an acquaintance, if not a friend, of a refugee like me, a stranger in a foreign country who would value any friendly act to fill the void left by the absence of loved ones from home. I now regarded Jo as someone who showed a touch of humanity; perhaps he had taken his own precious time and the trouble to find out where I had moved to. I thought it would be unfair to let him down, and agreed to accompany him to the *Swazi Spa*.

We had agreed he would bring me back immediately he had seen his uncle. But once he got behind the wheel he changed his mind, flooring the accelerator to increase speed. He had suddenly remembered his girlfriend in Manzini who he claimed also wanted to see his uncle. He said it had been a long time since he last saw his uncle, who had gone to England some time ago and was now back in Swaziland for a business meeting with some executives from the United Kingdom. I found elements of his story contradictory but dismissed them, thinking I had misunderstood the whole thing from the start. He was now silent, driving fast, possibly preoccupied with thoughts of his girlfriend in Manzini. Once there, he parked outside an elegant apartment, from which a small girl babbled something to him from a window. The words had no meaning for me; they seemed to mean something to Jo. When the girl attempted to come over to the car to see the visitor, Jo hurriedly retrieved her. Later I believed this was an attempt to prevent her from blurting out something to me that he would not have liked.

After waiting several minutes Jo's girlfriend got into the car beside him. She did not turn to look at or greet me, though I did notice her studying me through the rear-view mirror. Since she had found me in the car, I made no effort to initiate an exchange of greetings. More surprisingly, Jo, the friend who had requested that I accompany him, made not the slightest attempt to introduce us. Again, I found this most unusual, but then thought they might have had a quarrel.

We hardly spoke as we drove back from Manzini to Ezulwini Valley. When Jo and his girlfriend spoke, it was in English, which I later discovered was designed to hide their native tongue.

We pulled up at a parking lot reserved for guests of the *Swazi Spa Hotel*. The hotel was large and luxurious, probably rating as four star. At the hotel entrance, a man in uniform, very likely a porter greeted us with a slight bow. The hotel was packed with people, some rattling slot machines in the casino, others buying tokens for roulette, and some sitting quietly drinking. I looked for a place to sit; Jo bought some tokens for the slot machine; his girlfriend had mingled with the crowd in the passageway and disappeared.

Jo joined me, his hands full of tokens for the machines. There was nothing to be gained without venturing, he said. I said that even if I wanted to gain, I was doubtful whether I would opt for this type of venture. I watched him rattling the slot machines with their musical sounds, but no money was ejected. As he lost his last coin he screamed, 'Damn it,' and I knew he had lost his money.

I watched his reaction. He looked devastated, though he tried to suppress the expression on his face. His mouth seemed to have turned dry.

I reminded him of what he had said—nothing ventured, nothing gained—but he seemed unprepared for cracks that teased him rather than showed sympathy for his loss. He thought I was being unnecessarily sarcastic. I then reminded him that he had come to see his uncle, not to venture. At the mention of his uncle he immediately moved away from the slot machines and said he was coming back shortly. He returned with two full glasses of what looked like gin. He invited me to take one from his outstretched hands, saying his uncle had given us the gin.

'Where is your uncle', I asked.

'In the meeting,' he replied, adding that his uncle would be joining us shortly. I found this strange: his uncle buys us drinks without first asking what we drink. Still, I did not want to hurt my friend Jo by refusing his uncle's drink. Perhaps this is due to the African mentality of doing something for the sake of appeasing someone you feel you ought to respect.

I accepted the drink from Jo. But as I lifted the glass to say 'cheers,' I noticed the drink filled about three-quarters of the glass. Did this include the dilution, I wondered? Maybe. Asking saves a lot of guesswork; strangely, on this occasion, I failed to ask.

Before I could swallow my first sip, Jo announced that his girlfriend was in a hurry and had decided to take his car. He promised to take me back to Mbabane with his uncle before they returned to Manzini. I wondered whether his girlfriend had even seen his uncle, which was the sole purpose of her coming to Ezulwini. If the uncle was going to return to Manzini, why had she even bothered to come to the *Swazi Spa*?

These questions, like all the others, seemed to have no satisfactory answers. Foolishly, I dismissed them as other people's private matters which should not concern me. What a poor judge of character I was. I lifted my glass containing 'gin' and drank from it.

* * * * * *

Abduction

I lay on my back in surroundings that looked wet with dew. It was dark and silent, with the occasional sound of frogs from nearby ponds. I tried to lift my head but it was heavy; someone pushed me hard with a boot back to the ground. I thought I was dressed but couldn't be quite sure. I lifted an arm to mop my face, to detect if I had my spectacles on. I seemed to be still wearing them.

I was surrounded by people who spoke either Portuguese or English; I know both languages. The people around me looked like soldiers, with their guns pointed at me, but I could not figure out what they were. Was this a dream, a vision, a nightmare? Perhaps a terrible nightmare, I fearfully concluded.

Again and again I had this vision of men, three of them, one brandishing a pistol as they dragged me into a white Toyota car. The one with the pistol looked vicious and overweight. A jungle hat perched on his head, and he wore an overcoat. Another held what looked like a bayonet from a G-3 rifle. He looked like Jo, my companion for much of the day. The third man, a short fellow, pretended to be drunk and held a large red spotlight. I closed my eyes, and then opened them, unable to comprehend anything. Someone around me then ordered that I be lifted up.

Several pairs of hands held me and lifted me from the ground. I protested feebly that I should be left alone; the men hurled a barrage of insults at me. I now sat with my hands on my knees; soldiers cocked their guns, pointed them at me and surrounded me. Most of the soldiers had worn-out boots from which their toes protruded and their combat fatigues also looked worn-out. Many smoked tobacco rolled in paper and their bodies reeked of sweat; their mouths stank whenever they opened them to speak. Most seemed to have no contact with water for ages; they were dusty and clumsy in behaviour.

I was now sure this was no nightmare. I was being kicked by soldiers speaking Portuguese. I felt weak, perhaps from a hangover from the 'gin' I had consumed at the *Swazi Spa Hotel*. As it became lighter I surveyed the area. I spotted a distinctive building on the right-hand side. It had a vivid copper inscription in capital letters that read *Banco de Moçambique*. I stood for a

The Swazi OBSERVER

17c

Vol.3 No. 125 Matsapha, Monday, February 13 1984. Swaziland's National Newspaper. The Paper for The People.

TANZANIAN REFUGEE 'KIDNAPPED'

Observer Reporter.

A TANZANIAN refugee is believed to have been kidnapped by unknown people who took him across the border to Mozambique.

Mr Ludovick Mwijage, a former schoolteacher in Tanzania was allegedly kidnapped on December 16 and driven to Mozam-

bique, according to a spokesman of the High Commission for

few moments, petrified. I had been abducted from Swaziland to Mozambique.

* * * * * *

A soldier pushed me with a rifle butt, urging me to keep moving. He ordered me to put my hands above my head and obey all orders. I counted nine soldiers; they were joined by nine more as we started moving towards a nearby *Frelimo* camp. The new arrivals were harsh, kicking and hitting me with their rifle butts, shouting *bandido,* a Portuguese word for bandit, the term then used by *Frelimo* to describe *Renamo* (National Mozambique Resistance) rebels.

Jo suggested to the soldiers that they handcuff me as I was 'too smart' and might try to escape. It is hard to describe how I felt towards Jo; revulsion is an understatement. I recall glaring at him with contempt, until *Frelimo* soldiers began to strike me again with their rifle butts, ordering me to keep moving.

Humans are a mystery. They can charm you, put on a special type of character, all to achieve their own ends. Once done, they return to their true colours. I could not come to terms with what Jo had done. Yesterday he pretended to be my caring friend, even entertaining my visitor, Lindiwe, whom I now thought might herself have been part of the abduction; now Jo was my kidnapper.

Frelimo soldiers now swarmed around Jo, congratulating him for his 'hard work,' though I doubt many of them understood what was really happening. One soldier in the new section that had arrived shouted 'Jenerali (Jo), you have pulled a big job,' Jenerali, or Jo, simply smiled. The fact that he was known to *Frelimo* soldiers by his *nom de guerre* suggested this was not the first mission he had pulled off.

We turned off on the right-hand side of the Swaziland/ Maputo road into what looked like a mission school with a large cathedral. It was now clear that I had been abducted to the Mozambican town of Namaacha. How we crossed Swaziland's fenced border remained a mystery at that stage.

I was led inside the mission school, now converted into a training camp, after sentries posted at the gate opened it for us. A once beautiful Catholic mission school was now a *Frelimo* army barracks, with the buildings falling apart. Classrooms had been turned into soldiers' sleeping quarters and *Frelimo* offices.

We entered one of the buildings overlooking the cathedral; it stank of urine and human excrement. Even as I was being led inside the building, three soldiers stood facing the wall urinating. I wondered how *Frelimo* soldiers managed to work in such an environment. I remember seeing a group of soldiers emerge from the cathedral with their uniforms wrinkled, almost as if they had slept in them. I doubted if the sanctity of the church was respected any longer.

The room I was taken to had a *Frelimo* soldier slumbering behind a manual typewriter. Next to the typewriter was a black telephone, one of the old types with a rolling handle for calling the operator. A set of bicycles was clumped together against the wall and above them, on a string, hung a dozen or so manacles. At the far end of the room there hung a picture of the now late Samora Moisés Machel, the first president of Mozambique, with his beard and gap-toothed stare. The floor was unswept and smelt of fungus.

The room had now become crowded with *Frelimo* soldiers, many of whom had emerged from the cathedral. Some of the soldiers knew nothing of what had transpired and wanted to know where I was 'going for training.' Apparently they thought I was a South African smuggled out of Swaziland for military training in a Frontline State or elsewhere.

One of their number, probably the man in charge, ordered my pockets to be searched. They found some *Emalangeni* bank notes (*Emalangeni* is Swaziland's currency), and from another pocket fished out my pocket diary and room key for the Youth Centre. I was particularly worried about my diary, which contained the names of several contacts in Tanzania who belonged to our group. I also recorded my daily activities which would no doubt prove useful to the people who ordered my abduction.

Surprisingly, the *Frelimo* soldier merely flicked through the pages of my diary then asked where my photograph was fixed—he thought it was a passport. The soldier was illiterate as he could not distinguish a diary from a passport. I told him in English that the book he held was a diary, but he did not understand. He flung it on the table, where my money and room key were. I was then ordered to sit down on the floor.

91

'Jenerali,' or Jo as I knew him, entered the room, talking slowly with his friends and a group of soldiers we had left behind. Then, quite unexpectedly and to my amazement, the soldier who had ordered me to be searched promptly ordered the leader of the abduction team to step forward. Jo, like a soldier about to receive a medal for bravery stepped forward. The *Frelimo* soldier duly ordered him to be thoroughly searched.

For the man who had described himself as the 'arresting officer,' such treatment was demeaning; it diminished his status before the prisoner he had arrested. The *Frelimo* man was a no-nonsense soldier. From Jo's back trouser pocket he removed a Tanzanian alien travel document and threw it onto the table with my other things.

I was disturbed to see my country's travel document in the hands of an abductor, particularly my abductor. Over the years the Tanzanian government had indiscriminately issued Tanzanian passports to people not entitled to them, usually 'freedom fighters' whose activities it supported. The *Chama Cha Mapinduzi (CCM)* regime felt it was appropriate to issue our national passports to 'freedom fighters' to provide them with cover from detection and to facilitate travel in the course of their 'liberation' duties. Some Tanzanians who favoured a non-violent approach were unhappy about this.

Tanzania's ruling *Chama cha Mapinduzi* (and then the only party) played host to 'freedom fighters' it recognised from southern Africa and elsewhere, including some of Milton Obote's exiled entourage after Idi Amin had deposed Obote. Tanzanian opposition forces used to argue that *CCM*, which gave directives of this nature without legislative approval, was by such action confirmed to be a state party and not a mass party, as *CCM* liked to claim.

Even more disgusting to me was the thought that people to whom Tanzanians had extended hospitality, and for whom we made great sacrifices, particularly economically, were engaged in dirty activities and even spying on Tanzanians. That brings back memories of the first treason trial in 1969, in which Potlake Leballo, then acting president of the Pan-Africanist Congress of South Africa which was then based in Dar-Es-Salaam, featured prominently as a state witness. Remember too, the involvement of another South African known as Dumisane Dube, in the

92

mysterious death in a road accident in 1984 of Tanzania's only popular Prime Minister, Edward Moringe Sokoine. A strongly held view in Tanzania has it that Sokoine actually was bumped off for reasons of political expediency. Moreover, it is claimed, a South African was employed in order to avoid having to use a Tanzanian. After all, that might have provoked tribal sensitivities in a unitary country.

After Jo, the next to undergo the *Frelimo* search was the fat man in an overcoat, whom I later came to know as Marwick. From under his arm the *Frelimo* man retrieved a pistol contained in a green cotton holster. This explained why he continued to wear an overcoat in such hot temperatures. Marwick had no money, nor any identification, which was perhaps understandable for someone carrying out the type of assignments he did. Better to cover your trail in case things go wrong.

I was surprised that a man could leave his home with his pockets empty to carry out a mission such as this. It was almost as if he had set out to commit suicide. Was he perhaps Jo's 'uncle' who had attended the 'business meeting' at the *Swazi Spa*? Or, was it the person whom Jo was looking for, when he was driving aimlessly around Two Sticks area? Maybe he was the man who had offered the 'gin' that caused me to black out, leading to my abduction.

The third man, who looked young and innocent, surrendered the red spotlight (my efforts to establish his identity came to no fruition). Unlike his two compatriots, he had small pieces of paper in his pockets, something which suggested he was an amateur in the abduction business. His eyes and face lacked the zeal and portentousness so evident in his colleagues.

The *Frelimo* official proceeded to ask Jo about my abduction. He wanted to know from Jo how he brought me through from Swaziland. Jo replied that it was through 'the normal route,' his eyes darting from me to his interviewer. He seemed unsure about whether I understood Portuguese and refused to answer more questions. He told the *Frelimo* man he would do so once I was taken out of the room.

Two armed *Frelimo* soldiers then led me, handcuffed, out of the building. By now it was clear to me that the 'normal route' Jo had referred to was the one used to smuggle ANC (African National Congress) people out of Swaziland to Tanzania via

Mozambique, for military training. Once out of the room, I heard Jo, speaking loudly as if to someone far away. He said the 'parcel' had been delivered to the border post at Namaacha. It seemed the *Frelimo* man spoke on the same line after Jo, but I could not work out whether they had spoken to the same person. I assumed they had spoken to someone in Maputo.

Later, I was returned to the same room. Jo and his group were leaving, saying they would return once they had recovered their car from the bush where they had left it. I assumed they would use the same route to return to Swaziland, since they did not have proper travel papers.

* * * * * *

A Whiff of Prison

Early the next day at about 7am, a short man in the dotted khaki uniform of *Frelimo* entered the room. The soldier who had ordered the body search the previous day called his juniors to attention. I considered that the order did not apply to me since I was handcuffed and could not come abruptly to attention. The short man was clearly in charge. He exuded an aura of authority and self-importance, so typical of people of his calibre when approaching a stranger. He wore no shoulder identification to signify his rank; a small red belt across his shoulder suggested his seniority.

He spoke Portuguese fast and fluently and seemed to have no manners at all. He seemed intent on displaying his power, barking out orders to his juniors as if they were his personal servants. He demanded to know my name, but I decided I wasn't going to speak Portuguese, which I knew, because I felt I had much to gain from learning what my captors were discussing.

'I'm sorry officer,' I said in English. 'I don't speak Portuguese.' He stepped towards me, silent and unimpressed, took a white cloth from his pocket and tried to blindfold me with it. He failed, as it was too short. He then stepped back and, in broken English, asked me my name. Much to my surprise, after telling him who I was, he introduced himself as *Commandante* Mateus (pronounced Mateushi). He said I was being held captive at the request of certain Tanzanian officials and that he was awaiting further instructions from them as to what he should do with me. Awaiting further instructions from Tanzanian officials!

'As an officer of the Mozambican armed forces,' I inquired curiously, 'I would have thought that you took instructions and orders only from your immediate Mozambican superiors, rather than from Tanzanian officials'.

It would seem that *Commandante* Mateus failed to grasp the implications of my cautiously guarded remark, as he did not reply. Instead, he went on to tell me that he had, that morning, telephoned Wilfred Kiondo, a Tanzanian diplomat, at *Ujamaa House*, the Tanzanian embassy in Maputo.

Kiondo, now retired, was notoriously fierce, filling even some of his colleagues with dread. Ironically, it seemed that he was only semi-literate and reputedly needed assistance from a *Daily*

News (the government-owned newspaper) reporter; also connected with the secret service; to write a report to his superiors.

He was a low-ranking police officer during colonial rule and joined the Tanzanian Intelligence Service (TIS) after independence. He had served in many places and spent some time with TAZARA (Tanzania Zambia Railway Authority), during the construction of the railway line by the Chinese. Later he was transferred to Maputo as a counsellor at the Tanzanian embassy. He had been the co-ordinator of the whole plan to kidnap me. Mateus said that he could not do anything further regarding my situation until he received instructions from Kiondo.

Two young *Frelimo* men then removed my handcuffs after Mateus ordered this. At his behest, they were to take me for breakfast at *Namaacha hotel*. He warned me not to attempt an escape as his men had been ordered to shoot me in the legs if I did. The two soldiers escorted me to the hotel where a waiter offered us a breakfast menu of only scrambled eggs and sausages. It seemed there was nothing else to offer.

I tried a piece of sausage and some egg, but I could not taste anything. One of the *Frelimo* men gobbled up his meal in no time then asked if I intended to finish my breakfast. When I replied that I had eaten enough, he drew my plate towards himself and devoured the lot.

Commandante Mateus arrived later and ordered his breakfast. The waiters reacted promptly and obediently. I could never work out whether this was because they held him in high esteem or whether they feared and loathed him. Perhaps all three? As we sat, Mateus warmed to me; he said he had been to Havana, Cuba, for military training and that Fidel Castro was a great 'revolutionary' leader who had achieved much for his country. I listened without offering any comment.

Mateus said he returned to Africa from Cuba. His official car, by his own account, was a BMW which he frequently used on shopping trips to Swaziland.

'You prefer shopping in Swaziland to Maputo?', I asked, smiling in order to encourage Mateus to talk.

'Yes!' he replied, adding that this was because most consumer items were not obtainable in Mozambique. He blamed this on 'imperialists' and the chronic shortage of foreign exchange in Mozambique. 'It's a problem, a very big problem,' he said, his pride visibly hurt.

'Then Mozambique is not like the Cuba you praise,' I said. Mateus nodded his head as he pushed away his plate with the remnants of his breakfast. Cuba, he said, was really a socialist country. Mozambique would one day be a 'truly socialist' country, given the guidance of 'our vanguard *Frelimo* party.' He wiped his mouth with a white cloth he drew from his pocket; the same cloth he had tried to blindfold me with earlier. He moved from topic to topic; my mind was far away, wondering what awaited me in Dar-Es-Salaam.

Two cars and a Land Rover had already arrived at the Namaacha *Frelimo* camp by the time we returned from breakfast. It was clear I was going to be taken to Maputo by road. One of Mateus' deputies beckoned to me to claim my personal effects from the table where they were mixed with those of my abductors. This particular officer seemed incapable of reading, or he just didn't care. He handed me Jo's passport, saying, 'Take your passport with you.' He knew I was the only Tanzanian around, and might have thought that the first Tanzanian document he spotted was mine. I used the chance to identify my captor and to note some of his personal particulars (if indeed they were true).

His name was entered as Malcolm Zhugo and, according to the document, he was a mechanic by profession. Not wanting to raise the suspicion of the *Frelimo* man, I quickly turned to the visa pages of the passport. Jo had travelled quite extensively: there were several 'entry' and 'exit' endorsements, mostly for Swaziland, but also of other southern African states. By having a Tanzanian travel document, Malcolm Zhugo enjoyed relative freedom of movement in Commonwealth countries in Africa.

I returned Malcolm Zhugo's passport to the officer and told him my passport was that small, black book on the table—my pocket diary containing my personal effects, including my room key and some money. I then pretended I had a sudden stomach ache and asked if I could be taken to the toilet. I needed to destroy several pages of the diary lest I incriminated people still in Tanzania.

The toilet was outside the camp's gate, which perhaps explained why the camp itself was littered with human excrement. Two armed *Frelimo* soldiers escorted me to a ramshackle latrine made of corrugated iron sheets. Inside, logs were placed on top of the pit, with a small, narrow space left in the middle for the user to position himself. One soldier, his AK47 ready, stood in front of the latrine, the other behind. They seemed positioned to prevent my possible escape. To my relief, they were less interested in what I did inside the latrine.

My room key from the Youth Centre in Mbabane was the first item to find its way down the pit. I was afraid my abductors might use it to gain entry to my room and remove documents that could be used against me. The next thing to go down the pit was my pocket diary, though only the pages which contained names and details of my contacts in Tanzania. I thought it unwise to dispose of the whole diary, yet I did not want to bring trouble for friends in Tanzania.

I tore out the relevant pages, chewed them, and then spat them into the latrine to ensure nothing could be retrieved. I satisfied myself that the diary now contained only names which could not be connected to me politically. I returned the diary to my pocket and left the latrine.

* * * * * *

Commandante Mateus arranged us into two cars which had arrived from Maputo. Two plain-clothes men, possibly Tanzanians, hovered around but did not take an active role in the proceedings. I was put onto a Land Rover positioned between two white Rada cars with radio communication equipment. Again handcuffs were snapped on and four armed soldiers sat around me at the back of the vehicle. Mateus sat in front; adjusting his military cap using the rear-view mirror, then signalled the convoy to get moving.

We passed many road blocks on the way to Maputo and I worried about security on the road. Those were the days when *Renamo*, a guerrilla movement opposed to the then *Frelimo* Marxist rule (*Renamo* later transformed itself into a political party after signing a peace accord with *Frelimo* in Rome, Italy, on October 4, 1992) had increased its rebel activities along this road, attacking convoys at random, whether of the military variety or otherwise. If that had happened on this day, I would probably have been a victim. Unarmed and handcuffed, I would have been helpless in a normal road accident; how much more so in a rebel attack?

Somewhere in downtown Maputo we pulled up at what looked to be an ordinary flat. Inside was anything but normal. People, some handcuffed, others not, sat around apparently unaware of when they would be released—if at all. Opposite one of the male rooms I noticed a young woman taking a shower in a group. I was ordered to sit on an empty mattress cover from where I watched the men in the crowded room sweating profusely.

Near me sat two young men who had been arrested for their religious activities, both clasping their bibles determinedly; they were not going to enter their graves without their bibles. I thought it rather poignant that someone should suffer so much just for a belief he holds. *Frelimo* had its own religion—Marxism— and seemed quite content to deny others their religious freedom in the name of Marxism. I wondered just how long it would take *Frelimo* to lose its own freedom as they encroached on the freedom of others.

Commandante Mateus returned with the two plain-clothes men I had noticed at Namaacha. Having ditched any trace of courtesy and tact, he proceeded to get rough, shouting in Portuguese as he pushed me towards the Land Rover that had brought us. It seemed somebody had given him good reason to hate me, and he wasted no time in showing it. I was 'intellectually arrogant,' he said, but Machava would knock this arrogance out of me.

I wondered what on earth Machava was. The trip in the Land Rover gave a foretaste of what it could be like: two soldiers laid me down in the back of the vehicle, pressed me down hard, and covered my face with a hat. The Land Rover screeched off and moved fast for some time; then we came to an abrupt halt and the driver cut the engine. I was taken out and ordered to sit down until given further orders. As I looked around, I noticed I was inside a prison compound. I was at Machava maximum security prison.

* * * * * *

Inside Machava

Wednesday afternoon, December 7, 1983, I felt weak and dejected as Mateus and his men ordered me to accompany them to the prison offices. In the corridor we passed several prisoners awaiting interrogation, most of them handcuffed with their hands above their heads. One coloured prisoner had fallen asleep or possibly collapsed from exhaustion, falling in the middle of the corridor. The *Frelimo* soldiers were unperturbed, scarcely noticing; some kicked him, demanding that he stand up, but none cared to lift him up. The man was perspiring profusely.

I was told to sit down on the floor facing my interviewer, a young *Frelimo* man flanked by two colleagues. The room was bare except for the chair the man sat on and a table on which there was a scrap of paper with my particulars, or possibly for the *Frelimo* man to write on. There was nothing else, not even a pin. He studied me, and then asked in English 'Are you Ludovick Mwichaje?' I replied that I wasn't, and his face was a mixture of bewilderment and anger.

'What do you mean?' he asked, frowning. I repeated that that was not my name. He looked at his colleagues, puzzled, then back at the paper. He studied it closer this time, and then broke into a triumphant smile: 'your name is misspelt,' he said, and I replied that I was not sure. He demanded I spell my name and, after some hesitation, I asked him whether he did not need to interview Ludovick Mwichaje before speaking to Ludovick Mwijage. I had wasted my time and he was quite clear. 'It's you we need,' he said.

The *Frelimo* man made notes of my personal particulars, including my address in Tanzania and Swaziland. Then, pointing with his pen to a blue prison uniform, he ordered that I change into it, as I was now going down to the cell. Since he spoke understandable English, I asked him about my legal status at the prison and whether the *Frelimo* government had any charges against me. He said I was being detained on the orders of the Tanzanian government. Some Tanzanian officials would soon be coming to speak to me, but he didn't know when.

'Tanzanian officials ordering me incarcerated in Mozambique seemingly without charge and....' He interrupted me.

'You will have to ask them that...' he snapped impatiently, tensing his body like a cat readying to pounce on a mouse. I grabbed the prison drab and changed into it.

At this point, the *Frelimo* man rose from his seat as he ordered that I be handcuffed again. I protested, arguing that since I would be in a prison cell there was no purpose in having me handcuffed. The *Frelimo* man said they had their own *modus operandi*; besides, he insisted, I was being held in Machava on the express orders of Tanzanian officials representing their government in Maputo.

* * * * * *

Machava contained about seven blocks which were known to the inmates as *pavilions*. I think it is one of the best fortified prisons in Africa. The high walls surrounding the prison were manned around the clock by a sentry armed with a machine gun.

Machava's *pavilions* contained cells on either side, separated by a large passageway. The cells were overcrowded. In *pavilion* No. 7, where I was held, some of the cells held as many as six prisoners. Prison seemed to be the only nationalised industry in Mozambique that was functioning. Prisoners who were not confined to their cells during the day would cling to the bars of the *pavilion* to breathe fresh air, and even this was a special privilege.

I estimated my cell was about 11 feet by 13 feet. There was no toilet, not even a bucket to urinate or pass motion; the floor was bare, without any blankets. There was nothing to read and strict instructions were issued that I should be locked in solitary confinement. I was only allowed to go to the collective toilet and at night the mosquitoes feasted on me and I could not scare them off because of my handcuffs. My diet consisted of boiled rice and fried fish. Sometimes there was simply no lunch or dinner because, as I was told later, there was a food shortage in Mozambique. In the mornings I would get black tea with a doughnut, but sometimes nothing at all. Every morning for ten minutes I was allowed out of my cell to pass water and wash my face; but washing my face proved difficult with handcuffs. Lights blazed day and night, their controllers oblivious to the lack of electricity elsewhere in Mozambique. I felt as if I was in a grave, buried alive.

* * * * * *

This was the second time I had been in detention, the first going back to August 1971 when I was a student teacher at Morogoro.

I had been detained at Morogoro merely for expressing a political opinion. I had been appointed editor-in-chief of Mhonda College's newsletter, which, as it turned out, never got off the ground anyway. Basically, the newsletter intended to reflect the thinking of the college community, using articles from students and staff. But, an English lecturer had insisted that all articles be censored before publication. I strongly disagreed, setting him and myself on a collision course.

When Idi Amin deposed Milton Obote in a Ugandan military coup in 1971, I took the liberty of writing an editorial comment on political developments in Uganda and the effect on neighbouring states. I had studied at secondary and high school in Uganda and took a keen interest in developments in that country. I held the view that Obote, whom the Tanzanian government chose to support, was his own worst enemy: he initiated a dictatorial trend in Uganda, abolishing opposition parties and declaring himself 'executive president'. His Uganda People's Congress (UPC) had become the only 'legitimate' party. Obote himself, some observers believed, was trying to emulate Tanzania's style of leadership.

So, in my yet unpublished editorial, I argued that Obote had actually allowed Amin to rise to power. After all, it was Obote who appointed Amin as chief of defence staff; yet he had the opportunity to give the post to someone better equipped than Amin. The editorial also touched on Nyerere's frequent condemnation of the new Uganda regime. Many students felt Nyerere was doing this merely to deflect attention from his own domestic problems and failures.

Though the editorial was never published, government had heard about it and they did not like it. I was ill-treated in my dormitory one day by three plain-clothes security men who had arrived in the company of the college principal and the English lecturer who was acting as censor. I was taken to Morogoro for detention, and the college was shut. The student government was dissolved and its entire leadership transferred to different colleges because, in the words of the college authorities, I had 'great

102

influence' over it.

After being heavily interrogated for several days by the Tanzanian Intelligence Service (TIS), it was decided that I should be charged in a court of law with 'common assault and causing actual bodily harm.' With this as the so-called holding charge, investigations into my actual political activities could continue.

By now, new allegations started to emerge. Claims were being made by the security services that I had been 'communicating' with Amin and that at the time of my arrest I had tried to destroy a letter which supported this claim. Elements in the state then tried every trick they could to bolster their claim that I had tried to 'communicate' with Amin. In fact, the authorities were claiming that whilst I was a student in Uganda, I actually had an audience with the Ugandan tyrant. It was an affront albeit untrue. For, when Amin overthrew Obote I was a student teacher at the very same college where I had been arrested. Additionally, I had spent the previous year in the National Service at Makutopora, Dodoma. However, with new, more serious allegations, bail became harder to get.

The case dragged on for many months, until I was able to convince Ndugu Kisesa, who was then the government regional security officer (RSO) for Morogoro that I had nothing to do with Amin. He ultimately recommended to the President's Office that the case be withdrawn, which it was. During the several weeks I spent in detention at that time I was often threatened with my life; my friends and parents were harassed by the security police. I believe I became a marked man, one to be closely watched, ever since then.

Even after the case was dismissed, I remained rusticated. It was only in the following academic year that I was conditionally reinstated and transferred to Monduli College of National Education in Arusha.

My reinstatement, however, had to be sanctioned by the Ministry of Education itself in Dar-Es-Salaam namely, by Sefania Tunginie, who then was the Director of Education, Teachers' Training. I lost a whole year of my studies, the sort of price one had to pay then for expressing an opinion that annoyed the Tanzanian regime.

* * * * * *

103

My immediate neighbour in the 7th *pavilion* of Machava prison was a *mulatto* woman called Renete. She was on death row, allegedly for spying for *Renamo*. She spoke some English and, surprisingly, when I could briefly see her during my ten minutes for washing and passing water, she was always in good spirits, despite the death sentence hanging over her head. She spoke of an Italian boyfriend whom she seemed to have lost touch with since her incarceration. She was short and small, but beautiful.

One day, after being let out of her cell for a few minutes to use the toilet and wash, she refused to get back into the cell, demanding a mattress and a blanket. Renete was totally determined that she would not enter her cell until her demands had been met. A prison guard tried to push her into the cell but she would not budge. In the end she got her mattress and blanket. I greatly admired her courage. If Renete could be so resolute facing a death sentence, what about me? She became my inspiration.

Another foreign prisoner in our *pavilion* was a British citizen, Finlay Dion Hamilton. He was a director of *Manica Freight Services* and, according to him, had lived in Mozambique for more than two decades. *Frelimo*'s 'Revolutionary Military Tribunal' had sentenced him to twenty years in prison for allegedly aiding *Renamo* (an anti-*Frelimo* group) to blow up a fuel depot in Beira, Mozambique's second largest town. I saw him on several occasions in the morning when he was allowed out of his cell, and he seemed to be in low spirits. Once the *Frelimo* guards noticed that we conversed freely in English, he was transferred to *pavilion* No. 4.

Among the other prisoners were *Renamo* rebels who had accepted the *Frelimo* government's offer of amnesty if they surrendered. Instead of receiving amnesty, some were imprisoned in Machava. One such rebel was a young Zimbabwean man who had worked as a radio technician for *Renamo*. He claimed he had been trained in radio communications in South Africa. He said he had learnt of the government's amnesty offer from a leaflet he had picked up; he gave himself up and after interrogation was brought to Machava. He believed *Frelimo* had not honoured its promise. When I left Machava, his fate was still uncertain.

* * * * * *

On the fifth day of my incarceration in Machava, a prison guard rattled the padlock outside my cell; he called me out. I walked lamely ahead of him towards the prison offices. I had definitely lost weight due to the harsh prison conditions. A young man dressed in a white-sleeved shirt with a Nikon camera dangling over his chest stood next to the prison offices. He ordered me to sit on a stool in front of him. His incisors were sharpened. I thought he might be from Musoma, Julius Nyerere's home place. The man studied me for a while and then started questioning me in *Swahili*.

'Who are you?' he asked vaguely. 'Who did you send for?' I retorted. He stopped questioning me and instead asked me to pose for pictures. That done, I asked him if he was aware of my prison conditions and demanded to know if I was already serving a sentence. I also demanded to know what crime I had committed in Mozambique. He replied that he knew nothing about prison conditions, and even if he did, it was outside his power to do anything about it. His reply sounded very boastful.

I understood him; after all he was not a prison guard at Machava and probably did not understand what I was talking about. His job suggested he was a privileged person and I had no reason to believe he had ever been in prison, certainly not as a political prisoner. I thus seized the opportunity to warn him that the prison was like an infirmary. 'You should not think you're immune from going where you send others,' I told him. Briefly, I was telling him that what was happening to me today could happen to him tomorrow. Then added, seriously, that I wished I was the last to endure such treatment.

He looked at me with disbelief. 'Why are you saying all this?', he demanded of me. 'Well,' I replied, 'just to remind you that what we black Africans live under is like a tinderbox of frustration.' I reminded him that as long as African countries continued to follow one-party political systems, every African was a potential prisoner of conscience if not a refugee. He seemed momentarily stunned, condensing what I had told him. I was returned to my cell, convinced that he had got the message.

I don't particularly believe in miracles but that evening, December 11, 1983, a miracle happened; a *Frelimo* guard opened my cell door and commanded that I follow him. In front of the prison offices a group of men dressed in civilian clothes stood conversing in Portuguese. They seemed in jovial mood, slapping each other playfully, laughing and shaking hands frequently. One of them, a short man dressed in crimplene tailored trousers, held out his hand to greet me; the others watched silently. As we shook hands, I had the sudden feeling that my status was about to change, possibly for the better; this was, after all, the first time since I was incarcerated in Machava that I had shaken hands with a prison official. And the man whose hand I had just shaken seemed to be a senior official; he spoke to the rest of the group with authority. As it later turned out, the man was in fact the head of Machava Prison.

He instructed one of his juniors to remove my handcuffs and ordered that my civilian clothes be given back to me. However, the prison official in charge of prisoners was nowhere to be found. The chief of Machava decided that we go anyway, in my prison outfit. I was taken to a waiting Rada car fitted out with radio equipment. In front and behind were two army jeeps, their machine guns pointed at the Rada car. I sat in the back, my hands buried between my thighs to allay any fears that I might try to escape by overpowering my guards. Heavily armed *Frelimo* men sat on either side of me.

The head of Machava sat behind the steering wheel; beside him sat a short man in plain-clothes, his face marked with *Makonde* tribal marks. We moved in a convoy, one military jeep leading, the other trailing us. We moved in silence. Nobody cared to tell me where we were going nor did I bother to ask. I had resolved that whatever my fate, I would face it with a smile. The bottom line, as far as I was concerned, was that my suffering was for something I wholly believed in: democratic values and social justice.

We pulled up in front of an elegant multi-storey building in downtown Maputo. Opposite were houses surrounded by a fine garden from which the Mozambican flag was hoisted. I assumed this was the house of a senior state official. More than a dozen *Frelimo* soldiers armed with AK-47s stood in front of the multi-story building. The head of Machava disappeared into the building, leaving his lieutenant and two armed men with me in the car. Minutes later a soldier beckoned us into the building.

I was led into a large room on the first floor. It had a thick, expensive, red carpet, with walls decorated with paintings of various kinds. It was a self-contained double room. An armed

Frelimo soldier sat on a chair facing me and beside him was a table with a telephone. The soldier stood to attention whenever I entered or left the room. He seemed unaware of my status.

Before leaving, the head of Machava, speaking in fluent *Swahili* (he learnt the language in Tanzania when he was a refugee during the liberation war) introduced me to his proxy, the head of Matola Prison. The Matola Prison chief was to stay with me in my new quarters. He too spoke *Swahili* very well and was *de facto* commander of the troops deployed at the building.

The head of Matola Prison told me he was surprised at my sudden change of status. He admitted it was the first time in his career that a prisoner had been brought from prison to a state lodge. The room I was in, he informed me, was where the late president Mobutu Sese Seko of Zaire (now Democratic Republic of Congo) had slept during his last visit to Mozambique. Having established where I was now being held, I concluded that it was too good to be true.

Paradoxically, the *Frelimo* people seemed not to trust each other, despite their shared hardship and supposed solidarity. Perhaps it is characteristic of guerrillas not to trust each other. For example, the head of Machava kept his opposite number, the chief of Matola Prison, in the dark about my name, the reasons for my imprisonment, and indeed, the reasons for my transfer from prison to a state lodge. Yet the Matola Prison chief was part of my guard and overall commander of the unit guarding me. Additionally, extra troops were deployed at the lodge without advance warning being given to the Matola Prison chief. He later told me that when he was called from Matola Prison, he thought it was to collect a prisoner from Machava Prison who had not first been 'processed', as he termed it, at Matola Prison.

He was genuinely astounded that I had been brought directly to a state lodge, and that nobody in authority was prepared to explain why. This situation worked enormously to my advantage: I, the captive, had to explain my ordeal to my uninformed captor. I have never been able to establish the reasons for my sudden transfer from prison to state lodge. Was it the result of my calculated lecture to the official who had taken my photograph, or was it mere coincidence?

* * * * * *

107

Life at the state lodge was a far cry from the harsh realities of life in the streets of Maputo. The closet in my room contained perfumed soaps, Russian toothbrushes and toothpaste, electric shavers and expensive after-shave lotions; such items were then hard to come by in Maputo. Staff at the lodge were all dressed in white uniforms and were highly disciplined. A Goan woman, or Portuguese woman of Goan origin, seemed to be in charge of the chefs in the kitchen. Downstairs in the dining room four armed soldiers stood to attention every time we had our meals. Even when we had finished eating and I decided to remain seated, the soldiers would remain at attention until I had left. I realised then that African leaders were captives themselves: these soldiers were rehearsing what they were inevitably required to do whenever there was a state visit.

My new quarters also had a balcony overlooking the sea. Often I sat there with the Matola Prison chief after meals or a siesta. Whenever I moved to the balcony a staff member would ask me what I wanted to drink. To my surprise, when I ordered double whisky on the rocks, it was brought promptly and it was pure Scotch whisky. This contrasted sharply with Machava Prison, where prisoners did not even have adequate food or with the streets of Maputo, where consumer goods were in short supply, if not impossible to obtain. From the comfort of my new quarters, Mozambique seemed to be a country with two divergent economies.

* * * * * *

Because of his assigned duties, the Matola Prison chief slept in a room next to mine. As I settled in at the state lodge, we developed a good understanding of each other. He looked much poorer than his post suggested: on days that he guarded me, he never changed his clothes. Perhaps this was because he had been summoned at short notice for his new duties and had not had time to bring spare clothes. His clothing was virtually worn out. The shirt had patches on the sleeves and collar and his trousers were patched between the thighs.

Despite his shoddy appearance, he was an affable and sociable official. Frequently he praised the kindness of the Swazi people, recalling a trip he had made to Swaziland as part of an advance party for a visit by the late Samora Machel. He said he had enjoyed the pleasure of seeing King Sobhuza II, the revered Swazi king who died in 1982. 'And all the shops were full of consumer goods,' he kept saying. His frequent references to Swaziland and its relative economic success suggested that he yearned for political and economic change in his own country. He gave the impression that he was disillusioned with Mozambique's malfunctioning centrally-planned economy.

The Matola Prison chief was anxious to know what had happened to me, and was deeply touched and sympathetic when I told him. He believed that my abduction was known to only a select few top *Frelimo* officials, because the act itself was a transgression of international law. He wondered if there was anything he could do for me apart from setting me free, which was not possible.

I grasped the chance. I asked him if he could mail a note to Mbabane, Swaziland, notifying the UNHCR that I had been abducted. He agreed, and said I should write the note in the toilet in my room and leave it above the cistern, where he would pick it up later. He had access to my room and occasionally he used the toilet when we were on the balcony.

Thereafter, I went to the toilet, tore a piece of paper from my pocket diary, which had been returned to me after I left Machava, and wrote a short note for UNHCR in Mbabane. I decided to address it to an official I remembered, for fear that the Mozambicans might be censoring mail destined for abroad and addressed to international organisations. I flushed the toilet to fool the guards into thinking I was using it.

After returning to the balcony, the Matola Prison chief went to the toilet and retrieved the note. He stayed there a short while, and then flushed when he came out. Later, when I asked why I could not give him the note on the balcony since it was only us there, he replied with a smile: 'This is *Frelimo*, where anybody spies on everybody.'

* * * * * *

Journey to Tanzania

Early in the morning of December 16, 1983, a squad of eight *Frelimo* men in civilian clothes arrived at the state lodge. I could clearly detect their revolvers, hidden under their jackets. The head of Machava Prison, dressed in a tailored, crimplene suit with a badge of Samora Machel pinned on the lapel, was their commander. This time the convoy of three Rada cars, all fitted out with radio equipment, headed for Mavalane Airport, at the air force base. Some civilians, mostly women (possibly wives of *Frelimo* soldiers), joined us as we boarded a military aircraft through an opening at the tail end. So far, no one had formally told me where we were going. However, the chief of Matola Prison had informed me the previous night that Samora Machel, on his return from a tour of the provinces, had approved my repatriation to Tanzania, as requested.

A tall, stout, vicious looking man dressed in camouflage fatigues (I later established he was Mozambique's acting head of intelligence) boarded the plane to arrange our seating. He removed me from a window seat to one some distance from the emergency door, probably for security purposes. During the flight the *Frelimo* men spoke nothing of their mission. I thought this might be due to the presence of women and their children, or possibly because they had been tipped off by their seniors that I understood some Portuguese.

The women passengers disembarked at Pemba, south of the border town of Mtwara. We lunched there on boiled rice and fried fish. It seemed this was a readily available Mozambican dish as I remember it being a fairly common dish at Machava Prison. The rest of the journey to southern Tanzania was short. I remember how some of the *Frelimo* men kept fingering some US Dollar bills, checking for the security line. It seemed most of them had never seen a Dollar bill before.

Throughout the flight from Maputo to Pemba and onwards I had not been handcuffed. Now, as the military plane began descending, the head of the escort team went to the cockpit. When he returned, he ordered that I should be handcuffed. I immediately realised that I was already in Tanzania, my country.

* * * * * *

The aircraft touched down on the airfield. A lone fire-fighter, a young man in khaki uniform, stood motionless as he gazed at the taxiing plane. The pilot cut the engines and five men came through from the cockpit, pistols in their hands. I recognised the one wearing spectacles as a senior employee of the then government-owned *Air Tanzania* airline. I knew him only as Luvena.

Luvena took off my spectacles and blindfolded me. The other two men held me tightly and led me from the plane to a Land Rover parked nearby. They laid me back downwards on the back of the Land Rover, pressing hard on me. Though I had never met them before, they treated me as if they had a score to settle; they hurled insults at me saying I was a 'swine,' 'traitor,' 'bastard' and common criminal. Whatever derogatory terms they could think of, they used quite generously.

The Land Rover sped off like an ambulance transporting a casualty to hospital. It cut several corners before the driver stopped abruptly. The two men who had been pressing me to the floor of the vehicle marched me into a building and again they laid me on my back, blindfolded. An hour later the blindfold was removed to reveal a tiny room containing a small, portable fan which my two guards used to cool themselves. They sat against the only door, which was shut, facing me. The only glass window was sealed with old newspapers, keeping the fresh air out and preventing detainees from seeing outside. The walls were bare but for one *CCM* poster with a picture of Julius Nyerere, fist clenched, urging his subjects not to be wasteful for fear of an impending food crisis in Tanzania.

Later, a man I was to get to know as Mlawa entered the room. He ordered me stripped and took my clothes for a thorough search, leaving me only in my underpants. When I inquired from my guards why I was being stripped, one snapped that I should 'shut up.' He said if I uttered another word, they would 'teach me a lesson.' Out of reach of the fan's cool breeze and with the door and only window shut, I began to sweat profusely as I awaited my fate.

At about midnight, Mlawa ordered the guards to blindfold me again and take me to a larger room next door for interrogation. I was paraded in only my underwear before five men, my interrogators,

111

including the man who had blindfolded me on the aircraft, Luvena. I realised for the first time that people can respect institutional authorities only if those authorities respect an individual's rights; people cease to respect those same authorities when they use their power to erode an individual's inherent rights. The fact that men from the President's Office paraded me before them in only my underwear removed any semblance of the belief I once held that such people were noble, aristocratic servants of my land. I believed they did this to political detainees to dehumanise and demoralise them.

I was later to establish that I was being held at the offices of the government's regional security officer (RSO). At that time the RSO for Mtwara was a man called Brighton and he was present during my underwear parade. Unfortunately, I failed to establish the identity of the remaining two interrogators.

I also noticed quickly that four of my interrogators referred to their fifth colleague, Mlawa, as 'chief' from their headquarters in Dar-Es-Salaam. And Mlawa addressed his colleagues with a noticeable measure of authority. He sat at a separate table which was covered with a green flannel table cloth, making notes on a writing pad like a magistrate recording court proceedings. In front of him was a black attaché case containing a myriad of papers; sometimes he would refer to the papers and make a note. It seemed he had not shaved for more than two days and his tailored, black *safari* jacket was a poor fit and did not match the trousers. He had an expensive Rado wrist watch which he looked at very frequently and his Italian shoes also looked expensive. He also had a solar calculator which he had trouble operating.

On the wall above Mlawa hung a picture of Julius Nyerere in a *safari* jacket, smiling. I could not reconcile his smile with the behaviour of his men, parading me around almost naked and handcuffed. This contrast seemed to vindicate a saying of my community: *'Abalungi nibo banuk'omukanwa'* (i.e. It is usually people of fabulous beauty who stink in the mouth.) Rolled up manila cards were plastered on the remaining walls, apparently to conceal what was written from the captive's eyes. The window curtains were usually drawn and a large air-conditioner built into the wall frequently malfunctioned as the power often failed.

* * * * * *

112

Interrogation

When God shuts the door, He opens a window. One thing that worked immensely to my advantage was that Mlawa, my chief interrogator, was scarcely literate. Perhaps it was this that made him overzealous; and his over-enthusiasm might explain his rapid rise to the upper echelons of the Tanzanian Intelligence Service, over the heads of his better educated colleagues. I later established that the man had built himself a large house by Tanzanian standards, one that a medical doctor or a university lecturer could only dream of, no matter how hard he worked. With so much to lose if the system changed, Mlawa had a vested interest in flushing out dissenting elements ruthlessly.

Mlawa often asked unintelligible questions during interrogation; some of his better educated juniors posed sharper questions. He blindly gave away his own organisation's sources, as well as names of operatives who had gathered some of the information before him. He was convinced that what his organisation claimed to know about our political activities was true and that I should accept this as the case and tell more. He consequently closed all avenues of obtaining anything new from me, and would order that the two police guards assault me if he thought I was being 'uncooperative'.

This lack of 'cooperation' was to implicate innocent people; people whom the Intelligence Service perceived as government opponents. Included among these unfortunates were Dr Vedastus Kyaruzi, a former Secretary General of the Commonwealth Health Secretariat; an Assistant Commissioner of Police called Swebe who was then staff officer at the Ministry of Home Affairs; a prominent Nairobi-based Tanzanian herbalist known as Mushobozi and many others whom I knew nothing about, let alone shared political views with.

Despite being forced to implicate people I did not even know, Mlawa's 'leading questions' served a useful purpose: they betrayed his own informers and colleagues. For example, he would ask me a question on a particular subject. To find out how much he knew about the subject, I would initially hesitate and then simply reply that I knew nothing. This would prompt him to shout angrily that I had been heard saying certain things. His 'you were heard saying' replies eventually served to remind me whom I had actually talked with about that subject. This helped me form my own defence, given that I had obtained some idea of how much they knew of our activities. This strategy worked for me.

Mlawa's 'leading questions' helped me to identify people who had spied on us in Tanzania and in exile. A leading figure in this respect was Colonel Ahmed Mkindi.

Not only did Mkindi report back on our activities he thought one was involved in, he also implicated innocent people who had nothing at all to do with our political activities.

Mkindi's favourite tactic was entrapment: presenting himself as one being persecuted by the system. I remember that he had come to see me in Swaziland around mid-April, 1983, a few weeks after the Tanzanian government had sealed off its eight borders in order to catch 'economic saboteurs.' The real purpose, of course, was to prevent perceived government opponents from fleeing the country, and also to manufacture a scapegoat for Tanzania's ailing economy: the government had already established, by interrogating several dissidents it had arrested in January that year that the main cause of growing dissent was economic hardship and rampant corruption.

Mkindi had approached me in an agitated mood that day. He implied that his own brother had been arrested in Arusha in possession of one US Dollar, during the so-called corruption purge. We agreed that it was terribly unfair to arrest and detain a citizen for possessing a US Dollar, while the real thieves in the government hierarchy who siphoned off hoards of money and deposited it in foreign banks were walking scot-free. Mkindi then asked me if I knew anyone in the Dar-Es-Salaam police whom he could approach about his brother's unfair detention. In good faith, I recommended that he speak to Swebe, whom I said I had known as an impartial law enforcer when he was based in Kagera region as a regional staff officer. I had recommended Swebe to Mkindi believing that, in the pursuit of justice, Swebe would help him. Instead, Mkindi had listed Swebe as a government opponent; during my interrogation I was being forced to implicate Swebe.

Nestor Rweyemamu, a former athlete and regional commercial and industrial officer in Arusha, was another man whose innocence I tried to defend. Mkindi had told me that he

(Mkindi) wanted to go into business full-time because he was becoming disillusioned with his employer—the government. He claimed that each time he tried to get a business licence he was forced to walk a bureaucratic minefield and consequently he could not get his import-export business going. Thus, he wanted to know if I knew anyone in commerce who could show him how best to obtain his licence.

I replied, quite forthrightly, that if a senior diplomat based in Harare had no contacts in commerce, it was ridiculous to expect a Tanzanian refugee in Swaziland to have such contacts. He pleaded with me, offering the excuse that his long absence from Tanzania had put him out of touch with people at home. I mentioned the name of Nestor Rweyemamu, unaware that I was being recorded. I told Mkindi I was unsure if Rweyemamu could help, and that I didn't know where he had been transferred to. Moreover, I said this was a simple matter to worry about, unlike someone unfairly imprisoned for possessing a US Dollar. I had asked him to just forget about the business licence.

During my interrogation Rweyemamu's name cropped up in the context of what I had discussed with Mkindi. This clearly gave away Mlawa's source. Another rude shock came by the name of Yahya Hussein, the so-called Tanzanian astrologer who had invited me to his room and paid for my accommodation the day I arrived in Mbabane. My telex message, Amos Chiwele's letter and my air ticket cover, all of which disappeared from my bag in Hussein's room, lay open in front of Mlawa and his men. Mlawa also had information on the conversation Hussein and I had had.

As for Dr Kyaruzi, I was reported to have been seen entering his clinic in Bukoba before I took flight; Mlawa claimed that I had delayed there too long to have just gone for medication. When I denied I knew the doctor, Mlawa stood up in a fit of hurt pride and shouted that I had been seen in Swaziland 'grieving' after being told that Kyaruzi's wife had died. He also claimed that I was heard to remark that the doctor's wife had been ill for some time— and, indeed, she had been ill for a while.

Then Mlawa fired this question: why would I grieve for someone I did not know? And why did I remark that Kyaruzi's wife had been ill for some time if I did not know the doctor? Once again this could be traced to a conversation between Yahya Hussein and me. Indeed, it was Hussein who gave me the news of the death of Dr Kyaruzi's wife.

Mlawa was also given to fabricate information in order to intimidate or perhaps to create the impression he knew a lot. One such claim dated back to December 1982 when, according to my interrogators, myself and a certain unnamed people were 'heard' talking about issues that could 'endanger' the life of the former party chairman, Julius Nyerere. Yet, if there was any truth to that, Mlawa could not say why we were not apprehended immediately, especially since what we were supposed to have discussed was extremely serious. Given the arbitrary powers of detention vested in the Intelligence Service, it is absurd to believe we would not have been arrested there and then.

Mlawa had his men also torture me when I was 'uncooperative:' they would tighten my handcuffs and refuse to allow me to wash for up to a week. On one occasion they wanted me to implicate the prominent Nairobi-based Tanzanian herbalist Mushobozi. Mlawa claimed that Mushobozi had been seen driving me to the offices of the then Kenyan vice president, (later president) Mwai Kibaki, and that he had been seen handing me a huge envelope, presumably containing money. In short, Mushobozi stood accused of supplying money for furthering dissident activities in Tanzania.

Of all the people mentioned during my first three weeks of interrogation at Mtwara, Mushobozi was the most puzzling. I had never seen the man nor heard of him before my abduction; nobody had even mentioned his name before. Where his name came from and why the Tanzanian Intelligence Service seemed so keen to implicate him I will never know. But after a week of torture, with my left arm already festering from the tightened handcuffs, I gave in and implicated him.

I now admitted that the envelope Mushobozi was supposed to have handed to me did, indeed, contain money to sponsor dissident activities. It was a nightmare that was to live with me, perhaps forever. Mlawa seemed pleased that day; he allowed that I be taken blindfolded to the bathroom for a shower, the first since my abduction. Guards, their pistols pointing at me, watched as I bathed. I was also given medicine for my festering arm wound, and my handcuffs were later loosened.

'I will order them to treat you better if you keep cooperating like this,' Mlawa said. Later he boasted that his men operated in Nairobi as they did in Dar-Es-Salaam, apparently with a free hand, and that they would be going for Mushobozi at once. My 'fellow traitor,' as Mlawa termed Mushobozi, would be joining me at any time. Poor Mushobozi: I didn't even know his first name.

Two weeks later, after I had been transferred to Dar-Es-Salaam, Mlawa returned looking visibly annoyed. 'Mushobozi's house was searched,' he told me in an agitated mood, adding that nothing had been found to incriminate him. If this was true, I wondered how the Tanzanian security police could enter another sovereign state unless they were working closely with their colleagues there—in this case, the Kenyan Special Branch.

Mlawa repeatedly asked me in a frustrated tone why no evidence had been found on Mushobozi. I wanted to tell him that I had implicated an innocent man because I was under duress, but decided against that, not wanting to endure another torture session. Instead, I suppressed my sense of guilt and told Mlawa that perhaps Mushobozi had been smart enough to cover his trail.

Had Mlawa been an intelligent man in search of the truth, rather than trying to force acceptance of what he wanted, he would have concluded from my face that it was untrue Mushobozi had been involved in any political activity. Instead, Mlawa kept on saying that Mushobozi 'is using you ... people.' Mlawa then rattled off some speculative talk that Mushobozi was one of the principal figures opposed to Nyerere's *Ujamaa* system, and that he was using us as 'loudspeakers' for his paymasters in the Central Intelligence Agency (CIA) and other anti-socialist forces.

I listened and watched as he lapsed into an abyss of hypothesis and false assumptions. 'We will get the bastard,' Mlawa said. I prayed they didn't. It was nightmarish for me to think I had implicated an innocent person I had never seen or heard of before. I could not even describe his appearance: during interrogation, Mlawa would describe him and I would simply reply 'exactly' or 'sure' to the description. It was an unfortunate incident that I will have to live with all my life. Later, after my release and escape, while I was living in Portugal, I named my son Mushobozi, after the man I was forced to implicate in a serious case. My son was born in Swaziland while I was in detention. Unfortunately though, later, and for some inexplicable and extremely puzzling reasons, my son, Mushobozi, was later secretly taken to South Africa where he had his names and date of birth changed. More disturbing, it is now maintained that my son was not even born in Swaziland but rather South Africa, where he is now a citizen. Understandably, the South African authorities issued him with a new birth certificate attesting to his 'actual' place of birth. Whether this strange twist of events is connected to my case, or for that matter, the political views I espouse, I will never know for sure.

What I do know, however, is that the next day after my abduction from Swaziland, Imelda, the mother of my son, received an invitation, in Maputo, by the wife of John Kilunga.

Kilunga was a Tanzanian official based in Maputo but whose job description was unknown—at least to me. However, like most of Nyerere's spivs he seemed to live reasonably well, his shoes always shining and frequently behind the wheel of a red Volkswagen Golf car, cruising between Maputo and Mbabane.

We met on various occasions, mostly at the residence of Patrick Makanza, the Attorney-General, but we barely spoke with each other. How Kilunga's wife got to befriend Imelda, and why, is a million Dollar question.

However, it was an interesting co-incidence that the Kilungas should play host to Imelda only a day following my abduction; and that at the end of Imelda's visit to Maputo, it had to be Kiondo, the diplomat directly involved in my abduction, who had to offer her a lift back to Swaziland.

Another item of some interest involves Inspector Myeni of the Royal Swaziland Police who worked at the Manzini Police Station. On Saturday, April 4, 1992, Inspector Myeni instructed me to appear in person at the Manzini Police Station, where he examined my travel document, took down my particulars and instructed me that I should have no contact whatsoever with Imelda.

I had, despite the obvious risks involved, come all the way from Europe in the hope of spending Easter with my son.

He had been enrolled at Sidney Williams School in Manzini and I had been paying his tuition fees direct from Europe. Money for his maintenance was deposited in the Trust Fund of the *Baphalali* Swaziland Red Cross Society; and so Imelda received a regular monthly payment from this organisation for his maintenance.

Prior to this arrangement, I was paying her a lump sum of money periodically for my son's maintainance, but she would spend this quickly and attempt to make me pay more by methods I deemed unacceptable. Therefore, this arrangement was deemed to be convenient for all parties concerned. However, Inspector Myeni's restraining order appeared to abrogate this arrangement altogether. Consequently, I turned to the Social Welfare Office in Manzini for help and advice. I discussed the matter with Dudu Zwane, a social welfare official who was of the opinion that the best way was to find a boarding school for my son where I could visit him without having to go where he now lived with his mother.

This meant, amongst other things, that I would have to remit my son's maintenance through the same social welfare office in Manzini instead of the *Baphalali* office.

At this point, Dudu Zwane paid Imelda a visit at her flat to explain to her the new arrangement to which, according to her, she concurred.

However, while I was looking for a boarding school as proposed by the Manzini Social Welfare Office, my son was abruptly taken from the Sidney Williams School. Even Sibongile Shongwe, the headmistress whom I knew personally, did not know where my son had been taken or why Imelda had suddenly decided to take him away from her school.

Whereas my son's removal from Sidney Williams School puzzled me immensely, the reasons which Inspector Myeni gave to justify the order perturbed me beyond belief. He told me that Imelda requested the restraining order as she was 'scared' of Tanzanians. This was a result of news reports that a Tanzanian psychiatrist, a certain Dr John Spokes Madelege, who has since been released, was convicted in Swaziland for the murder of his wife, Sheila. Obviously, Dr Madelege's case had nothing to do with me, or the relationship with my young son whom I had come specifically to see.

Consequently, I started to tie the loose ends together. Some strange things had happened to me whilst I was in Swaziland some of which until now I am still unable to uncover the truth due to practical problems.

Nonetheless, sources close to the Tanzania Intelligence Service (TIS) now indicate that 'someone' close to me in Swaziland

April 2, 1992, the author with his son shortly before secret sojourn to South Africa. He has never seen his son since then.

Circa 2009: The author's son in South Africa where he works as a data technologist.

was 'instrumental' in the expedition of all this. Who this 'someone' is, is a task I will be working on for some years to come.

However, it is the issue of my son's assumption of new identity in South Africa on which Inspector Myeni declines to comment which will forever remain disturbing.

This is because it was soon after Inspector Myeni's order that my son was taken from Swaziland without my knowledge.

Consequently, it took a couple of years, a great effort and money, to establish the country into which my son had been taken.

Having established this, I immediately sent letters by courier to both the Social Welfare Office in Manzini and the Station Commander of Manzini Police Station where Inspector Myeni previously worked.

I needed to inform the Social Welfare Office of my son's new address so that money for his maintenance could be forwarded to Imelda.

Since, as explained, Imelda had left Swaziland without a forwarding address, all the cheques I had been sending for my son's maintenance had been laying in Manzini Social Welfare office.

As for the station commander, I wanted him to bring to the attention of Inspector Myeni the consequences of his restraining order.

More importantly, I needed to state my side of the story formally as Inspector Myeni had not given me the opportunity when he summoned me to his office to issue the order.

Indeed, it was this latter aspect that puzzled me; namely that a police inspector was taking it upon himself to issue an indefinite restraining order instead of a law court; and significantly, without hearing my side.

Whether Inspector Myeni really knew anything about all this or whether he was unwittingly used by powerful forces working against me by destroying everything left which was dear to me is hard to tell.

However, although I now knew the whereabouts of my son, I could not visit him there due to security considerations. I have invariably wondered whether the decision to take my son to South Africa, and without my knowledge, was reached with this aspect in mind.

The acquisition of a new South African birth certificate;

moving from Swaziland without informing me, despite knowing where I was; the assumption of new names there, seem to confirm my suspicion.

Later on I was to get letters from there asking for more money in addition to what I was already sending each month for the maintenance and tuition fees. These were purported to come from my son.

However, they later turned out to be forgeries emanating from sources other than my son.

After realising this, I passed copies of these forgeries to the Royal Swaziland Police, in Manzini, and also to the Social Welfare Office there for further information and further scrutiny. Naturally, the money these letters requested and which I obligingly sent lined the pockets of those behind the letters, and not my son.

Today, I cling to my treasure of forged letters in the hope that some day I will have DNA extracted from them (especially from the back of the envelopes which the forger(s) licked when sealing them) thereby putting an end to the riddle of forgery to rest.

Furthermore, if the South African authorities issued my son with a new birth certificate on the basis of forged documentation, such as an affidavit, for instance, then a record does exist of the person(s) who presented them to the competent authorities.

If, on the other hand, no such record exists, that would give a clue as to the nature of forces involved.

Of course, knowing the forces behind this will not better the relationship with my son, who might equally have been affected by all this in more ways than one. However, it would be a great relief, certainly, for both my son and I, to know the truth, ultimately.

It was now three weeks since I arrived at Mtwara from Mozambique and Mlawa had concluded that the initial interrogation was over. 'I am trying to beat the deadline,' he said sardonically. But the nightmare was not yet over; conditions of my detention remained harsh and I had no outside contact. Finally, Mlawa brought me a sixty-page statement, urging me to sign it without even reading the contents. Even if I had read the statement it would have made no difference since the entire contents had been extracted from me under duress and nearly all of it was false.

Nevertheless, I had assumed that when the statement was presented to senior officials in the *Ikulu* (State House), they would read it thoroughly and evaluate it. I strongly believed that because the statement showed I had said 'yes' to everything and State House officials would be compelled to raise some doubts. I expected they would send an evaluator, a better educated (or an intelligent) person than Mlawa, to come and talk to me, without using coercion and intimidation. The idea, I speculated, would be to try and establish the truth.

It was at the hoped-for moment that I intended to tell senior authorities exactly what had happened. But to my complete surprise, nobody else ever came to interview me again. This meant that my statement had not been properly evaluated at the *Ikulu*; or if it had, they clearly took it to be the truth.

Mlawa came to see me several days after I had been transferred to Dar-Es-Salaam from Mtwara, to extract more confessions using his familiar cowboy tactics. Throughout my captivity I wondered how many more victims of Nyerere's regime had been forced to sign statements obtained under duress and through physical torture. I wondered then if anybody would put together a book describing their plight, in order to give the world community a glimpse of human rights abuses under Nyerere's rule.

* * * * * *

Journey to Dar-Es-Salaam

Around midnight, December 27, 1983, I heard strange movements outside my cell; movements of people, security personnel and cars. They seemed to be moving heavy items in trucks outside; it sounded like petrol tanks and jerry cans. Although as a captive I was unable to see the outside world, I had managed to work out the impending moves against me by observing the sights and sounds of the building and my interrogators. On this particular night the movements outside convinced me I was about to be moved, though I couldn't work out where to. I had also worked out how to interpret the foot movements of my interrogators: from the way someone paced the floor, I could tell not only who it was but also what he might be up to.

So it was that after midnight I was blindfolded again and led to a Land Rover, once again by the same two guards who had watched me since I arrived back in Tanzania. I was laid down on my back in the back of the vehicle, between two petrol tanks and some jerry cans. I still wonder today what would have happened had we been involved in an accident, with me blindfolded and handcuffed stuck between containers of volatile liquid.

The Land Rover zigzagged as it rounded corners, possibly to confuse me about where we were heading. After a short drive on the tar, we joined a dirt road and travelled for many hours until we stopped somewhere: my escort party wanted to buy mangoes. Outside, I could hear people speaking *Swahili*; some asked for a lift but were told there was no room in the vehicle. The Land Rover was apparently covered with a tarpaulin and those innocent people requesting a ride could not have imagined what 'cargo' lay underneath, nor who owned the vehicle.

We set off again on yet another long journey, this time until about midnight, when we pulled up at an intelligence branch house (better described as a detention centre). We had a short sleep, until about four o'clock, when we took to the road again. Our journey lasted three days, and we slept at various detention centres on the road to Dar-Es-Salaam, all of which were run by the political (or secret) police.

We arrived in Dar-Es-Salaam on the fourth day, but it

seemed we were early. I was taken to yet another detention camp in the capital for an evening meal. By now I was completely exhausted and in physical pain as a result of the rough road we had been driving (and because of the manner in which I had been transported). For four consecutive days I had been blindfolded and in handcuffs, lying back down on the hard floor of the Land Rover, stuck between petrol cans, and travelling on bumpy roads. The blindfold was so tight that whenever I tried to move my eyes, I would see only green stars twinkling.

At about midnight on the day of my arrival in Dar-Es-Salaam, my police escort once again headed towards the city. Before reaching my next detention centre, they did the usual zigzagging and confusing U-turns, then reversed the Land Rover close to the building I was being taken into. I climbed down from the Land Rover; two secret police guards, pistols ever ready, led me inside; there we found Mlawa waiting.

I was at the notorious Oyster Bay detention camp, otherwise known in opposition circles as 'Gestapo Headquarters.' It was here that my ordeal of being held incommunicado for 478 days began.

* * * * * *

The Dark Side of

Nyerere´s Legacy

The Perils of Indifference

'Of course, indifference can be tempting—more than that, seductive. It is so much easier to look away from victims...It is, after all, awkward, troublesome, to be involved in another person's pain and despair. Yet, for the person who is indifferent, his or her neighbours are of no consequence. And, therefore, their lives are meaningless. Their hidden or visible anguish is of no interest. Indifference reduces the other to an abstraction'.

Eli Wiesel, April 12, 1999

As usual, Mlawa ordered his men to strip me; they left me in my underwear. I was put into a room containing a wooden bed with a foam mattress and a stool. Apart from its obvious purpose, the stool was also used by prisoners to alert guards that they wanted to use the toilet: you banged it until the guards came to attend to you. The two large windows were sealed with a heavy cloth material and the door was permanently closed, which was surprising for a room with no other inlet for fresh air. The lights blazed day and night. I was not allowed anything to read; visitors were never allowed at Tanzanian detention camps, Oyster Bay included. I was virtually cut off from the outside world.

Next to my room was a toilet and next to it, a bathroom. Whenever I used the bathroom, a guard kept a close watch. It was claimed that some detainees had previously tried to commit suicide by drowning themselves in a basin full of water. Next to the bathroom was another room for a detainee; beside it was a small torture chamber, directly opposite my room.

Detainees being held in the rooms never saw each other, although we all used the same toilet and bathroom. If two internees banged their stools simultaneously, signalling that they wanted to use the toilet, one would be told to wait until the other had finished and been returned to his room. Only then would the second detainee be permitted to go to the toilet.

Almost every week I could hear the screams of internees being subjected to electric shock torture and beatings; sometimes their pitiful screams carried on throughout the entire night. I could never sleep with torture victims' cries for mercy piercing the night.

Experience is life's best teacher. What I was enduring at one of Nyerere's detention camps was a nasty experience, but it taught me more about the man so much revered the world over as the most 'enlightened' and 'liberal' African leader; one who upheld the rule of law and propagated the principles of human rights and equality for black South Africans. Nyerere often lambasted the white minority South African government for its scant regard for the rights of the black majority. I now started to wonder if the world was aware that Nyerere's frequent condemnation of South Africa's excesses were designed, in part, to deflect attention from his own human rights abuses.

Perhaps it will never be known how a man of Nyerere's

intellect and stature could regard criticism of his policies by his usually docile subjects as a personal threat, and not just as a *bona flde* challenge. The British, mandated by the League of Nations to administer Tanganyika (now Tanzania), never erected a single detention camp like Oyster Bay. On the contrary, they showed remarkable tolerance, even towards subjects who demanded independence. Tanzania had no political prisoners during British rule; nor were there any political refugees. In fact, the British left behind the very best they had: a fine infrastructure and a political system which worked well in England and elsewhere where Her Majesty was revered.

From the perspective of a young Tanzanian contemporary, the problem with the British was not that they held on too tightly or for too long, or even that they removed mineral and other resources; rather, the problem was that they let go too suddenly, without adequate planning for the transfer of power. There was no mass education, no awareness of the machinery involved in self-government. Tanganyikans, as we were known then, knew nothing of other countries' mistakes and successes; were unfamiliar with the concept of being able to defend one's own freedom and the idea of democracy; what they knew was the despondency and apathy that had been a necessary ingredient in colonialism. In short, we did not have a gradual transition to independence.

Furthermore, no precautions were taken or agreements initiated to ensure Nyerere could not impose his will on the people as easily as he did; or to prevent him abrogating the constitution with the ease he did. No precautions were taken to ensure the survival of democracy; as a consequence, it was snuffed out before it could take off. If Tanzania is owed a debt by anyone, it is best measured in terms of what we lost against what we got in return—and I am not referring to mineral resources, but to our loss of liberty and self-esteem. To phrase it aptly: we attained political independence and lost our freedom!

The human rights situation in Nyerere's Tanzania was compounded by the ambivalence of Western donor countries: they propped up a failed experiment (*Ujamaa*) with billions of Dollars, believing it might work; yet they failed to condemn unequivocally the human rights abuses in Tanzania. Financial support, notably from the Scandinavian countries, ensured the survival of Nyerere's regime; survival which ultimately gave rise to rampant corruption and oppression.

It is difficult to understand how the world community could so readily condemn South Africa's human rights abuses whilst keeping ominously silent when African leaders committed similar excesses on their black subjects. South Africa's minority whites refused to grant political rights to the black majority, and they were persistently denounced by the world for that. But when Nyerere's sole ruling party, with less than three million members in a country of some thirty million, outlawed all other political groups—that was acceptable. There was no denunciation of this injustice!

It must be understood that justice does not simply mean arresting an individual and bringing him before a court to answer for his alleged offence. Justice, being a major component of democracy, embodies the concepts of human rights and civil liberties. The detention of government critics was the order of the day under Nyerere who, as explained in the introduction to this account, exercised power not through institutions but as a single man. Clearly, no one could expect justice to prevail in such a system.

Freedom and justice are interlocked; justice derives from freedom; you can't have justice without freedom first. Similarly for equality, a person denied equality will not enjoy much freedom and the reverse is also true. Justice is therefore founded upon the recognition of the rights of all mankind to protection of life, liberty and property; it also rests on the recognition of freedom of conscience and expression, and, more importantly, freedom of association. These precepts form the basis of genuine democracy and justice.

In the final analysis, we know there is freedom in any given society only if those who dissent are free to do so. Selective freedom—that which applies only to supporters of a given regime and members of a single privileged political party—cannot be regarded as freedom by any stretch of the imagination. The four freedoms expounded by the former US President, Franklin D. Roosevelt, in 1941, have particular relevance at this point, especially for African countries where police tyranny substitutes for the due process of the law[1]. The result of this tyranny is the elimination of the ideals of freedom and equality, a characteristic of regimes like Nyerere's in which personal power predominated.

This might surprise some, but it is true that terrible human rights violations blot Nyerere's supposed impeccable record: the torture of political detainees, the mayhem in his detention camps and harassment of perceived political enemies, were all daily occurrences under his rule. But Nyerere's much vaunted *Ujamaa*, through which the regime exercised near absolute control over the populace and media, ensured that few of these abuses ever came to light.

From my own experience of detention in Tanzania and the experiences of hundreds of others who endured similar and worse abuse—unsung heroes who suffered silently—I feel duty bound to provide a detailed picture of what occurred under Nyerere.

I haven't listed these events in chronological order, but in order of importance and on the basis of unbiased reporting. As mentioned earlier, these incidents were not widely talked about when they occurred, but they are well documented. They represent not all, but some of the documented cases; the suffering of scores of lesser known people has yet to be documented and made public.

It is paradoxical that in most black African nations, Tanzania included, it is sometimes as dangerous to be a friend of the regime as its enemy. A Tanzanian example: On October 19, 1968, Nyerere, then president, ordered several members of his Parliament expelled, and detained others without trial. Their crime: criticising his policies during a budget debate. Among the victims were Eli Anangisye and a one-time friend of Nyerere, Joseph Kasella-Bantu, MP (Nzega East). The others were former trade union leader and former high commissioner to the United Kingdom, Christopher Kassanga Tumbo; FK Chogga, MP, (Iringa South); J Bakampenja, MP, (Ihangiro); GR Kaneno, MP, (Karagwe); FL Masha, MP, (Geita East); SM Kibuga, MP, (Mufindi); and WR Mwakitwange, MP (Nominated). Several hundred people were detained without trial that same month; up to sixty in the Kilimanjaro region alone.

---

1 In the State of the Union address delivered to the United States Congress on January 6, 1941, President Roosevelt proposed four points as fundamental freedoms humans everywhere in the world must enjoy. These are: freedom of speech and expression; freedom of religion; freedom from want and freedom from fear.

DAR ES SALAAM 22263
FAST, RELIABLE & EFFICIENT SERVICE BETWEEN MTWARA, RUVUMA, MBEYA REGIONS To DAR ES SALAAM & VICE VERSA
Value of your money!

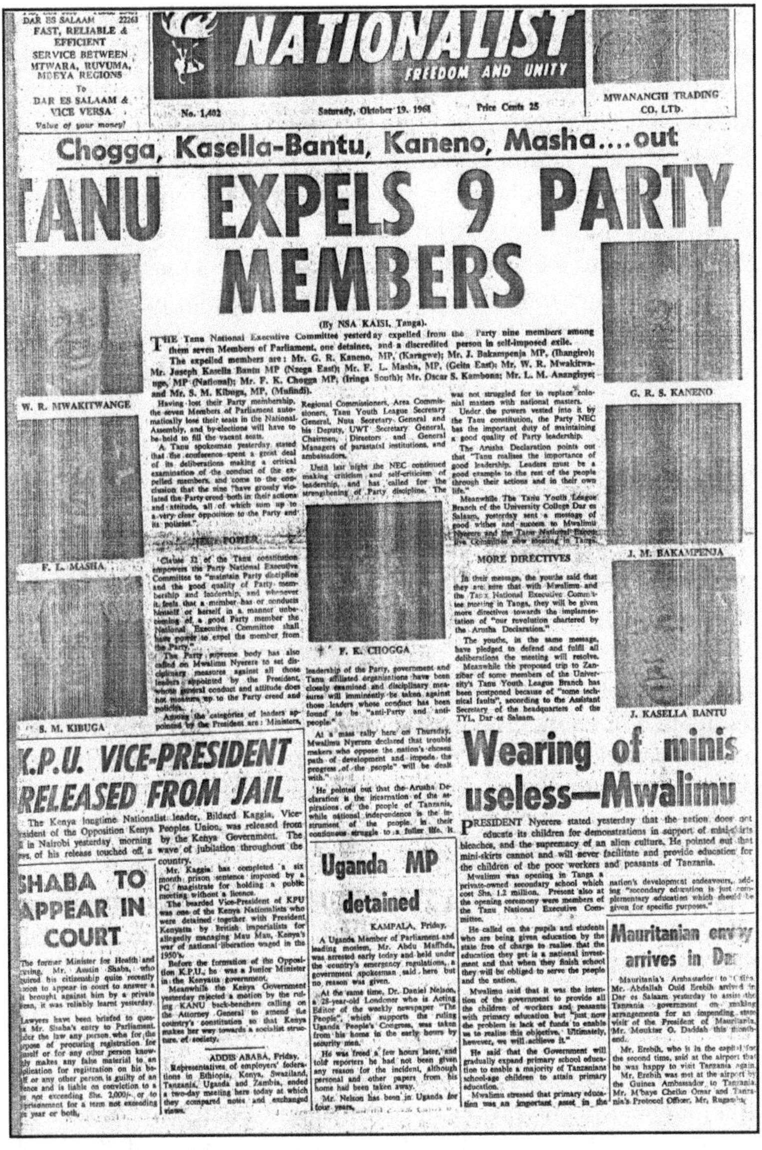

NATIONALIST
FREEDOM AND UNITY

No. 1,402 Saturday, October 19, 1968 Price Cents 25

MWANANCHI TRADING CO. LTD.

Chogga, Kasella-Bantu, Kaneno, Masha....out

TANU EXPELS 9 PARTY MEMBERS

(By NSA KAISI, Tanga).

THE Tanu National Executive Committee yesterday expelled from the Party nine members among them seven Members of Parliament, one detainee, and a discredited person in self-imposed exile.

The expelled members are: Mr. G. R. Kaneno, MP, (Karagwe); Mr. J. Bakampenja MP, (Ihangiro); Mr. Joseph Kasella Bantu MP (Nzega East); Mr. F. L. Masha, MP, (Geita East); Mr. W. R. Mwakitwange, MP (National); Mr. F. K. Chogga MP, (Iringa South); Mr. Oscar S. Kambona; Mr. L. M. Anangisye; and Mr. S. M. Kibuga, MP, (Mufindi).

W. R. MWAKITWANGE

F. L. MASHA

S. M. KIBUGA

Having lost their Party membership, the seven Members of Parliament automatically lose their seats in the National Assembly, and by-elections will have to be held to fill the vacant seats.

A Tanu spokesman yesterday stated that the conference spent a great deal of its deliberations making a critical examination of the conduct of the expelled members, and come to the conclusion that the nine "have grossly violated the Party creed both in their actions and attitude, all of which sum up to a very clear opposition to the Party and its policies."

NEC POWER

Clause 32 of the Tanu constitution empowers the Party National Executive Committee to "maintain Party discipline and the good quality of Party membership and leadership, and whenever it feels that a member has or conducts himself or herself in a manner unbecoming of a good Party member the National Executive Committee shall have power to expel the member from the Party."

The Party supreme body has also called on Mwalimu Nyerere to set disciplinary measures against all those leaders appointed by the President, whose general conduct and attitude does not measure up to the Party creed and policies.

Among the categories of leaders appointed by the President are: Ministers, Regional Commissioners, Area Commissioners, Tanu Youth League Secretary General, Nuta Secretary General and his Deputy, UWT Secretary General, Chairmen, Directors and General Managers of parastatal institutions, and ambassadors.

Until last night the NEC continued making criticism and self-criticism of leadership, and has called for the strengthening of Party discipline. The

F. K. CHOGGA

leadership of the Party, government and Tanu affiliated organisations have been closely examined and disciplinary measures will imminently be taken against those leaders whose conduct has been found to be "anti-Party and anti-people."

At a mass rally here on Thursday, Mwalimu Nyerere declared that trouble makers who oppose the nation's chosen path of development and impede the progress of the people" will be dealt with."

He pointed out that the Arusha Declaration is the incarnation of the aspirations of the people of Tanzania, while national independence is the instrument of the people in their continuous struggle to a fuller life. It was not struggled for to replace colonial masters with national masters.

Under the powers vested into it by the Tanu constitution, the Party NEC has the important duty of maintaining a good quality of Party leadership.

The Arusha Declaration points out that "Tanu realises the importance of good leadership. Leaders must be a good example to the rest of the people through their actions and in their own life."

Meanwhile The Tanu Youth League Branch of the University College Dar es Salaam, yesterday sent a message of good wishes and success to Mwalimu Nyerere and the Tanu National Executive Committee now meeting in Tanga.

MORE DIRECTIVES

In their message, the youths said that they are sure that with Mwalimu and the Tanu National Executive Committee meeting in Tanga, they will be given more directives towards the implementation of "our revolution chartered by the Arusha Declaration."

The youths, in the same message, have pledged to defend and fulfil all deliberations the meeting will resolve.

Meanwhile the proposed trip to Zanzibar of some members of the University's Tanu Youth League Branch has been postponed because of "some technical faults", according to the Assistant Secretary of the headquarters of the TYL, Dar es Salaam.

G. R. S. KANENO

J. M. BAKAMPENJA

J. KASELLA BANTU

K.P.U. VICE-PRESIDENT RELEASED FROM JAIL

The Kenya longtime Nationalist leader, Bildard Kaggia, Vice-President of the Opposition Kenya Peoples Union, was released from jail in Nairobi yesterday morning by the Kenya Government. The news of his release touched off a wave of jubilation throughout the country.

Mr. Kaggia has completed a six month prison sentence imposed by a PC magistrate for holding a public meeting without a licence.

The bearded Vice-President of KPU was one of the Kenya Nationalists who were detained together with President Kenyatta by British imperialists for allegedly managing Mau Mau, Kenya's war of national liberation waged in the 1950's.

Before the formation of the Opposition K.P.U., he was a Junior Minister in the Kenyatta government.

Meanwhile the Kenya Government yesterday rejected a motion by the ruling KANU back-benchers calling on the Attorney General to amend the country's constitution so that Kenya makes her way towards a socialist structure of society.

ADDIS ABABA, Friday.

Representatives of employers' federations in Ethiopia, Kenya, Swaziland, Tanzania, Uganda and Zambia, ended a two-day meeting here today at which they compared notes and exchanged views.

SHABA TO APPEAR IN COURT

The former Minister for Health and Housing, Mr. Austin Shaba, who acquired his citizenship quite recently is soon to appear in court to answer a suit brought against him by a private citizen, it was reliably learnt yesterday.

Lawyers have been briefed to question Mr. Shaba's entry to Parliament. Under the law any person who for the purpose of procuring registration for himself or for any other person knowingly makes any false material to an application for registration on his behalf or any other person is guilty of an offence and is liable on conviction to a fine not exceeding Shs. 2,000/- or to imprisonment for a term not exceeding one year or both.

Uganda MP detained

KAMPALA, Friday.

A Uganda Member of Parliament and leading moslem, Mr. Abdu Maffhda, was arrested early today and held under the country's emergency regulations, a government spokesman said here but no reason was given.

At the same time, Dr. Daniel Nelson, a 28-year-old Londoner who is Acting Editor of the weekly newspaper "The People", which supports the ruling Uganda People's Congress, was taken from his home in the early hours by security men.

He was freed a few hours later, and told reporters he had not been given any reason for the incident, although personal and other papers from his home had been taken away.

Mr. Nelson has been in Uganda for four years.

Wearing of minis useless—Mwalimu

PRESIDENT Nyerere stated yesterday that the nation does not educate its children for demonstrations in support of mini-skirts bleaches, and the supremacy of an alien culture. He pointed out that mini-skirts cannot and will never facilitate and provide education for the children of the poor workers and peasants of Tanzania.

Mwalimu was opening in Tanga a private-owned secondary school which cost Shs. 1.2 million. Present also at the opening ceremony were members of the Tanu National Executive Committee.

He called on the pupils and students who are being given education by the state free of charge to realise that the education they get is a national investment and that when they finish school they will be obliged to serve the people and the nation.

Mwalimu said that it was the intention of the government to provide all the children of workers and peasants with primary education but "just now the problem is lack of funds to enable us to realise this objective. Ultimately, however, we will achieve it."

He said that the Government will gradually expand primary school education to enable a majority of Tanzanians school-age children to attain primary education.

Mwalimu stressed that primary education was an important asset in the nation's development endeavours, adding "secondary education is just complementary education which should be given for specific purposes."

Mauritanian envoy arrives in Dar

Mauritania's Ambassador to [illegible] Mr. Abdallah Ould Erebih arrived in Dar es Salaam yesterday to assist the Tanzania government on making arrangements for an impending state visit of the President of Mauritania, Mr. Moukhtar O. Daddah this month-end.

Mr. Erebih, who is in the capital for the second time, said at the airport that he was happy to visit Tanzania again.

Mr. Erebih was met at the airport by the Guinea Ambassador to Tanzania, Mr. M'baye Cheikh Omar and Tanzania's Protocol Officer, Mr. Rugang[illegible]

By the illegal powers he granted himself after he had usurped sovereign authority, Nyerere could expel from his sole ruling party any member of parliament deemed critical of his regime. Loss of party membership entailed automatic loss of one's parliamentary seat. In this manner, Nyerere could expel an elected official from Parliament, as this illustration shows.

When a report about these detentions appeared on October 2, 1968, in the widely circulating *Daily Nation*, a Kenyan newspaper, the government promptly ordered the arrest of Tanzanian journalist Melek Mzirai Kangero, for filing the report. Thereafter, repression of real or imaginary opponents of Nyerere's regime intensified.

Prior to this incident, in December 1967, Nyerere ordered the arrest of the former vice president of Zanzibar, Abdallah Kassim Hanga. Nyerere then had Hanga paraded before a mass rally at the national stadium in Dar-Es-Salaam, criticising him publicly in the most virulent terms. Hanga stood before Nyerere handcuffed like a prisoner, unable to defend himself. Hanga's crime: opposition to Nyerere's regime of personal rule and his desire to establish a pervasive and entrenched cult of personality similar to that of Kim Il-Sung, the late North Korean despot, who is supposedly the country's 'Eternal President'.

An even greater shock to the public than the mass mockery of Hanga was the fact that he had returned from exile in Guinea, after being assured by Guinea's President Ahmed Sékou Touré and Nyerere himself that he would be welcome and 'free' at home. Hanga, of course, was never to be 'free.' Three years after being humiliated in public, Hanga and his former Minister for Education and ambassador to the United States, Sheikh Othman Sharrif, were killed in Zanzibar by the Karume regime in circumstances that the mainland authorities and, indeed, Nyerere himself never explained.

Before their murder, a group of elders from Mbeya region, where Sheikh Sharrif had worked as a veterinary officer, pleaded with Nyerere not to return the two men to Zanzibar. Nyerere refused, insisting that the men would have a 'fair' trial in Zanzibar. The *Swahili* weekly *Ulimwengu* (The World) demanded in its editorial of November 19, 1967 that, in view of the fact that Tanzania had a freely elected Parliament and a legal and judicial system, the detainees should be charged with specific offences and brought before the competent courts of the land. Moreover, the newspaper said, this was especially important in view of Nyerere's own declared devotion to the concept of human rights. Nyerere's government responded by detaining the editor, Otini Kambona, holding him for a decade without charge or trial. Otini Kambona's brother, Mathias, was also detained for several years without charge. According to the London *Daily Telegraph* of July 10, 1997, the two brothers were only released following repeated representations from human rights campaigners and the intervention of Robert Muldoon, the then Prime Minister of New Zealand. Now the pattern of criminal abuse of public governmental power by Nyerere, shifted to top gear.

On October 27, 1969, the party newspaper *Uhuru* (Freedom) carried a story on the front page to the effect that fourteen people had been arrested for allegedly 'plotting' to overthrow 'the government of peasants and workers'. A 'Special Military Court', the paper added, had sentenced four people to death. These included Idrisa Abdallah Majura, Mohamed Pandu, Idd Hassan and an army major called Lazaro Williams.

Ostensibly, on the day preceding the *Uhuru* newspaper report, the Tanzanian authorities had paraded Major Williams before a public rally, claiming that he had a list of 'co-conspirators' which he was to read out to the public. The 'co-conspirators' on Major Williams' list were now being connected to Abdullah Kassim Hanga, whom Nyerere had personally paraded before a mass rally at the national stadium in Dar-Es-Salaam, a year before.

Visibly terrified, his hands shaking, Major Williams proceeded to read from the scripted speech, to the effect that Idrisa Abdallah Majura, a schoolteacher whom the Tanzanian Intelligence Service (TIS) had arrested earlier in his home village of Kiziba, Bukoba, was the 'courier' between the 'plotters'. The script did not elaborate any further as to Majura's intention and motive in his alleged role as a 'courier'.

However, Major Williams did read out additional names of alleged 'plotters', namely, Yusuf Hamis Mashaka, Mkubwa Juma Hamadi, Mkuza Juma Mkuza, Musa Vuai Musa, Badru Haji Cecic Makame, Abdurahim (aka Handsome) Abdallah Ali Mwinyi Tambwe Halua, Haji Mlinge, and Mngwali Ussi. This latter group, the authorities announced, had been sentenced by the same 'Special Military Court' to 'ten years imprisonment'.

Strangely, the mass rally was not told where and when the 'Special Military Court' took place, nor were the names of military judges who presided over the case revealed. The evidence on which the 'plotters' were convicted was also withheld. Also, there was no mention of the legal representation afforded the condemned prisoners, if at all they were provided any, as one would expect.

Dar-Es-Salaam, Tuesday, January 16, 1968: President Nyerere initiates the show-trial process by parading Abdullah Kassim Hanga (seated between two police officers) at a mass rally at the national stadium after accusing him of 'boasting' about leading a coup to oust Sheikh Karume's brutal regime. Some observers, however, believe Nyerere was infuriated in part by Hanga's association with Oscar Kambona, Nyerere's former right-hand man who later became a vocal critic of Nyerere's intractable one-man rule. Hanga had apparently stayed at Oscar's residence in London whilst en route to Tanzania from exile in Guinea.

Sheikh Abeid Karume (left) and Julius Nyerere (right). Behind (centre) is Abdallah Kassim Hanga, the man the two leaders wanted to forget.

Such details should have been regarded as essential in view of the fact that the case involved capital punishment. To date, none of the fourteen men arrested, including those the authorities said had been sentenced to 'ten years imprisonment' has ever been seen again.

In a move designed to curtail the independence of the Judiciary, Nyerere ordered that a learned magistrate, A. Ngitami be detained for acquitting a defendant that the government wanted convicted and imprisoned. Magistrate Ngitami was later released after members of the Bar, led by the then Chief Justice, Mr. Justice Phillip Telfer Georges, a foreign expatriate from Trinidad, had protested. From this point on, courts of law in Tanzania gradually witnessed the erosion of judicial independence. At this juncture, some judges who made decisions which displeased Nyerere were removed from the Judiciary altogether and re-assigned elsewhere.

Then came the iniquitous legislation of 1970 in which an amendment to the colonial-inherited penal code was rushed through Parliament to make provision for the death penalty for persons convicted of treason. The new legislation was deliberately retrospective, which meant it would apply to the persons it had been designed to punish. This was done after the arrests of Bibi Titi Mohamed, a former Member of Parliament, Michael Mowbray Kamaliza, a former Minister of Labour and then the head of the country's only Trade Union, Gray Likungu Mattaka, a former News Editor of the newspaper of the ruling party, Captain Eliya Lifa Chipaka and his brother John, Colonel William Chacha, then Tanzania's Military Attaché in Peking and Lieutenant Alfred Philip Milinga (Milinga was later cleared of all charges). The government accused them of treason and misprision of treason (knowing of an intended treason and doing nothing), and in October, 1969, Nyerere announced they would stand trial for crimes against the state. In March, 1970, a bill was passed (Act No 2, 1970) amending section 39 of the former penal code. Sentences handed down under the new Act could be applied retrospectively, thus making the seven defendants who had been arrested six months before the legislation was changed, liable for the new penalties. In a legal sense, this action was not compatible with the principles of natural justice. Moreover, the rule against retrospective application of the law is supposed to be the basic tenet of all legal systems.

Nyerere's regime also persistently absolved itself of any

involvement with the brutal reign of the fanatical nationalist, Sheikh Abeid Amani Karume in Zanzibar. There, torture of political opponents was widespread; some opposition figures mysteriously disappearing. Yet the Nyerere regime routinely sent mainlanders and natives of Zanzibar, resident on the mainland, to Zanzibar knowing that they would be tortured. According to a strong-worded letter which appeared in a Tanzanian newspaper, the *Business Times* of July 10, 1992, people, including amongst others, Ali Khalifa, Maalim Mohamed Matter, Harun Baharun, Sayyid Hassan Sheikh, Mohamed A Abbas, Ali Jaffer, Sayyid Mohamed Adnan, Hashim Haji Abdullah, Hashim Mohamed, Abdulatif bin Brek, Maalim Haruna, Mzee Mbaba who died in prison, are known to have been sent to Zanzibar after being arrested by the Tanzanian Intelligence Service (TIS) on the mainland on unspecified charges.

Between 1969 and 1970, Nyerere's regime consigned Bibi Titi Mohamed, the Chipaka brothers, Gray Likungu Mattaka and Michael Mowbray Kamaliza, amongst others, to Zanzibar, specifically for torture. At some stage they were held at Zanzibar's most notorious torture chamber, 'Kwa Bamkwe' otherwise known as 'Kwa Mandera', which was within the Zanzibar city centre prison. For more than five months these detainees rotated between several Zanzibar prisons; other Zanzibar political detainees suffering the same fate, although some survived Karume's reign of terror.

Why would a revered figure like Nyerere allow his own political detainees to be taken to Zanzibar for torture if his government truly loathed Karume's excesses? How can we believe that Nyerere and Karume's regime were not partners in brutality, when today Karume's minions, the perpetrators of terror, are walking scot-free in Tanzania? Some even hold senior government posts offered them by Nyerere, or obtained on his recommendation. Why did Nyerere's government close its ears when the call went out for the perpetrators of crimes against humanity to be brought to trial?

And what of those in senior party positions and top government posts who were involved in the forced marriages scandal? Salmin Amour, former president of Zanzibar, is known to have taken part in a forced marriage in September, 1970. Amour's 'wife,' a woman of Persian origin, re-married her fiancé later in

Copenhagen, Denmark, after she finally succeeded in breaking free from the man she was forced to marry. This marriage was against her will and that of her parents.

But, it was the horrendous abuse that the victims endured whilst in the bondage of their 'husbands' which shocked the civilised world.

Apparently, information about these abuses was able to reach the outside world after letters written by the victims were smuggled out of Zanzibar, presumably during the victims' visits to hospital for medical treatment.

In an article entitled 'The Plight of Four Unwilling Wives,' published by the *Guardian* newspaper of London, on March 21, 1972, Linda Christmas quoted one of the victims describing their plight as follows:

'Our situation is very grave and has now reached beyond the bounds of human endurance. Some of us have even attempted to commit suicide but were saved in time. We have been anxious by waiting patiently for the last one and half years in the hope that succour is forthcoming but regret that this succour looks like a mirage; but our hopes and spirits are high as we look ahead with hope and confidence that we have the support of the world for our cause which is right; and right will triumph in the end'.

'We suffer loneliness, away from our parents, relations and friends. Our loneliness is only broken by abuses and beatings from the so-called husbands; and on certain occasions the beatings became so severe that I had to be admitted in hospital for treatment. I am now physically and mentally exhausted with the tortures'.

Yet, the United Republic of Tanzania (which includes Zanzibar) acceded to the United Nation's 1956 Supplementary Convention on the 'Abolition of slavery, the slave trade and institutions and practices similar to slavery'

Such practices, it must be emphasised, include *inter alia* servitude, including abduction.

Thus, it is a very sad irony that the very same state, should adopt and enforce a policy which is totally the opposite of the Convention to which it acceded.

How many more minor and mid-level government and *CCM* officials who committed similar crimes against minority groups in Zanzibar still hold public office? What of the young women whose lives they ruined? Will the government compensate the victims? What of the parents of young virgins who were jailed and caned because they refused to allow their daughters to enter forced marriages with 'indigenous' Zanzibaris? Ironically, almost every member of the Zanzibar Revolutionary Council (ZRC) ended up grabbing as 'wives' women of Persian, Indian and Arab origin, the very groups that were supposed to be oppressors of the 'indigenous' Zanzibaris.

Even today the *CCM* government remains reluctant to purge its ranks of elements which ordinary Tanzanians claim were involved in the mysterious disappearance, in Zanzibar, of real or perceived political opponents. Many of the culprits are secure in their positions today, thanks to the *CCM* policy of '*kulindana*' (protecting each other). Brigadier Abdallah Said Natepe (now retired), was, for many years, Nyerere's Minister of State in the Union government. This means that Nyerere entrusted Natepe to oversee the intelligence and security affairs of Tanzania.

However, Natepe, together with the late Brigadier Seif Bakari Omar, whom Nyerere had appointed Deputy Minister of Defence in the Union government, were both alleged to have been instrumental in the mysterious disappearance of scores of people in Zanzibar.

Other officials alleged to be linked with these enforced disappearances include the rest of the inner circle of the so-called Committee of Fourteen, namely Ramadhani Haji, Mohamed Abdallah Ameir (Kaujore), Mohamed Mfaranyaki, Khamis Darweshi, Said Idd Bavuai, Hamid Ameir, Hafidh Suleiman, Pili Khamis, Said Washoto, Khamis Hemed Nyuni and Yusuf Himid.

Others include Edington Kisasi, a former Commissioner of Police; Hassan Nassor Moyo, a former Minister of Education; Ibrahim Makungu, a senior intelligence official and Brigadier Khamis Hemed of Tanzania People's Defence Force (TPDF).

The last named officer is further alleged to have headed a squad responsible for disposing of thousands of dead bodies in dry wells which were located in Bambi; an isolated area on the main island of Zanzibar. These were people who were killed during the bloody revolution (referred to in the introduction) and its aftermath.

These officials may well be innocent of the crimes they are alleged to have committed, but as long as the *CCM* and its government continue to protect them from facing their accusers, and consequently denying them their constitutional right to defend themselves before a court, the public will believe that they are indeed guilty.

The Tanzanian government has persistently refused to allow forensic experts to examine the Bambi wells and to institute a Truth and Reconciliation Commission (TRC). This could establish the truth behind these and other killings; where the victims are buried (if at all they were). This refusal seems to indicate that the government is intent on suppressing the truth, thereby perpetuating the agony of the victims' families.

One example as to how far the *CCM* government is prepared to go in order to protect these alleged perpetrators of crimes against humanity is that of Juma Ameir Juma.

Ameir Juma was, until late 1997, a minister-counsellor at the Tanzanian High Commission in the United Kingdom.

Trained in both intelligence and interrogation by the former East German secret police, the *Staat Sicherheit Polizei* (*Stasi*), Juma Ameir Juma worked at the earlier mentioned torture chamber 'Kwa Bamkwe' prior to being awarded a diplomatic post in the United Kingdom[2]. He practised his profession with maximum zeal and enthusiasm. Scores of victims were tortured there, the majority of them died as a result of their injuries.

Rashaad Mohamed Rashid, who currently lives in Copenhagen, Denmark, and who was held at 'Kwa Bamkwe' between 1966 and April 1973 remembers how on direct orders of Juma Ameir Juma inmates were routinely flogged with electric cable until they succumbed.

'Despite my own inhuman treatment by Juma Ameir (Juma) which included whippings and threats of acts of sodomy against my human person…I remember three of my fellow inmates namely Abas Ahmadia, Salim Abdallah and Saleh Abdallah, dying as a result of the protracted torture by Juma Ameir Juma and his confederates…'

Indeed, Rashid's charges are corroborated by another former inmate of 'Kwa Bamkwe', Mohamed Said alias Mtendeni.

---

2 http://www.information.dk/11941

Mtendeni was arrested on the morning of April, 8, 1972, by Juma Ameir Juma himself supported by two associates armed with sub-machine guns. Upon arriving at 'Kwa Bamkwe' Juma Ameir Juma ordered Mtendeni to take off his clothes and he, Juma Ameir Juma, '...personally flogged me with *mpera* (a guava cane) until I fainted...'

Mtendeni describes in graphic terms, how Juma Ameir Juma would be heard to say, 'The white people say money speaks, but I say it's *mpera* which speaks'.

Mtendeni further narrates how Juma Ameir Juma ordered Noorbai Issa, another internee, to be bound and later hoisted with the same rope in a simulation of hanging. Noorbai Issa howled for mercy, says Mtendeni, but Juma Ameir Juma merely laughed at his howling, until the rope was finally loosened and he fell heavily to the ground.

Even so, Mohamed Said Mtendeni survived Juma Ameir Juma's barbarism and fled to The Gulf upon his release where he lived in exile until recently. As a result of Juma Ameir Juma's prolonged, physical torture, one of his legs has never functioned normally again, despite undergoing extensive treatment.

During the period he spent in Juma Ameir Juma's so-called security cells, Mtendeni remembers some of his fellow inmates who fell by the wayside—also due to protracted torture. These included army lieutenants Ali Othman and Mikidadi A. Ali.

In addition, the latter victim's brother, Ali A. Kayaya was briefly held at Juma Ameir Juma's 'Kwa Bamkwe' although unlike his unfortunate brother he survived.

All told, Mohamed Said Mtendeni's list of those fellow inmates who died as a result of torture includes Mohamed Abdallah Saghir and a certain Ali Salehe.

A further victim of Juma Ameir Juma's unprecedented, horrifying torture is Hashil Seif Hashil, a naturalised Danish citizen. He tells a similar story to those of other Juma Ameir Juma's victims.

Hashil was arrested on the mainland by members of the Tanzanian Intelligence Service (TIS) sometime in April 1972. After being held incommunicado for nearly six months, a team of seven torture experts from Zanzibar were sent to the mainland.

According to the account published by the Danish

newspaper *Information* of September 11, 1997, Juma Ameir Juma was among those seven.

According to *Information*, '...Hashil was handcuffed and blindfolded' as the seven officials took him with another detainee to some detention centre: 'I did not know where we were going. We drove for approximately half an hour (from where we were being held), and I could hear that we drove by the sea. At the time we arrived at a house (detention centre) my blindfold was removed. The house was scary; there was blood over the walls'.

Furthermore, according to the *Information* newspaper, Hashil was flogged by Juma Ameir with an electric wire until he passed out. He adds that this was '...because they could not make me do what they wanted me to do'; that is 'put my signature on a piece of paper below a large number of names, to testify that people on the list were working against the government'.

Hashil was released with a group of other detainees after being held in detention without trial for over six years, finally making it to Denmark. This followed a concerted campaign to get him and other fellow detainees released by Amnesty International (AI).

Other victims of Juma Ameir Juma's physical torture include Mohamed Abdallah Baramia alias Kikono, Ibrahim Mohamed Hussein, Ibrahim Mohamed Sudi (who has difficulty in walking, his legs suffering severely from Juma Ameir Juma's torture and still bearing scars as a result), Isaack Juma Harakati alias Mteswa, Hamis Abdallah Ameir and Musa Shaaban.

Consequently, when the *Africa Analysis* of June 27, 1997, carried a story indicating that Juma Ameir Juma was to relocate to the Tanzania embassy in Stockholm, Sweden, a group of his victims hurriedly contacted the Netherlands Institute of Human Rights (SIM) of the University of Utrecht asking them to submit the case on their behalf to the International Criminal Tribunal for the former Yugoslavia[3].

However, the Yugoslavia Tribunal in The Hague has only jurisdiction over crimes committed in the former Yugoslavia after January 1, 1991.

Nonetheless, the Netherlands Institute of Human Rights

---

3 See *BT* (Denmark), September 28, 1997 (p 5). Also, see opposite page.

FAMILY

mirror

Tanzania foremost general interest newspaper

DAY AND NIGHT
PHARMACY LIMITED
P.O. Box 70103
DSM (NAMANGA BR.)
TEL: 667114,
FAX 112440 TLX: 41816
BUSINESS HOURS:
7.00 AM - 1.00 AM
INCLUDING SATURDAYS,
SUNDAYS & PUBLIC HOLIDAYS

ISSN 0856 - 2407 NO. 218   24 - 30 OCT., 1997   PRICE T.SHS. 200/=   KShs. 20

Danish newspaper reports on Tanzanian diplomat who 'tortured' prisoners:

Victims want him prosecuted at The Hague's Court

By Mirror Reporter

A Danish newspaper has reported that Juma Ameir, a diplomat whom Tanzania plans to move to its embassy in Stockholm (which also covers Denmark) runs the risk of being accused of crimes against humanity at the UN International Court in The Hague.

• *Tanzania vil give ham diplomatstatus i Danmark:*

Ofrene: Han er en tortur-bøddel

B.T. the Danish newspaper that reported on the Tanzanian diplomat's past deeds. Picture on the paper shows one of the victims, Hashil Hashil.

The newspaper, B.T. in its issue of September 28, 1997 reports on page 5 that the controversial Juma Ameir is currently working as his country's counsellor at its London embassy, "but according to the news magazine *Africa Analyses*, is going to be moved to the embassy in Sweden, covering the whole of Scandinavia".

The Danish popular evening daily continued," The high-ranking diplomat has, according to Tanzania refugees, a sinister past as leader of the torture chamber in the Kwa Manders prison in the island of Zanzibar, which is situated off the Kenya and Tanzania coasts in the India Ocean".

The newspaper which the *Family Mirror* has obtained a copy of, quotes Ludovick S. Mwijage, journalist and writer as telling it that a number of people "disappeared under Juma Ameir, who was tortured, some also, by the notorious East

Ludovick Mwijage

Quote of the Week

"*Regional co-operation is inevitable in this region. Smuggling is a clandestine form of regional co-operation. When governments fail to organise proper trade regimes, others will act*".

· Yoweri Kaguta Museveni, President of Uganda, in an interview during a visit to Kibale in Western Ugandan December 6, 1995.

Tanzanian diplomat

From page 1

German communist secret police, the "Stasi". Mr. Mwijage now lives in Copenhagen, Denmark.

B.T further reports that in a letter to the Danish Centre for Human Rights, Mwijage, whose release from a Tanzania prison was obtained by the International Red Cross, describes the brutal atrocities used in the torture chamber in the 1970s." In Mr. Ameir's torture chamber, electric wires were attached to the testicles of men, which often caused

ire.

"We have collected documentation and testimonies from survivors" Mwijage further said in his written testimony to the Centre, "and we are going to present this material to the UN International Tribunal in the Hague next week (i.e. early October 1997) demanding that he (Ameir) be accused for crimes against humanity."

The Danish newspaper further quotes Mwijage as saying that the Tanzania government which employed Ameir

as confirming to the press that Juma Ameir was being transferred to Sweden and thereby gaining diplomatic status in Denmark. But when the newspaper sought from the Ambassador the date of the transfer, he first denied any knowledge of Juma Ameir, Later, according to B.T., the ambassador admitted knowing the name. "But I know nothing

Torture victim Hashil Hashil showing his "torture" scars

templated to recall Juma Ameir. The source who did

VIP treatment

From page 1

House of Representatives, senior sports officials and more than 25 journalists who covered the tour.

Regional and District Commissioners of Pemba were 52 Mkoani Port to welcome Mr. Raza on his arrival and also on his return to Zanzibar. He took a group of 30 people, including 20 journalists. He paid for their transport and accommodation plus their allowances in Pemba.

gungas and cash.

Political observers and journalists who joined the tour have been surprised with the VIP treatment accorded to Mr. Raza which reduced ministers and regional commissioners to mere junior civil servants.

"The protocol in Zanzibar is upside down. Perhaps this is what one should expect from a government which is both democratic and revolutionary," commented one of the

A newspaper report on Juma Ameir Juma, at the time the minister-counsellor at the Tanzania High Commission in the United Kingdom, who used to tell detainees he physically tortured: 'The white people say money speaks but I say it's mpera (guava cane: author's note) which speaks'.

did advise the victims to file a complaint with the country where Juma Ameir Juma was living i.e. the United Kingdom, and see whether prosecution on a national level was possible. Since the United Kingdom has ratified the Convention against torture, which obliges it to establish jurisdiction over torture, Juma Ameir Juma's victims were hopeful that Juma Ameir Juma would face his accusers in an open court; a privilege he denied his victims.

However, as the victims presented the appropriate British authorities with the background to the case and collected evidential material, the Ministry of Foreign Affairs and International Co-operation in Dar-Es-Salaam hastily recalled Juma Ameir Juma back home and cancelled his posting to Sweden.

It is difficult to understand that if Juma Ameir Juma was innocent of the crimes he is alleged to have committed, then why recall him with such haste to where he enjoys total protection from prosecution? It would seem more appropriate for him to face his accusers in a neutral country.

The *CCM* government still owes the world an explanation for the disappearance of people such as Abdulaziz Twala, who was Finance Minister in Zanzibar, Salehe Sadalla Akida, who was Minister for Labour, Roads and Energy, Aboud Nadhif, the then Principal secretary of Trade and Industry, Mdungi Ussi Mcha, who was Deputy Minister for Education and Jaha Ubwa Jaha, who was Deputy Principle Secretary for Trade and Industry.

Other detainees who disappeared include Amour Zahoro, Mohamed Salim Jinja, Mohamed Salim Hilal, Suleiman Hemed Suleiman, Fadhil Hemed Salim, Soud Mohamed Nassoro, Seif Ali Nassor and Mohamed Amour Mohamed.

Others are Khamis S. Seif, Ahmed Mohamed Salim, Salum A. Mohamed, Kamis Masoud Kamis, Juma Maulid Jimrindo, Mohamed Pandu Mcha, Salim Ahmed Seif, Salim M. Nassor, Mohamed K. Khamis, Salim H. Salim, Said Humud Ali, Hemed Said, Mohamed Juma and Mohamed Makame Hatibu.

Still more who were detained, only to disappear were Hamza Mohamed Said Ali, Fumba (aka Pemba boy), Makame J. Msorima, Mwanga Said, Mohamed Hamud, Ame Makame, Kassim Mohamed, Abbas Mohamed Mdonga, Abdulla Suleiman, Said Dahoma (Kombanyongo), Mohamed Kassim, Ali Mzee Mbalia, Suleiman Salim and Ahmada (aka Mgazija). The majority of these political detainees were known to be staunch supporters of government and the Union, but they had annoyed a few people in power by demanding the introduction of democracy, social justice and accountability. The authorities had them arrested; to date no explanation has been forthcoming about their mysterious disappearance from prison, despite concerted efforts by concerned members of their families and the public at large to obtain clarification of their fate from the authorities.

Indeed, on May 8, 1992, a Tanzanian newspaper *The Business Times* carried on its front page a petition signed by some sixty people calling on the Union president, then Ali Hassan Mwinyi, himself a Zanzibari, to at least formally clarify the fate of these political detainees. The petitions were ignored by President Mwinyi.

However, it is the case involving nineteen men, including, amongst others, Mohamed Hameza, Sharrif Ahmed, Mzee Wazir, a fisherman from the Zanzibar island of Tumbatu, Said Ali, Salum Seif, Mohamed Khamis, Mohammed Hamed, Musa Ali, Mohamed Juma, Said Hamoud Alei, Salum Nassor and Sultan Nassor which best illustrates the level of criminal abuse of authority by the late Nyerere's regime.

These men were arrested on the night of September 20, 1970, on charges that they were 'plotting to overthrow the Zanzibar Revolutionary Government' by force of arms.

In 1971, and in blatant violation of international law and judicial principles, the Tanzanian government had the alleged plotters paraded in handcuffs at the Maisara Suleiman ground in Zanzibar. Brandishing his ceremonial stick menacingly over the heads of terrified prisoners, the first vice president of Tanzania, Sheikh Karume, announced to the world that the nineteen prisoners had been condemned to death by a 'Special Military Court' that had previously condemned Major Williams and his group to death.

As in the case of Major Williams, the first vice president gave no indication as to when and where the 'Special Military Court' took place; neither did he provide details with regards to the legal representation afforded the accused nor the names of judges who supposedly presided over the 'Special Military Court' which had condemned the accused to death.

All Sheikh Karume would say was that two of the accused,

namely, Said Ali and Mohamed Hemed, had received 'military training' in Dubai and Saudi Arabia respectively. He added that the 'plotters' had told interrogators (most definitely at 'Kwa Bamkwe') that they were supported by the governments of the United States, Britain, and Kenya. Dubai, Saudi Arabia, America.... Britain...it seemed Byzantine if not absurd.

Indeed, according to *Drum* magazine (East Africa edition) of July 1971, Sheikh Karume was quoted admitting as much: 'The plotters' he said, 'worked for themselves'; and the paraded men seemed to be ignorant of the geographical location of the countries that supposedly backed them. Their familiarity with fire-arms seemed non-existent.

However, that did not prevent a Tanzanian army captain from informing the rally that the nineteen men, fourteen of whom who had never left Zanzibar in their entire lives, were only an 'advance party'. Fifty four others he said, like someone rehearsing a song, lived abroad, mainly in neighbouring Mombasa. That, in essence, was the state 'evidence' against the accused that sealed their fate, but the issue of the 'Special Military Court' that convicted them lingered.

This is because Zanzibar did not, and does not, have an independent army, apart from the Tanzania People's Defence Force (TPDF) of which Nyerere, as president, was its Commander-in-Chief. Therefore, in terms of command responsibility, no such 'Special Military Court' could have gone ahead without the express approval of the Commander-in-Chief i.e. Nyerere.

However, Nyerere let the Maisara Suleiman ground show trial proceed, and, to be sure, members of the Tanzania People's Defence Force (TPDF) and the Field Force Unit (FFU) from the mainland descended on Maisara Suleiman ground in droves, and only a few hours before the prisoners being led to their fate they could be seen hassling the grim-faced prisoners to face the cameras.

In contrast, this is the same Nyerere who, in a bid to demonstrate his 'compassionate' nature to the world, hurriedly flew to the Zambian capital, Lusaka, in 1997, to plead for the release of Dr Kenneth David Kaunda.

The former Zambian president was being held in a Lusaka prison on charges that he knew of preparations to stage a *coup d'état* in October, 1997, against the then Frederick Chiluba government, but had allegedly failed to inform the Zambian authorities. Consequently, following Nyerere's intervention, Dr Kaunda was moved from jail and placed under house arrest at his Kulundu residence in Lusaka until he was released on June 1, 1998, after all charges were dropped.

However, unlike those Tanzanian citizens whose lives were in actual danger having been sentenced to death by a kangaroo court, Dr Kaunda's life was not in immediate danger as he was to be subjected to the due process of the Zambian law.

Ironically, in 2001, a High Court in Tanzania set free a group of political detainees who had been languishing in jail for over three years on the charges of 'treason'. These included Juma Duni Haji, Ramadhan Shamna Abdi, Abdullah Said Abeid, Abbas Zam Ali, Said Zam Ali, Machano Khamis Ali, Nassor Seif Amour, Sharrif Haji Dadi, Hamad Masoud Hamad, Hassan Mbarouk Hassan, Hamad Mnanga Khalfan, Mohamed Ali Maalim, Pembe Ame Manja, Soud Yusuf Mgeni, Zulekha Ahmed Mohamed, Hamad Rashid Mohamed, Zeina Juma Mohamed and Hamza Makame Omar.

In acquitting them, the court observed that no charges of 'treason' can stand as Zanzibar is part of Tanzania. This means, one cannot conceivably 'plot' to overthrow part of Tanzania as were the allegations against the accused in this case.

Examining the execution of the prisoners who were paraded at the Maisara Suleiman ground and Major Williams' group in the context of the above ruling by the High Court, how can these atrocities be justified?

Whilst the issue of the Maisara prisoners still lingered, the authorities were announcing that henceforth, Zanzibaris of Comorian origin were to be expelled *en masse* from the islands. No reason was given for such a drastic move, except to say those who wished to stay in Zanzibar should apply for right of residence and/or citizenship.

Of course, this was not the first time that nationals of Tanzania had been deprived of citizenship by the whim of a ruler.

In 1968, Oscar Salathiel Kambona, the former Tanzanian Foreign Minister and one time Nyerere's right-hand man, was stripped off his citizenship at the personal instructions of Nyerere himself. This followed Kambona's defection to the United

Kingdom after disagreeing with Nyerere on various political issues. In depriving him of citizenship, Nyerere's regime contended that Kambona was a 'Malawian' from Likoma Island and thus did not qualify for Tanzanian citizenship. This was clearly untrue.

According to *Wikipedia*, an online encyclopaedia, Kambona was born (on August 13, 1928) on the shores of Lake Nyasa, in a small village called Kwambe near Mbamba Bay in the district of Mbinga, Songea, southern Tanzania.

His father, the Reverend David Kambona, belonged to the first group of African priests to be ordained in the Anglican Church of Tanganyika.

Apparently, Kambona first met Nyerere when he was attending school at Tabora Boys' Senior Government School (where he returned as a teacher in 1952) whilst Nyerere was teaching at St. Mary's Catholic School in Tabora.

When Nyerere formed TANU (Tanganyika African National Union) Kambona became Secretary-General.

Indeed, after Tanganyika attained independence from Britain (on December 9, 1961), Kambona held important cabinet posts in Nyerere's own government prior to his defection to the United Kingdom. So, how then could Kambona not have been a Tanzanian citizen?

Kambona, during the army mutiny of January 21, 1964, had also saved Nyerere's government from collapsing and perhaps saved his life too.

In the early hours of the mutiny, the helmsman had abandoned the ship of the state and taken to his heels before ending up in a squalid mud hut several kilometres outside the commercial capital, Dar-Es-Salaam.

It was in that mud hut that Nyerere was to take refuge for a couple of days, leaving behind his right-hand man, Kambona, to deal with the mutineers.

By hiding in a mud hut rather than in a normal house, Nyerere perhaps thought that if the mutinying soldiers who were led by Sgt Francis Higo Ilogi came looking for him, they would start looking in normal houses as a mud hut would not be considered a likely place in which a sovereign head of state would choose to hide.

During the days of the mutiny, Nyerere was completely

powerless and, had Kambona wanted to seize power, he might have done so by exploiting the events of the moment.

Instead, Kambona remained loyal to Nyerere and, once the mutiny was over, Kambona brought Nyerere back to the commercial capital covered with a dusty overcoat, slumped in the back seat of an unmarked Land Rover.

When on March 31, 1964, a 40-strong advance party of the Nigeria battalion that was to replace 40 British Royal Marine Commandos, landed at the Dar-Es-Salaam Airport (now called *Mwalimu* Nyerere International Airport), they were greeted by none other than Kambona, whom Nyerere was later to deprive of his citizenship.

Apparently, the British Royal Marine Commandos, whom the Nigerian troops had come to replace, had been in the country on a peacekeeping mission following the described army mutiny.

Not surprisingly, Nyerere's loyal juniors, whom he had left behind to run the country on his behalf and, of course, to preserve the memory of Africa's 'great' man (in terms of the latter, they are doing a highly exceptional job, particularly where it serves their own interests), had been using similar tactics against individual citizens who, like Kambona, had served their country conscientiously but later fell out of favour with the powers that be.

In 2001, the *Awamu ya Tatu* i.e. the Third Phase government of President Mkapa, stripped some nationals of their citizenship (or rather, declared them as never having been Tanzanian citizens in the first place). These included Jenerali Ulimwengu, a noted member of society and former Chairman of the country's Sports Council; Timothy Bandora, former ambassador to Nigeria; Anatoli Amani, former *CCM* chairman of Kagera region; Mouldine Castico, former *CCM* Publicity Secretary in Zanzibar and Kabendera Shinani, a radio journalist.

Most of these later regained their citizenship ostensibly after being compelled to apply for it; however, prior to this, the Permanent Parliamentary Committees of External Affairs and Defence and Security respectively, issued a joint statement on November 9, 2001, calling on the Mkapa government not to give them back their citizenship in the supposed interests of Tanzania's 'defence and security.' What security?

It was an open secret that some of these fell out of

government favour because of their firm stand against institutional corruption, or simply manifested sympathy for the opposition.

Others, in fact, were deprived of their citizenship after they openly expressed concern over the January 2001, mass killings in Zanzibar and Pemba.

According to news reports, some 40 peaceful demonstrators were shot dead as scores of others fled the islands to neighbouring countries[4]. Apparently, the demonstrations were held in protest against the controversial Zanzibar election in 2000, which was flawed and marred by widespread irregularities.

Incredibly, following this recent mass slaughter of unarmed civilians, nobody was ever held accountable, thanks once more to the *CCM* culture of *kulindana* i.e. protecting each other.

Furthermore, in a move reminiscent of a 'reward' for those who might otherwise have been held responsible for the shootings by virtue of their positions; and who did not attempt to stop the killings, President Mkapa promoted a significant number of senior police officers only a few months later.

Consequently, the families of the victims and the public at large started to wonder whether whoever ordered the killings was not 'well protected' and/or whether he did not act with 'full authority' of the president. Admittedly, this may have been conjecture.

However, as long as those responsible for that mass slaughter are not identified and punished for what they did, these perceptions will invariably persist.

Nevertheless, it was Kabendera Shinani's public humiliation which was to end tragically by his suicide. Like his mother, who hails from Bukoba, Shinani had never been anything other than being a Tanzanian citizen.

He attended elementary school at Mugeza in Bukoba before joining Bukoba Secondary school.

After completing Form IV, he worked briefly for *Mahakama* i.e. the Judiciary in Kigoma region. However, he had to leave this job due to poor wages and went to work as a radio journalist in neighbouring Rwanda, subsequently becoming a *BBC*

---

4 http://news.bbc.co.uk/2/hi/africa/4237526.stm

Swahili correspondent.

During the Rwandan genocide, Shinani opted to return home to Bukoba with his family, although he remained a *Swahili* correspondent for the *BBC*.

Shortly after being declared not to be a Tanzanian citizen, the police in Bukoba formally charged him with registering a vote in the 2000 election when he was 'not a citizen'. However, this was not Shinani's first time to vote in the country as he had voted before, prior to taking up the new job in Rwanda.

Reliable sources now contend that all this happened after Shinani allegedly implied in one of his reports, that Wilson Mutagaywa Masilingi, President Mkapa's former Minister of State (Good Governance—indeed!) had actually lost Muleba South constituency to his rival.

True or not, this kind of information did not necessarily have to come from Shinani. As I indicated earlier in the introduction, most *CCM* Members of Parliament who were able to retain their constituencies did so with the apparent help of *takrima* (the supposed traditional African hospitality).

By being able to use the money that the Mkapa government fraudulently took from the bank (also referred to in the introduction) many *CCM* parliamentary candidates were able to gain advantage over the opposition candidates. Sometimes, it was just paying out the opposition candidates from contesting the election.

According to *East African Business,* of April 7, 2008, 108 million Tanzania shillings (about 87,000 $US) was 'offered' by a person suspected of involvement in the EPA scandal, to retain the Kigoma Urban constituency which was held by the opposition, *Chama cha Demokrasia na Maendeleo* (*CHADEMA*), for ten years.

The money, the paper added, was used to woo both *CCM* and *CHADEMA* voters to vote for the *CCM* candidate.

Consequently, the Kigoma Urban seat went to *CCM*, and the former *CHADEMA* candidate defected to *CCM*. Shortly afterwards, the defector became a member of the East Africa Legislative Assembly for the ruling party to which he defected, i.e. *CCM*.

Additionally, the paper added that part of the EPA money went to Songea Urban, where a *CCM* parliamentary candidate was facing a tough challenge from a rival opposition candidate.

Then, there was an undisclosed 'substantial amount' that was reportedly paid to an influential sheikh (now deceased) so that he could get his Moslem followers, who seemed to favour the opposition over the *CCM*, to vote for the latter party.

These are but a few examples; incidents like this were widespread during the 2005 election campaign to attempt listing here.

It nonetheless became common practice after President Mkapa's government had legalised *takrima*, under which offering cash, or other presents to voters became perfectly legal.

This was despite the very obvious pitfalls inherent in the practice and universal protestations from the public.

In January, 2005, the Legal Human Rights Centre of Tanzania, together with the National Organisation for Legal Assistance and the Lawyers' Environmental Action Team, jointly filed an application in the High Court challenging the validity of *takrima*. They contended that *takrima* was, amongst other things, a negation of fundamental freedoms and constitutional rights.

On March 8, 2005, the electronic *IPP Media* of Tanzania quoted former Prime Minister, Joseph Sinde Warioba, adding his voice to the debate and denouncing *takrima* as a 'distortion' of African traditional hospitality that some day might '…cause a big disaster'.

Although the above petition succeeded, there were attempts by the Kikwete government to challenge the decision, wishing it to be overturned in favour of *takrima*. Consequently, if Warioba's fear of an impending *takrima* 'disaster' was, God forbid, to become a reality, then it would occur after those whom it was designed to benefit had already benefited enormously from it.

All told, despite Shinani's alleged reporting of the election results for Muleba South constituency, it is not being suggested that Wilson Masilingi was in any way involved in his death. Indeed, there is no conclusive evidence linking the issue of *takrima* directly or indirectly to Shinani's suicide. However, the resulting stress and unwanted public humiliation following the government's decision to deprive him of citizenship, whatever the reason, contributed to Shinani taking his own life.

One would have thought that following this unfortunate

incident the Tanzanian authorities would have been compelled to put a stop to this nonsensical practice that is tantamount to official blackmail. However, they did not!

Instead, on October 27, 2003, Ali Mohamed Nabwa, the Managing Editor of *Dira* (Compass), and an *aide* to the late Vice President Dr Omari Juma, was formally declared not to be a Tanzanian citizen.

Therefore, in order for Nabwa to be able to remain in his own country in the interim, the government granted him a 'special permit', renewable after every three months.

However, less than a month after being stripped off his citizenship, on November 24, 2003, Nabwa's weekly tabloid, *Dira*, was banned by the government for allegedly 'unfolding old wounds' and for 'following up the origins' of Zanzibar's former dictator, Sheikh Karume.

The government did not provide details as to what those 'wounds' were, but by mentioning them, it seemed the government was indirectly acknowledging that such 'wounds' do, indeed, exist. Unfortunately, for the government, some 'wounds' are too dangerously septic and foul smelling to be left untreated for so long. Setting euphemisms aside, it seems apparent that the 'wounds' was a reference to enforced disappearances and extra-judicial, political killings, both past and present, which Nabwa's newspaper, *Dira*, had attempted to bring up for public discussion.

On the other hand, it would seem hard not to discuss the 'origins' of Sheikh Karume, or for that matter, that of mainland rulers, when the rulers themselves initiated the discourse by expelling Comorians *en masse* from Zanzibar (referred to *supra*) or by subjecting individual citizens to severe emotional stress and public humiliation on the account of their supposed original roots. Whilst that may seem a matter of opinion, the banning of *Dira* newspaper provided a clue as to why Nabwa's citizenship had suddenly become a matter of apparent difficulty.

Nyerere also had little liking for intellectuals expressing their free mind. When an American-based Tanzanian academic, Loyd Binagi, was reported to Nyerere as having expressed an opinion contrary to his (Nyerere), he promptly sent his former bodyguard, a certain Kalumanga, accompanied by Peter Bwimbo and Robert Baruti who has since retired, to arrest the academic.

Whilst interned, Binagi was mishandled by the trio to such an extent that a kettle (*birika*), filled with hot water was applied to the academic's body.

In retrospect, it seems Nyerere's dislike of free thinking dates back to the time when he introduced the National Service programme in Tanzania in the mid-sixties.

Definitely, the programme was fiercely opposed in 1966 by university students who, in consequence, took to the streets to openly register their opposition to it.

However, Nyerere appeared not to have been angered by the protest much as what was expressed during the protest.

Indeed, many of the placards which the students wielded during the demonstration bluntly declared that '*afadhali ya mkoloni*'(which if loosely translated: 'the colonists were better').

Angered by this statement, Nyerere ordered the university closed and embarked upon overhauling the entire educational system from elementary to university level.

In elementary schools, the textbooks now contained political material that seemed designed to indoctrinate the young minds. School atlases bore his image and the cult of personality was ostensibly taking root.

However, it was admission to the university which underwent radical transformation. Nyerere declared that the university was for 'mature people' who ought to have had a working experience prior to applying for admission to it. This meant that the university would no longer accept direct admission of students from high school as had previously been the practice. The political motive was clear: to forestall future opposition from the educated young.

For, unlike unmarried young students from high school, people who joined the university after years of working experience had families and would be cautious not to engage in protests at the university without considering the repercussions their families may suffer as a result of their actions.

Additionally, all mature entrants to the university from then on, had to be members of his ruling party, who nonetheless had to be vetted by members of '*Usalama wa Taifa*' (*UwT*). This was an added precaution which ensured that those who joined the university were obedient to him. It was from here that the culture of political obedience started to take hold amongst the country's intelligentsia, at least insofar as that generation was concerned.

However, Nyerere did more than this. With the educational system bequeathed to Tanzania by departing British colonial authorities almost scrapped in its entirety, Nyerere was able to push through his 'reforms' in earnest. For example, regions that produced students with the highest pass mark saw most of their students not selected for tertiary education despite having passed with a higher score.

Nyerere declared that only a few students with such a high score would be taken, to allow students with a lower pass mark in other regions to be given the opportunity for tertiary education. It would seem absurd for many that a student with an eighty percent pass mark could be dropped in favour of one with a forty percent pass mark, in the name of what Nyerere called 'equality' in education.

Some observers believe this had nothing to do with Nyerere's declared passion for 'equality' but that he wished to have educated people who would obey him. Indeed, some of them continue to obey him to this day.

For example, it is not uncommon for some lecturers at the University of Dar-Es-Salaam (UDSM) to commence their opening remarks with reference to Nyerere: 'Like the father of the nation consistently cautioned this nation (the most commonly used phrase is *Kama baba wa taifa alivyotuasisi*) so goes the opening remarks. Then if the lecturer happens to be teaching biology, a discipline far detached from political science, you could get something like this: 'Biology is the study of living organisms…you should all, always, bear in mind how the father of the nation asked us to approach the study of this discipline…', the lecturer might conclude by tenderly stroking the image of Julius Nyerere embossed on a *kitenge* shirt he is wearing.

Visualise for a moment the impact of such introductory remarks on young minds, especially when the same or similar remarks are repeated again and again through the media. Whether parents in Tanzania (or elsewhere in Africa) have the right to know about the quality of education given to their children is a matter for future academic debate.

However, what is clear (albeit puzzling) is that, the

kitenge shirt the lecturer might be wearing, would have a slogan *'Watanzania Tumuenzi Baba wa Taifa'*. Ostensibly, the slogan seeks to remind Tanzanians of their supposed duty to 'preserve the memory of the father of the nation'.

In reality however, Nyerere's memory cannot be 'preserved' in the context of the 'father of the nation'.

This is because Nyerere did not bring a new nation-state into existence, such as Muhammad Ali Jinnah, who founded Pakistan in 1947, or Sheikh Mujibur Rahman, who founded Bangladesh in 1971.

Uniting Tanganyika and Zanzibar (the two countries that have existed since time immemorial), or, for that matter, achieving independence for his people, does not make Nyerere 'father of the nation'—and this should be clear.

Of course, there are several revered political leaders who are today referred to as father of the nation. These include *inter alia* Sir Seewoosagur Ramgoolan, the first post-independence prime minister of Mauritius, and *Mahatma* Gandhi of India, for example.

However, Sir Seewoosagur was not an autocratic ruler, and, of course, *Mahatma* Gandhi never aspired to political office.

Even Nelson Mandela's honorary title of *Madiba* was not bestowed upon him as a result of his long campaign against apartheid. Rather, *Madiba* as it happens is an honorary title which is adopted by elders of Mandela's clan.

Even if the title had been conferred upon Mandela as a result of his long political activism (or for being the first black South African president), perhaps it would still have been amenable to critical appraisal. This is because a statesman like the Reverend Dr Martin Luther King Jr, whose non-violent campaign achieved much the same for African Americans, did not have an honorary title of the sort.

More tellingly, in Western democracies, leaders who were behind the establishment of modern-day nation-states are commonly referred to as Founding Fathers. It is in very rare circumstances where such leaders are referred to as father of the nation.

It goes further. Since the notion of *primus inter pares* and dictatorship cannot co-exist, the principal objective of a dictator is thus invariably to project himself as a supreme leader who is indispensable to the nation he rules.

It is not surprising therefore that leaders in democratic societies do not bestow on themselves honorary titles whose principle aim is the promotion and sustenance of an individual ruler's supreme image (or cult of personality). Perhaps such a thing would be inconceivable in a democracy, given that such titles are commonly associated with dictators, some of them notorious: the Führer, Il Duce, Caudillo, Dear Leader, The Most Beloved Son of the People, Ngwazi, Osagyefo, Uncle Bob and other tyrants of similar repute.

It is due to these and other factors that I have described (and continue to describe) that I refuse to accept that a ruler who usurped sovereign authority and established a regime of personal power would qualify for an honorary title of 'father of the nation'.

There is a perception that each generation ought to discover its mission, fulfil it or betray it. This is a new century whereby contemporary African political leaders no longer feel the need to carry ceremonial sticks, fly-whisks or white handkerchiefs as symbols of their authority.

Consequently, there would be no harm caused if Tanzania's forces of reason and reform critically appraised the continued use (and misuse) of the honorary titles that Nyerere bestowed upon himself following his imposition of personal rule.

I am certain those who wish to revere him nonetheless, can do so in a conventional manner; exactly in the same way the people in developed countries revere their leaders, ostensibly without being obsequious.

If, on the other hand, acquiescence to authoritarian dominance, sycophancy and unquestioning flattery are more rooted in Tanzania's own social culture than in the cult of personality that Nyerere created, then our social culture as well should be critically appraised so that 'respect' for rulers can be clearly distinguished from sycophancy.

After all, culture is a developing aspect of society; and so acquiring some positive aspects of other people's culture in order to enrich one's own is not only appropriate but an imperative process in promoting social growth and human development. This is more so, in a world that has increasingly become more integrated and interdependent than in the past eras.

Thus, our interaction with the rest of the world should enable us to identify some negative aspects of our culture that hold us back. Such a change requires a starting point.

If we don't, our peers may fail to comprehend some peculiar aspects of our culture under which we dance for dictators; regard them as if they are a father to us, and address their wives as 'mama'.

Not only that, but it seems our peers may not even tell us how strange they think this is, so as not to appear racist.

All told, another casualty of Nyerere's 'reforms' was English which, ironically, Nyerere himself mastered well.

Suddenly English was now being labelled as *kasumba ya kikoloni* (colonial mentality/hangover) which was no longer considered an important subject.

Some apologists tend to argue that promoting *Swahili* in place of English was important in moulding Tanzania's national unity.

However, this does not explain why the school syllabus had to contain a lot of political material; or, for that matter, does it explain why books and materials for adult education, which was funded in part by such organisations as UNESCO, had to contain ideological propaganda.

Indeed, during colonial rule when English was taught alongside *Swahili*, Tanzania's social cohesion was not in peril. There is also evidence to suggest that English was not taught at the expense of *Swahili*. Nyerere, who spoke both languages perfectly well (in addition to his first language, *Kizanaki*) is himself a good example in support of this argument.

In addition, in the rest of Anglophone Africa where English was taught, and continues to be taught alongside local languages, their countries have not disintegrated as a result of this.

Thus, denying people the opportunity to learn a language that would give them access to valuable knowledge (and communication) because a ruler dreads the prospect of being challenged if he allowed it (or because the ruler wishes to stand out as the most intelligent person in the country), is something Tanzanians, and all people of good will, should question.

Indeed, had the British colonial administration pursued this line of thinking, probably Nyerere himself might not have had a good enough education to give him the ability to challenge the *status quo.*

The 'creative unity' articulated by Karen Blixen, and to which I referred in the introduction, is not simply about diversity. It is also about free thinking, as people can have diverse views and opinions only if they can think freely.

Today the international community is attempting to grapple with the deadly effect of indoctrination in the form of terrorism. It remains to be seen whether political indoctrination of the type outlined above could, in the long term, have a similar effect as indoctrination conducted in religious *madrassa.*

I wonder whether the international community should not formally promote free thinking as a basic fundamental right, for all peoples of nations, which should not be tempered with by local potentates.

Then again, that would depend on how free thinking is quantified within this context. However, would that not be appropriate, particularly during this time when brain-washing has spawned a new threat to global security?

Whatever the answer to that question may be, Nyerere's 'reforms' caused the entire educational programme to plummet, as can be clearly discerned today. Not surprisingly, as recently as February 2009, the Kikwete government was contemplating ways of re-introducing at least two Advanced Level (A-Level) schools in each district; a very positive move, but one which might take a long time before it can benefit the majority of students in the country.

All in all, most of the 'reforms' were later abandoned following the arrival of information technology (IT) and other inevitable factors, but not before they served Nyerere well. It would not surprise me if today, those in Tanzania who are enthusiastically canonising Nyerere, were not the product of the educational system I have just described.

Nonetheless, it was Nyerere's continued use of show trials (in cases with a clear political dimension) instead of law courts, which will continue to baffle historians.

Whether Nyerere preferred this method in the belief that it would have a demonstrative effect (i.e. of punishing one person in order to teach a thousand others), will be a matter for future academic debate. In the meantime though, that debate commences with the following fourth, and the biggest, show-trial in Tanzania's political history.

At a public rally in Nachingwea, southern Tanzania, on March 16, 1975, Nyerere's government and *Frelimo* put on a show-trial some 240 Mozambican political dissidents, including some former *Frelimo* leaders for their alleged 'crimes' against *Frelimo*[5]. They included, amongst others, a Presbyterian minister, the Reverend Uria Timoteo Simango.

The charismatic minister had been the vice president of *Frelimo* since its inception was formally proclaimed in Dar-Es-Salaam on June 25, 1962, under the leadership of Dr Eduardo Chivambo Mondlane.

This followed a merger of three nationalist movements namely, National African Union of Independent Mozambique (*UNAMI*), African National Union (*MANU*) and National Democratic Union of Mozambique (*UDENAMO*).

When Dr Mondlane was assassinated in Tanzania on February 3, 1969, Rev Simango automatically became acting president of *Frelimo*. However, his leadership was quickly challenged and less than two months after Dr Mondlane's assassination, his leadership was replaced by a triumvirate comprised of Rev Simango himself, Samora Machel and Marcelino dos Santos.

Ostensibly, the bomb which killed Dr Mondlane was concealed in the fourth volume; part of a set of five volumes; devoted to 'social philosophy' by Georgi Plekhanov.

Of course, *Frelimo* blamed Dr Mondlane's assassination on *Polícia Internacional e de Defesa Estado* (*PIDE*) i.e. International and State Defence Police.

However, the government of Dr Marcello Caetano in Lisbon denied this. Instead, it blamed 'extreme left wing factions' within *Frelimo* for the death of its leader. It added that Dr Mondlane was 'a moderate, a man we could eventually talk to, and his disappearance is a loss.'[6] Not everybody, of course, believed that version.

What was not in doubt though was that, towards the latter part of 1969 there were persistent reports of *Frelimo* cadres dying of unnatural causes.[7]

It would seem this is what prompted Rev Simango,

---

5 Africa Research Bulletin, March 1-31, 1975, (p.3567, B-C).
6 http://www.time.com/time/magazine/article/0,9171,900625-2,00.html
7 see Journal of Southern African Studies, Vol. 2, No 1 (Oct., 1975), pp. 66-82

amongst other things, to issue a document entitled *The Gloomy Situation in Frelimo*.

In this document, which was first published in edition No. 41, *Mozambique Revolution*, October-December 1969, Rev Simango accused his own movement of carrying out 'many unnecessary executions of fighters and people'. He added that, 'Personally, I cannot agree to be part of crimes against our people'.

This appeared to indicate that Rev Simango was intent on dissociating himself with the people he virulently assailed as 'criminals' whose hands were 'full of blood'.

So, when in November 1969 Rev Simango was expelled from the Central Committee of *Frelimo*, it seemed he had already made up his mind to quit *Frelimo* a month earlier—hence releasing the above-mentioned document.

Four months later, in April 1970, Rev Simango went to Egypt where he and colleagues of the same ideological inclination remained politically active.

According to *Wikipedia*, an online encyclopaedia, Rev Simango returned to Mozambique in 1974, after the Carnation Revolution in Portugal (of April 25, 1974) and established a political party, National Coalition Party (*PCN*), with the view to contesting elections with *Frelimo*.

However, Machel's *Frelimo* which shared the transitional government with Portugal would not let him do that as it was totally opposed to multi-party elections (the Portuguese colonial authorities ultimately handed over sole power to *Frelimo*).

Sensing his life might be in danger, Rev Simango fled Mozambique to neighbouring Malawi. Several months later he was abducted from there by agents of *Frelimo*'s *Serviço Nacional de Segurança Popular* (*SNASP*), i.e. National Service for People's Security, who had been working closely with their Tanzanian counterpart, *Usalama wa Taifa* (*UwT*).

On March, 15, 1975, Rev Simango, together with Paulo José Gumane, the leader of *UDENAMO* but who had since joined the National Coalition Party (*PCN*), appeared briefly before Samora Machel, in Nachingwea, southern Tanzania, a day before he (Rev Simango) was made to read out a 20-page forced public confession.

The following day, March 16, 1975, Rev Simango was

again paraded with other Mozambican dissidents who had taken part in the seizure of the radio station in Lourenço Marques (Maputo) in September 1974. These included, amongst others, Basilio Banda and Dr Faustino Kambeo.

Also paraded were, amongst others, Paulo Unhai, Holomulo Chitofo (Adelino) Gwambe (Gwambe co-founded *UDENAMO* with Gumane) and Lázaro Nkavandame.

Since the prisoners had already been sentenced by an invisible court, it would seem the principal objective of the show-trial was to publicly humiliate the prisoners before their execution; a warning perhaps to those opposed to *Frelimo*'s policies.

The show-trial itself was not dissimilar to the other three in both manner and form. As in the preceding show-trials Rev Simango was forced to read out his scripted confession to the public, in which he implicated himself (and others) in the assassination of Dr Mondlane. This was one of the bizarre twists of this show-trial.

For, in *The Gloomy Situation in Frelimo*, which can now be viewed on *Macua blog*, Rev Simango gave details of several meetings which took place at Oyster Bay, Dar-Es-Salaam, at the residence of Janet Rae Mondlane, the widow of the assassinated *Frelimo* leader.

These details revealed the meetings to have taken place between the end of February and early March 1969. They also revealed that these meetings were attended by *Frelimo* officials from the southern part of Mozambique. These included, amongst others, Armando Guebuza, Joaquim Chissano, Samora Machel, Marcelino dos Santos, Aurelio Manave, Josina Abiatar Muthemba, Francisco Sumbane and Eugénio Mondlane.

According to the document, in the course of these meetings, it was concluded that Rev Simango himself, Silverio Mungu (later brutally murdered), Mariano Masinye and Samuel Dhlakama; all of whom hailed from the northern part of Mozambique; were enemies of southerners and 'were responsible for the death of Dr Mondlane and, therefore, should be eliminated'.

Apart from the tribal issue, it would appear that no conclusive evidence was ever adduced in support of these serious allegations. That, of course, did not prevent the Central Committee of *Frelimo* which met six months later from concluding that 'Simango should be subjected to popular justice in Mozambique (i.e. paraded in public)[8].

Now then, were some participants of these meetings also members of the invisible court which decided which people were to be subjected to 'popular justice'? Where these members now seeking to enforce the decision taken during those meetings or the decision of the Central Committee? Did the same people sit on the Central Committee as well? Did Rev Simango bring this matter into the open to highlight the danger he faced and how lawless *Frelimo* had become? Did the mutual mistrust between the cadre from northern and southern part of Mozambique reflect factions within *Frelimo* to which the Caetano regime had referred?

For discernible reasons, the Tanzanian authorities decline to answer inquiries regarding this and other less publicised subsequent show-trials which took place in April and May respectively.

Indeed, on Monday, March 20, 1975, four days after the referral show-trial, another group of about fifty Mozambican prisoners (including some who were previously paraded) were again paraded before Samora Machel at Farm Seventeen, Nachingwea. These included, amongst others, Joana Francisco Fonseca Simeão, another key opposition figure but who had joined the National Coalition Party (*NCP*).

Like Rev Simango, Joana Simeão had also committed a particularly serious *faux pas* (actually 'treason') when the political party which she led before joining the National Coalition Party (*PCN*), *Grupo Unido de Moçambique* (*Gumo*), or the United Group for Mozambique, advocated a free-market economic system and competitive democracy. Indeed, according to the *Daily News* of Wednesday, April 23, 1975, Joana Simeão admitted during the referral show-trial to have formed *GUMO* in order to 'represent the people of Mozambique'. This statement, however, prompted Samora Machel to ask her angry almost as if she wasn't even a Mozambican: 'Who are you to represent the interests of the Mozambican people?'

Others who were paraded on that particular day included Venancio Guambe, Paulo Emílio Margueza, Mario Munene, Veronica Aniyiva, Pedro Mondlane (a cousin of the late *Frelimo* president Eduardo Mondlane), Basilio Calisto Maculuve, the

---

8 *Africa Watch* report, *Conspicuous Destruction*, July, 1992, (p 16)

leader of *Fromoco*, one of the numerous political groups formed in Mozambique after the April 25, 1974, Carnation Revolution in Portugal, Manuel Mumba, José Eugénio Zitha, a medical student at Lourenço Marques University, and many other people from all walks of life who were being rounded up in Mozambique for a variety of alleged political crimes and brought to Tanzania to be publicly humiliated.

On Monday, May 12, 1975, President Julius Nyerere, accompanied by Zambia's President Kenneth Kaunda, both dressed in the dotted khaki uniform of *Frelimo*, took part in another show-trial at the regular show-trial venue at Farm Seventeen, Nachingwea, at which a group of Mozambican prisoners was paraded before them. These included the Reverend Uria Simango, Paulo Gumane and Lázaro Nkavandame (*Tempo*, June 1, 1975), all of whom had previously been put on show-trial multiple times.

All told, Rev Simango's confessed involvement into the assassination of Dr Mondlane, was further undermined by evidential facts emanating from independent sources.

These sources, including the *Time* magazine which I cite *supra*, indicated Rev Simango to have been also a target of assassination.

In actual fact, Rev Simango had been sent a book bomb similar to the one which killed Dr Mondlane. This was reportedly wrapped in the second volume of Plekhanov books, whilst Marcelino dos Santos was sent Volume 1, also wrapped in the same way.

Indeed, according to a declassified State Department document dated March 24, 1969, Thomas R. Pickering, the then deputy chief of mission, at the US Embassy in Dare-Es-Salaam, confirmed that a third book bomb which had been addressed to Rev Simango (then acting president of *Frelimo*) had been intercepted.

He added that the bomb had been sent to Rev Simango whilst on a tour of duty in Nachingwea, and had been addressed to the *Frelimo* training camp post office where it was intercepted and defused.

However, Pickering noted rather curiously, 'Only a few people knew that Simango would be away in Nachingwea.'

He further observed that the squad from the Criminal Investigation Department (CID), which had been sent to Dar-Es-

Salaam post office to look out for bombs addressed to *Frelimo* officials, 'missed the bomb sent to Simango', until when it was discovered there in Nachingwea. This would seem to imply that the bomb had been sent to Nachingwea from (or, through) the Dar-Salaam post office, where the CID squad had ostensibly been deployed to intercept suspicious packets.

To some observers these, when combined with other contradictory elements of this case, made Rev Simango's 'confession' controvertible.

On the other hand, it would seem difficult to discern how such a 'confession' would have been obtained from him (or from other prisoners) without coercion or duress; especially when examining the circumstances surrounding his defection from *Frelimo*; and, crucially, his abduction from exile.

Indeed, testimonies of former political detainees as contained herein show torture to extract confessions to have been routine in Tanzania (where Rev Simango was interrogated before being put on a show-trial), therefore it is safe to assume he would not have been treated differently.

All told, at the end of his scripted 'confession' Rev Simango supposedly 'asked' Machel to send him to *campos de reeducação* (re-education camps) where he would atone for his confessed litany of 'crimes' against *Frelimo*.

Apparently, 're-education camps' were internment camps that were operated by *Frelimo* and reminiscent of Joseph Stalin's *Gulags*. During Machel's tyrannical rule, thousands of people were interned in these camps and many were said never to have come out alive.

These included, amongst others, prostitutes, drunkards, petty criminals and those Machel and his underlings perceived as 'social deviants'; or, shall we say *Xiconhoca, o Inimigo*, to borrow the parlance which used to characterise a popular Mozambican cartoon.

Precisely, 're-education camps' were in addition to traditional prisons and other maximum security prisons such as Machava, which I described earlier.

In 1978, Colonel Mbuta, of Tanzania People's Defence Force (TPDF), happened to visit some of these camps while on a tour of duty in Mozambique. Later, in a casual conversation at

In this picture, José Eugénio Zitha is seen being paraded by Samora Machel at Nachingwea. He was also extra-judicially murdered after the Nyerere regime sent him back to Mozambique. In 2008, his son lodged a complaint with the African Commission on Human Rights (Communication 361/08: JE Zitha & PJL Zitha, represented by Prof Dr Liesebeth Zegveld v Mozambique), which found in favour of Mozambique.

Sunday, May 11, 1975: Presidents Nyerere (right), Kenneth Kaunda (centre) and Samora Machel (left) stand to attention as their national anthems are sung upon arrival at Nachingwea in southern Tanzania, where they were to take part in a show-trial the following day.

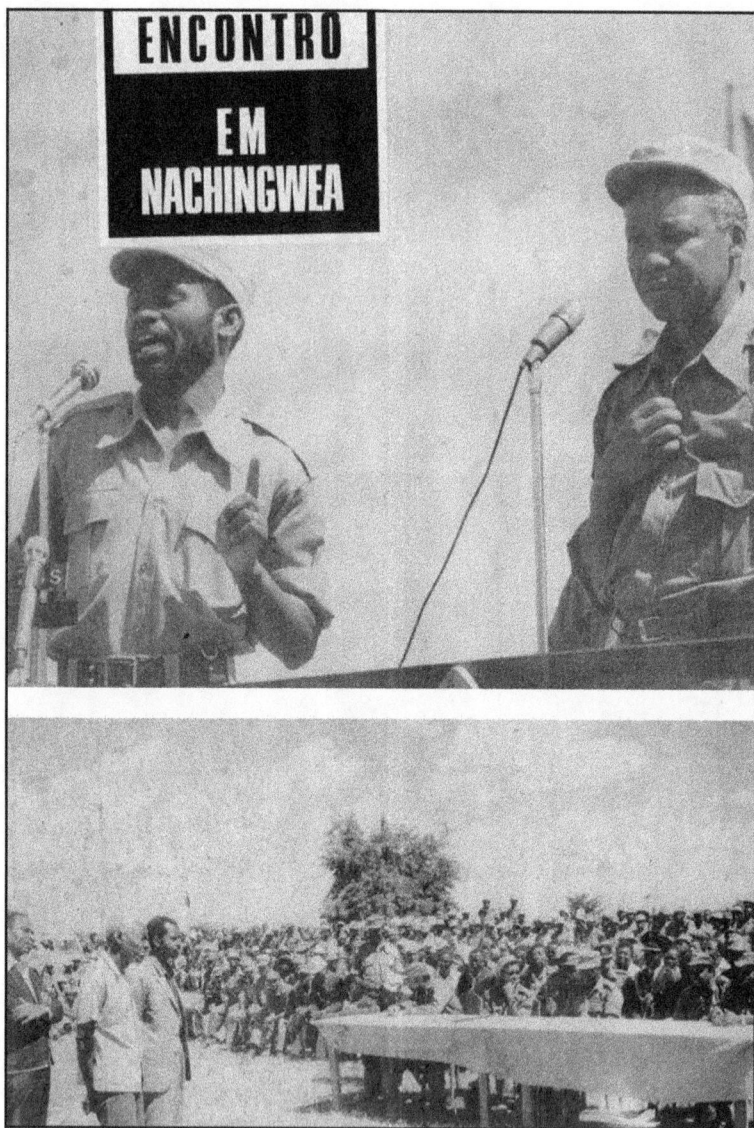

Farm 17, Monday, May 12, 1975: Nyerere (right in the above illustration) addresses a partisan crowd in *Swahili* that had congregated there for that day's event. Machel (gesticulating on the left) translated Nyerere's speech from *Swahili* to Portuguese. In the illustration below, Nyerere (seated between Machel, on the left, Zambia's Dr Kaunda, on the right) had Gumane—behind Nkavandame (right)—and Rev Simango (left) paraded before them.

According to the *Daily News* of April 23, 1975, groups of Mozambican political prisoners whom it referred to as 'traitors' were being conveyed to Farm 17 at Nachingwea by government Land Rovers at brief interludes. As they alighted from the Land Rovers, Machel would randomly pick one out, firmly grasp his or her arms, then make his rounds back and forth with the victim in front of a partisan audience that verbally assailed them. The next four pages show pictures of some of the prisoners who were humiliated in this way before their ultimate fate.

a cocktail party that was hosted at *Hotel Turismo* in down town Maputo, he somewhat banteringly cautioned colleagues and friends not to mistake them for holiday camps. They were, he said, 'hell on earth'.

His honest views could not save him from a tragic accident however. Barely a month after making such remarks, he died with others in an unexplained accident whilst still on a tour of duty in Mozambique.

After the 'confessions' from the prisoners had ended Machel, who, after becoming president, liked to address his audience from the balcony and dressed in military uniform like Benito Mussolini, took the floor.

He spoke forcibly, shaking as he wagged his accusing finger at the prisoners whom he kept referring to as *'inimigos do povo'* (enemies of the people); or, as *'reaccionária'* (reactionary), a phrase Machel used quite liberally when referring to Paulo Gumane who previously had been *Frelimo*'s deputy General Secretary.

The prisoners who were ringed by Machel's fighters and elements of the Tanzania Intelligence Service (TIS) looked on seemingly totally dejected, as the entire world seemed to have completely abandoned them.

At the end of the show-trial, the prisoners were taken away in National Service vehicles which were provided by the Nyerere regime; vehicles which transported them to locations where they were later to be dispatched to their imminent fate.

As with the other show-trials that preceded this one, no one knows to date where the victims were buried, if at all.

Additionally, to this day both the Tanzanian and Mozambican authorities refuse to clarify the circumstances surrounding the arrest and later execution of Celina Simango, the wife of Rev Simango.

So far, the only established circumstances are those under which Celina Simango was transported from Nachingwea to Mozambique, where she was later executed.

Indeed, according to reliable sources, after the Nachingwea show-trial had ended, some political prisoners including, amongst others, Rev Simango, his wife Celina, Raúl Casal Ribeiro, his wife Lucia Casal Ribeiro and their two daughters, had been separated from other prisoners.

It is unclear why the organisers of the show-trial chose to separate these prisoners from the rest.

Since all prisoners were of particular interest to the authorities, one can only speculate that they were either separated because they were considered to be of far more interest to both Tanzania and *Frelimo*. Otherwise, if it was a mere precautionary measure, then surely this would have applied to all prisoners?

Whatever the case may be, it was only after they had been separated from other prisoners that they were transported from Nachingwea to the shores of Lake Nyasa. From there, they were taken by boat to Metangula Naval Base in Mozambique, before finally being taken to the notorious M'telela 're-education camp' which was located in Niassa Province.

João M Cabrita, an investigative journalist and writer who interviewed a former inmate of M'telela 're-education camp', asserts that Celina Simango and Lucia Casal Ribeiro were executed at this camp, a few years after their arrival there. Ostensibly, the witness who saw some of the killings whilst interned there told Cabrita that the two women were dispatched not long after their husbands had also been killed.

From the factors outlined *supra*, it would seem apparent that *Frelimo* was at that time intent on doing away with any meaningful opposition to it. Equally, it seemed intent on eliminating the entire political leadership of the National Coalition party (*PNC*). What is unfathomable to this day however, is why *Frelimo* wanted to kill these two innocent women as well.

Although it has now emerged that one of the women, Celina Simango, was in fact a '*Frelimo* militant', there is no conclusive evidence showing her to have been politically or otherwise opposed to *Frelimo* or its late leader, Samora Machel, whom critics have since dubbed 'Mozambique's black Nero'. Indeed, the Tanzanian government-owned newspaper, the *Daily News* of April 23, 1975, asserted that, unlike her husband Rev Simango, Celina had in fact 'refused to betray the struggle' (see illustration opposite page).

So given her publicly acknowledged loyalty to *Frelimo* and its leadership, why was she arrested, subjected to a show-trial at Nachingwea, then sent by the Nyerere regime to Mozambique, where she was unlawfully killed along with Ribeiro's wife Lucia?

that this man was a rea-
sonary?," Ndugu Samora asked
stazia after singling her
of the crowd.
Then one woman militant took
rgueza to task. "When you
ived in Beira you said you
nted to lead the people to inde-
adence. You and Unyal. What
e of independence did you
e in mind?"

VENANCIO Guambe,
the 22-year old tattooed
killer.

Margueza mumbled someth-
ing. "Why can't you answer?
This is the time to answer",
persisted the militant. She then
addressed the first question to
a friend of Margueza, a traitor from the first batch, Julius Razao. He answered
simply: "The people have won".
The parading of the 12 continued, and was only punctua-
ted by singing. Then it was
Jose Nyawunga's turn to be
taken around. He had run away
with a FRELIMO gun and joined the enemy ranks in 1969.
"Where is our gun?" one
militant from the crowd asked
him. When he failed to answer,
the crowd jeered at him. Another militant stood up and came
to face him.
"How was it in Boane? (the
Portuguese military head-
quarters in Lourenco Marques).
NYAWUNGA: I was arrested
by the Portuguese and forced
to Boane.
MILITANT: How could it be
that you were forced there when
they gave you a car to take
you to town for weekends and
house to yourself?
NYAWUNGA: Well it is the
revolution.
MILITANT: What kind of revolution? You used to say that
FRELIMO would not win. Who
as won now?

your meetings?" The old man
was then heading FROMOCO,
one of the numerous political groups formed in Mozambique after the April coup in Portugal.
Maculuve looked at the militant, his lips quivering, his
grey hair matching his grey
suit, and said: "I have suffered for Mozambique. I fought
in order to gain independence
just like you have. I was de-
ported in 1960 to Portugal for
my political activities". He stayed in Portugal until 1962, he
said.
The third and last group
to be paraded was also
brought to the scene in the
Landrover. It included one
Sambule who joined Frelimo
in 1967. He was later sent to
Cabo Delgado in Mozambique
from where he was recalled
in 1974.
"Do you know why we sent
him to Cabo Delgado? He was
found with a knife in a toilet
here at the camp waiting to
murder me," Ndugu Samora
said. The last group also
included Manuel Mumba who
had stayed in Mbeya for a
long time and knew about the
bomb that was being sent to
kill Mondlane in February
1969.
Towards the end of the parade, the traitors who were
paraded on March 16 were
also brought in to meet their
friends. They included Uria
Simango, who Ndugu Samora
let him pose with his wife,
Celina Simango, a FRELIMO
militant.

didn't have such people. These
people are our teachers. They

of the occasion, not only for
Mozambique, but the whole of
Africa.

URIA SIMANGO, one of the 240 traitors who were
paraded on March 16, beside his wife, Celina —
who refused to betray the struggle — when 24
more traitors were paraded at Nachingwea on
Monday. Celina Simango is a FRELIMO militant.

ELEVEN OF the 24 traitors paraded on Monday line up before President
Samora explained their crimes.

On Friday, July 16, 2010, I put that question by electronic mail to Sérgio Vieira (also known as Sérgio Maria Castelo Branco da Silva Vieira).

Vieira, a left-learning intellectual, once served as director of Machel's office; and a controversial one at that which, some say, kept tabs on perceived political dissidents. Also, he headed the Ministry of Security, amongst other posts, the functions of which were reportedly more demanding than that of the former.

All told, when in the mid-1980s the Machel regime was desperately attempting to cover-up for the atrocious crimes to which I refer, it turned to Sérgio Vieira as someone who could perform such a delicate task with skill and portentousness.

And the implicit trust in Vieira, by the regime he served, was not only conveyed to him verbally, but also in the Order of Action No 5/80 from the minister of security, then Jacinto Veloso, which I reproduce below.

MINISTRY OF SECURITY
Order of Action No 5/80
FROM: DI
TO: DB and CHIEF BO

In the spirit of the customs, uses and traditions of the armed struggle for National Liberation, the permanent Political Committee of *Frelimo* has adjudged, and condemned to be executed by shooting, the following deserters and traitors to the people and the National Cause, who have already been executed:
URIA SIMANGO
LÁZARO NKAVANDAME
JULIO RAZALO NLIA
MATEUS GWENGERE
JOANA SIMEÃO
PAULO GUMANE

In order to forestall possible negative reaction, national or international, which may arise in consequence of the execution of these counter-revolutionaries, the permanent Political Committee has decided to publicise this act as a Revolutionary decision of the *Frelimo* Party, and not as a judicial Act.

It is therefore necessary to compile a dossier stating the complete criminal history of these individuals, as well as their confessions to the elements of the DD/SI who interrogated them, statements by witnesses and deeds of trial and sentence.

Apart from this dossier, a communiqué must be issued which will be read by the Comrade Commander-in Chief, in which he will announce the execution of the above-mentioned counter-revolutionaries.

It was decided to nominate a committee to compile the dossier and to prepare the public communiqué.

The Comrade Commander-in-Chief has decided that the above-mentioned committee will be headed by the Comrade SÉRGIO VIEIRA, and will have as additional members Comrades ÓSCAR MONTEIRO, JÓSE JULIO DE ANDRADE, MATIAS XAVIER and JORGE COSTA.

THE STRUGGLE CONTINUES
MAPUTO 29/7/80
THE MINISTER OF SECURITY
JACINTO VELOSO[9]

After decades of arguments and counter-arguments over the authenticity of the Order, finally in mid-June, 2010, Vieira, in his usual intellectual candour, confirmed its existence to the media[10]. Admittedly, it was at this juncture that I felt inclined to put that question directly to him.

In doing so, I made it clear to him that although the victims were Mozambican nationals, their fate was sealed in Tanzania.

I had no doubt in my mind that Vieira would realise that, these politicians could not have been killed if the Nyerere regime had not handed them over to his political masters; or if it had refused to allow the show-trial to proceed on Tanzanian soil, and if indeed it had not provided logistical support to transport the prisoners to their imminent death.

All told, on Saturday, July 17, 2010, I received a terse response from Sérgio Vieira which stated as follows:

'As a private person and someone who left government office since 1987, I am not [in a position] to answer. Please contact the government', he politely advised me.

However, as Maputo strives to consolidate nascent

---

9 *Scope* (South Africa), February 11, 1983 (pp. 34-35)
10 O País (Mozambique) June 25, 2010 (Special Supplement, pp 29-30)

democracy, Vieira and confederates may find that the government to which he referred me would rather have them held individually accountable.

If the Mozambican government were to do this, it would be emphasising individual responsibility whilst simultaneously trying to remedy past wrongs, ostensibly without losing too much face.

On the other hand, leaving public office does not (and should not) preclude public officials alleged to have committed serious human rights violations whilst they held office from being held accountable; at least not as long as they remain *compos mentis*.

Nonetheless, Vieira's refusal to answer my question left me wondering whether the Machel regime executed these women for fear that, were they to live, they might become a rallying point for the opposition, in the absence of their executed husbands.

Yet, this too, did not make much sense, especially in the case of Lucia. For, her husband Raúl Casal Ribeiro had quit active politics way back in 1966.

What happened was that, until October 1966 when Filipe Samuel Magaia (*Frelimo*'s first armed forces commander) was killed upon returning to Tanzania from inspecting the frontlines, by another guerrilla known as Lorenço Matola, Ribeiro had been a Political Commissar.

Apparently, Magaia was assassinated under highly suspicious circumstances; and, although the Tanzanian authorities had made it known that his assassin had been put under lock and key, it was not long before he was seen walking scot-free in Kenya. How Matola managed to extricate himself from the claws of Nyerere's political police so easily is unclear, for sure.

What seemed clear however was that, had Matola been of particular interest to both Nyerere's regime and *Frelimo*, perhaps he might have been abducted from there, as were other perceived *Frelimo* dissidents whom I discuss in this account.

Anyway, following the assassination of Commander Filipe Magaia, Ribeiro left *Frelimo* around that time and settled in the northern part of Tanzania, where he led a completely quiet life.

However, that quiet life was to be permanently shuttered after being arrested with his wife, by Nyerere's political police-men who, as we already know, handed them over to *Frelimo*, which killed the couple.

Ironically, at the height of the Nachingwea show-trial, Machel had stated in no uncertain terms that 'we will not kill them (the prisoners)' because 'they are our educators'.

If Machel was expecting the prisoners he paraded to 'educate' him and his locums then for sure, he must have been mocking them, which was equally despicable.

For, having violated the prisoners' dignity in that cowardly manner, it is hard to discern how he truly envisaged that happening. Nonetheless, Machel did inform the rally that, 'If people like these (prisoners) take power in Mozambique, imperialism will take root in Mozambique.' Imperialism!? Is this what it was all about?

If imperialism as a political orientation is fundamentally necessitated by evolving political and economic factors, then it is difficult to discern how subjecting citizens to physical and emotional abuse could have prevented it from ever 'taking root in Mozambique'.

Whereas, that is a matter of opinion, the issue of Machel reneging on his promise not to kill the prisoners is not. Indeed, due to factors which compelled me to write this account, the need for clarity over this issue is more imperative than ever.

Some apologists of both the Nyerere and Machel's regimes like to argue that the two governments had 'credible intelligence' indicating that the South African security forces intended to raid the facilities in which the prisoners were being held, with the view to setting them free.

If that had happened, said one Tanzanian academic who was close to the late President Julius Nyerere, 'That would have helped the enemy (*Renamo*) enormously'.

But, this argument cannot be sustained especially when considering the nature and scope of the atrocities in question.

Indeed, even if any of that were true, it does not explain why *Frelimo* failed to move the prisoners to more secure facilities instead of executing them.

Also, it does not explain why the *Frelimo* government had not sought transfer of prisoners back to Tanzania, which, as it is, was farther from white-ruled South Africa than Mozambique was. After all, the prisoners in question were all initially interrogated and also paraded there, whilst many others had permanent homes there too.

Not only that, but now that the authenticity of the Order of Action No 5/80 (discussed earlier) has been confirmed how does *Frelimo*, and by implication Tanzania, reconcile the former argument with the latter fact?

Interestingly, some people who were so close to the late Mozambican dictator, have of late been appearing on *CNN* and other Western media outlets posing as 'human rights activists'.

Although these 'human rights activists' manifest attributes of shaking the entire body when speaking just like the late Mozambican dictator, they seem to have a decidedly selective memory insofar as human rights are concerned.

For example, they don't tell the world community why the prisoners I have just mentioned were extra-judicially executed by the man over whom they had enormous influence, ostensibly without a hearing.

They do not say why they remained silent when these atrocities were being committed by the same ruler; nor do they say why all of a sudden, human rights are now a matter of particular concern to them.

It has to be emphasised that these were not the only people to be killed extra-judicially by the Machel regime.

Many more people were routinely being executed after the Machel regime accused them of being *'candongueiros'* (dealers in contraband), which Machel blamed for the continued scarcity of basic commodities in Mozambique.

Others, of course, perished in other notorious detention facilities which I described earlier, whilst some did not survive in *Frelimo's* disastrous *aldeias comunais* (communal villages). Apparently, these were villages in which Machel had gathered the rural peasantry to work collectively for the greater good of all.

Additionally, it was there that Mozambique's rural people were supposed to acquire a 'new mentality' which was to enable them to understand Machel's utopian dreams of transforming his impoverished nation of 16.9 million into a proletariat paradise that was devoid of 'parasites' of any kind.

Indeed, it was those 'parasites', and the elements of the rural peasantry who found the whole idea alien to their natural way of life, plus those who legitimately declined to consent to being used as political guinea pigs, that did not survive in Machel's *aldeias comunais*.

It would seem imperative that these salient questions are addressed by these 'human rights activists'; lest informed viewers will invariably conclude they are using this as a distraction from the real issue of extra-judicial executions that were presided over by the president to whom they were so close.

It is possible that they (the 'human rights activists') have undergone a complete transformation rivalling the conversion of Saul of Tarsus (who later became St Paul), following his vision on the road to Damascus.

Should this be the case, then this aspect must be clearly accentuated by them in order to set the record straight and thus dispel the notion I have just described.

Nonetheless, another concerning aspect is that the atrocious crimes that were committed by the Machel regime are not as frequently discussed as, for example, Machel's own death.

On October 19, 1986, Machel's presidential jet, a *Tupelov TU-134* aircraft, crashed into the Lebombo Mountains, near Mbuzini, South Africa.

Although it was later established that the plane crash was caused by pilot error, there have been persistent rumours (peddled largely by grieving relatives of Samora Machel) that his death was not an accident but that it was a result of a 'conspiracy' to kill him.

To be sure, on January 19, 1999, a memorial at the site of the crash was inaugurated by the late president Nelson Mandela of South Africa and Mozambique's Joaquim Alberto Chissano, amongst others in attendance. The monument's main feature consists of thirty-five steel tubes symbolising the number of those who perished in the crash.

However, I suppose the general public, and indeed families of the victims of Nachingwea show-trial would like to see a similar monument erected there with 240 still tubes symbolising the number of people who were killed on orders of Machel himself, who presided over the so-called 'popular justice' on that material day.

I would like to make it clear that it is not my intention to sound flippant. However, I fail to discern how a section of pan-African media could be more obsessed with the life of a single dictator i.e. Machel, than the lives of scores of his victims whom he liquidated without a second thought, let alone subjecting them to the due process of the law.

It would seem appropriate that the killings of Machel and those of his victims should be addressed simultaneously and with equal rights and with equal emphasis. By doing this, black Africans would be demonstrating to the world that they do indeed value human life.

Valuing human life is not a selective affair; rather, it is inclusive in the sense that the life of Machel (or any other dictator) has no greater value than those of his victims; and this must be clear.

Whilst that perhaps is a matter of opinion, the extra-judicial murder of over 200 political prisoners is not. It must be noted that a negligible number of prisoners who were regularly brought from Mozambique to Tanzania to be put on show-trial at Farm Seventeen, Nachingwea, by Samora Machel in cahoots with the Tanzania authorities, are known to have survived. Rather, it is sure to form part of the ongoing 'investigation process' into Nyerere's planned sainthood, much as the other three show-trials which preceded the grand show-trial of March 16, 1975, will. Moreover, what I reveal in this account calls into question whether the current meme of 'black lives matter' should not in fact extend to black African rulers who shunned democratic traditions and the rule of law for ideological reasons. Are we, possessed of our right faculties, really to believe there is an ideology that sanctions the deprivation of due-process rights and violates the sanctity of a person? In other words, shouldn't 'black lives matter' even where an African potentate unlawfully shoots dead his own kind or they mysteriously disappear from his execrable dungeons?

Not so long ago, Benedito Luis Machava, a PhD student who was doing research for his dissertation on Mozambique's notorious *campos de reeducação* (re-education camps), told João Cabrita that he had come across the expression 'Tanzania individual'. This term was used whenever the governor of Niassa Province, Aurélio Manave, ordered the execution of prisoners after receiving instructions to do this from his political masters in Maputo. It was intended only to single out prisoners for execution who had previously been sent to Tanzania for show-trial. Moreover, it was an expression that was well known by the Nyerere regime given that virtually every single prisoner who was rounded up in Mozambique or abducted from neighbouring countries and brought to Tanzania was codenamed as such, since they were categorised as high priority opponents of *Frelimo*. Indeed, during the conversation at a cocktail party at *Hotel Turismo* (which I referred to earlier), both army colonels Frank Mbuta and Juma Maneno touched on this issue, albeit in hushed tones.

But it is the official silence that is most ominous—silence which clearly shows criminal culpability. Sanctions that are legally (or legitimately) imposed are never shrouded in secrecy.

Should anyone doubt this view point, then the words of Marcelino dos Santos, a Marxist intellectual and former deputy president under Samora Machel would help illustrate the scope of criminal responsibility pertaining to these executions.

In an interview with Emílio Manhique, a television journalist with *Mozambique Television* (*TVM*), on September 19, 1997, Marcelino dos Santos attempted to philosophise the atrocious Nachingwea crimes as follows:

'Because one must see that at that moment, and naturally, while we ourselves felt the validity of revolutionary justice, the one built and fertilised by the armed struggle of national liberation, there existed, nonetheless, the fact that one had already formed a state, albeit one where *Frelimo* was the fundamental power. So it was that, perhaps, which led us, knowing precisely that many people would not comprehend things well, to prefer to keep silent. But let me say clearly that we do not regret these acts because we acted with revolutionary violence against traitors and traitors against the Mozambican people'[11].

Traitors!? Today the *Frelimo* government has embraced both multi-partyism and a free market economic system: policies favoured by most of those it killed. So who is a 'traitor' in this regard? Those politicians who were extra-judicially executed by *Frelimo* or *Frelimo* itself which executed people with fine, political minds and whose policies it is enthusiastically implementing today?

---

11 http://en.wikipedia.org/wiki/Uria_Simango

Whatever answer to that question may be, it seems the world underestimated the scale of the Nachingwea atrocities.

For, according to the Portuguese Service of Voice of America (i.e. *Voz da América-Notícias*), of March 31, 2010, the number of victims of these heinous crimes is thought to exceed 300.

I have used the word 'thought' on purpose because so long as both the Tanzanian and Mozambican governments pig-headedly refuse to publish the list of names of people they routinely put on show-trials, or of how many died of natural causes whilst interned in both countries, and, more specifically, how many detainees were unlawfully shot dead by the authorities in Mozambique after being sent back there by the Nyerere regime, the public will invariably rely on such figures as published by independent media outlets.

Whatever the case may be, with the number of victims of these atrocities rising, people are now questioning the right and legitimacy of Nyerere's regime to abduct people who fell outside Tanzania's jurisdiction; people who were neither Tanzanian nationals nor enjoyed the legal protection of the Tanzanian state, for what that was worth; and, crucially, people who had not infringed any Tanzanian laws.

Hopefully, Major Joseph Butiku might someday elaborate on these troubling aspects of these cases. For, Major Butiku, now chairman of *Mwalimu* Nyerere Foundation, had for many years been responsible for directing the activities of Nyerere's six political police organisations.

It is widely believed that by virtue of his position, he was privy to most decisions which were taken with regard to the victims discussed in this account. If he wasn't, then he should be able to know who was.

As I contend in the introduction of this book, matters pertaining to civil rights and civil liberties are an international onus; so, by giving a clear explanation of what exactly happened, Major Butiku would not be doing anyone a favour but fulfilling his obligation to the international community on behalf of the political masters he served so conscientiously.

Nonetheless, it was the abduction from Nairobi, Kenya, of the Reverend Father Mateus Pinho Gwenjere (also spelt as Gwengere), by Nyerere's political police agents, which might be of interest to the Catholic Church, which today is enthusiastically campaigning for Nyerere's canonisation.

Fr Gwenjere, a vocal critic of *Frelimo*'s policies, was abducted from Nairobi in October 1975, almost five months after the staging of several show-trials to which I refer.

And it is beyond doubt that Julius Nyerere, who reportedly sanctioned his abduction (his political police, *Usalama wa Taifa* (*UwT*), had no authority to abduct people from other countries without Nyerere being informed in advance because of the potential international repercussion) before finally handing him over to *Frelimo*, knew beforehand that the priest would be murdered. After all, Nyerere must surely by then have been aware of what had happened to groups of political prisoners his regime routinely handed over to *Frelimo* after their public humiliation on Tanzania soil.

It seems the systematic harassment of the bespectacled priest by Nyerere's regime intensified shortly after the assassination of Dr Mondlane. George Roberts analysed the assassination comprehensively in his paper 'The assassination of Mondlane: FRELIMO, Tanzania, and the politics of exile in Dar es Salaam'. Indeed, Roberts's analysis of events leading up to the assassination of Mondlane is substantially the same as what Tanzanian officials familiar with the investigation told US officials.

Indeed, according to another declassified State Department document dated February 13, 1969, a senior officer of the Criminal Investigation Department (CID), a certain Manikam, had informed US diplomats in Dar-Es-Salam that Fr Mateus Gwenjere had been detained in connection with the assassination of Dr Mondlane.

Manikam further informed US officials that the Tanzanian authorities believed Fr Gwenjere was behind the attack on *Frelimo* headquarters in 1968 which resulted in one death. He added that the priest was further suspected of orchestrating disturbances that same year at the Mozambique Institute.

Nevertheless, other well-informed observers thought many of the allegations levelled against Fr Gwenjere may in fact have been a result of his opposition to *Frelimo*'s policies, as well as other structural issues identified in George Roberts's paper, more than anything else. The minister himself was probably aware of this, which is why, when the opportunity availed itself, he immediately fled Tanzania to Kenya.

However, while still residing in Dar-Es-Salaam, Nyerere's political police outfit, *Usalama wa Taifa* (*UwT*), had instructed one of its agents known as JHK Matola (no relationship to Lorenço Matola, a Mozambican, who carried out the assassination of Commander Magaia) to befriend the affable priest. The agent dutifully did this, albeit posing as a 'dissident' opposed to Nyerere's regime of personal rule: the very same entrapment tactic which I described in the fifth chapter of this book.

So after Fr Gwenjere had fled to Kenya, where Matola was now stationed, the latter sent him a handwritten note proposing they meet at his (Matola's) residence. Aware that as a minister of religion, Fr Gwenjere was like a social worker—in fact, he was involved in work for the welfare of Mozambican refugees when he lived in Tanzania—Matola made a point of appealing to that human touch in his note, a copy of which is now in the hands of João M Cabrita, author of the authoritative work 'Mozambique: The Torturous Road to Democracy'. So Matola commenced his missive in *Swahili* to Fr Gwenjere this way:

'Father (sic) Ngwenjere, I did not come to see you yesterday because I've pain in my left arm, my condition is bad. So far, I've not taken the tickets for the trip to Mombasa because I haven't seen you. Would you please come to my place as soon as you read this missive. It would be a very good thing if you came early. Thanks.
JHK Matola,
Jamhuri Estate,
House No K 17 "A"
9/10/75'

Apparently, the purpose of the Mombasa trip was for the Nyerere political police agent to introduce Fr Gwenjere to other like-minded exiles, both Mozambican and Tanzanian, whom the agent claimed lived in the coastal town of Mombasa.

For this reason perhaps, the minister was not apprehensive about being in the company of two other 'Tanzanian dissidents' who were in fact members of Nyerere's dreaded political police. After introducing them to the unsuspecting Fr Gwenjere, the trio got into a green Ford Cortina with the registration number KMK546 for the sojourn to Mombasa. But instead of driving straight to Mombasa, the car sped towards the much closer Tanzanian border town of

Namanga, Arusha. There, a well-prepared platoon of Nyerere's men was waiting to give the Catholic priest a very, very warm welcome back.

Unfortunately, it was to be his last as he was executed in the manner described in Order of Action No 5/80, after the Nyerere regime handed him over to *Frelimo*.

Another case that springs to mind is that of Adelino Sirres Pires, a professional hunter who endured horrendous abuse at the hands of Nyerere's political police.

Apparently Pires was in Tanzania representing Hunters Africa, an American company which had taken over the operations of another company called Monterrey Big Game Hunters Club, which was owned by a group of Mexican industrialists.

Hunters Africa had concessions in Tabora. However, Pires had been in Arusha after seeing off former French President Valéry Giscard d'Estaing and his family who had been in the country on a hunting trip organised by Hunters Africa.

On the late afternoon of August 27, 1984, Pires was seized at his hotel by Nyerere's political police. They bundled him into a short-wheelbase Land Rover and then blindfolded him as they sped off to a nearby detention centre. There, Pires's hands and feet were tightly bound with rubber straps which nearly caused gangrene. His son, nephew and family friend who also worked for Hunters Africa at its Ugalla concession in Tabora had been arrested a day earlier and their treatment was not dissimilar to Pires's.

For fifty-five consecutive days Pires and his party were held at various detention camps before finally being flown to Mozambique in Nyerere's presidential jet to be interrogated there by *Frelimo*'s *Serviço Nacional de Segurança Popular* (*SNASP*), i.e. National Service for People's Security, on trumped charges that he was an arms smuggler for the Central Intelligence Agency (CIA).

Pires survived his harrowing experience—thanks, once again, to the pressure of some influential members of the international hunting community which resulted in his unconditional release.

Nonetheless, it later emerged that some people who wanted to take possession of Hunters Africa's equipment and steal its new operations in Tanzania were behind this episode. These were close friends of Nyerere's daughter Anna and were in cahoots

Flashback to 1982 in Santa Antonio: Adelino Sirres Pires (right) and French President Valéry Giscard d'Estaing. For fifty-five consecutive days he was brutalised by Nyerere's political police, but he survived his ordeal largely due to the intercedence of some influential members of the international hunting community.

with Muhidin Ndolanga, who at that material time was the general manager of the Arusha-based Tanzania Wildlife Corporation (TAWICO). Then, TAWICO was responsible for controlling all hunting in the country.

Another heinous abuse of Nyerere's power occurred following the bloody revolution in Zanzibar (referred to in the introduction) which resulted in the collapse of the government of Prime Minister Sheikh Mohamed Shamte Hamad, whom Nyerere subsequently imprisoned without trial. His foreign Minister, Sheikh Ali Muhsin Barwani, was also jailed without trial for ten years. Other senior Zanzibari politicians who were jailed without trial by Nyerere after the collapse of the government included Juma Aley, Dr Idarus Baalawy, Maulid Mshagama, Salim Kombo, Rashid Hamad, Abadhar Juma, Amirali Abdul Rasul and several others of Sheikh Shamte's ministers. Justice-minded Tanzanians and the world at large would have preferred that they be brought before a court of law to answer for the alleged crimes committed during their one month in office. Many Tanzanians remain unconvinced today that these politicians could have committed such serious crimes in only one month to put them behind bars for ten years. It is widely believed they were persecuted because of their Arab origin. Similarly, if we were to apply an identical mathematical equation that one month in office results in ten years in prison, how many years would CCM leaders get who have been in power for over forty years and who now overtly admit that 'we made mistakes' and surprisingly continue to make them despite public protestations?

But 'mistakes' is an understatement in view of the following incident. On the evening of Saturday, September 19, 1964, Mohamed Abdallah Ameir (Kaujore), a member of the Zanzibar Revolutionary Council (ZRC), shot dead five worshippers at *Ithnashiri* mosque in Kiponda in Zanzibar.

Kaujore's victims included eight-year old Ghulam Abbas Kassamali, Sayyid Abdulmuttalib Hashim Hussainy, Haj Abdul-Hussain Ramtullah, Mohamad Asar (Babu Haji) and Sayyid Ali Asghar. But because Kaujore was '*kigogo*' (a political heavy weight), no legal action was taken against him—thanks, once again, to the culture of '*kulindana*' (protecting each other).

It is difficult to see how justice could exist in a country

where the law does not provide legal safeguards against arbitrary arrest. This is particularly so in a situation where the president is asked to sign blank detention orders allowing political police officials to fill in the names of the people they want to detain; which

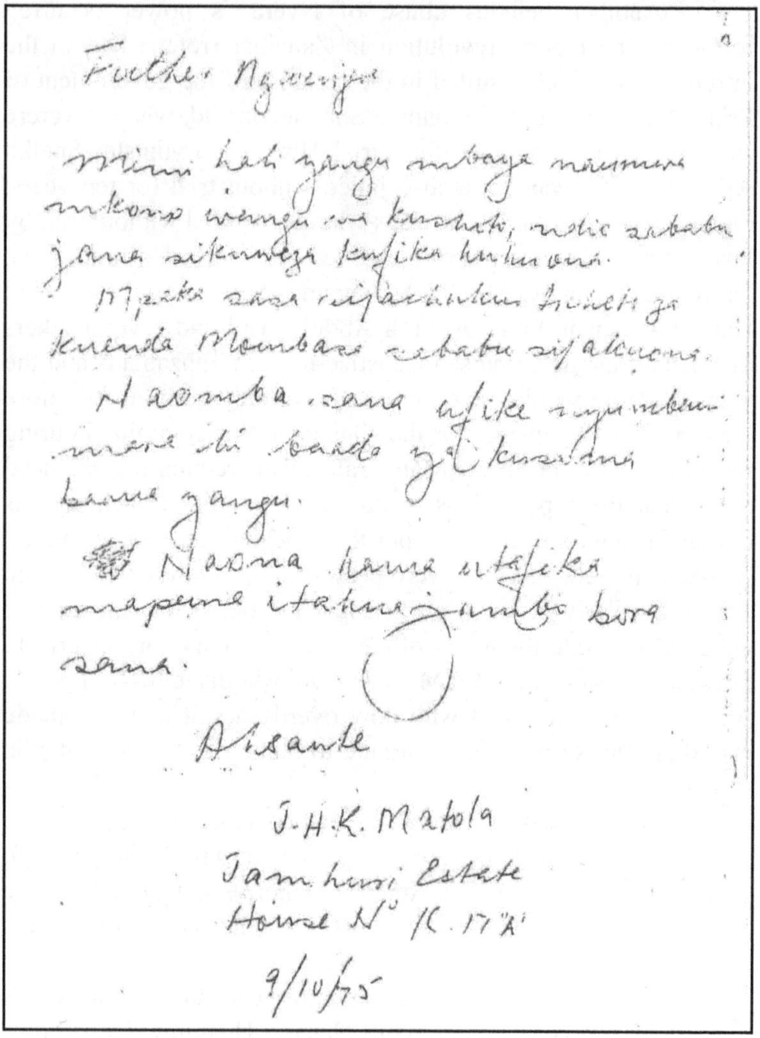

Father Ngwenjere

mimi hali yangu mbaya naumwa mkono wangu wa kushoto, ndio sababu jana sikuweza kufika kuku ona.

Mzuka sana nijachukua hadi za kuenda Mombasa sababu sij aleweni.

N aomba sana ufike nyumbani mimi iki baado ya kusikia hame yangu.

N aona hame utafika mapema itakuwa jambo bora sana.

Asante

J·H·K· Matola
Jamhuri Estate
House No K 17A
9/10/75

A copy of a note (above) which Nyerere's political police agent sent to Fr Mateus Gwenjere (pictured opposite page) shortly before his abduction from Nairobi, Kenya. The agent was then working with the East African Community (EAC) and resided at Jamhuri Estate House No K 17A. The car used in the abduction of Fr Gwenjere was a green Ford Cortina with registration number KMK546.

192

was a common practice under Nyerere. Under those circumstances, it is difficult to imagine how the liberty of the individual can be safeguarded or how to prevent detention motivated by vengeance or jealousy.

The death or torture of detainees at the notorious detention camp in Kigoto, in the Mwanza region, serves as a reminder of how Nyerere used his prerogative powers corruptly. In 1977, the government ordered villagers in Mwanza and the neighbouring Shinyanga region rounded up and detained for interrogation. The victims were apparently taken in for practising witchcraft, a charge with no scientific or legal basis and which the government does not even recognise. Moreover, witchcraft does not constitute a danger to the security of the state. Alhaj Ali Hassan Mwinyi, former Union president, then Minister of Home Affairs, resigned from the government accepting 'political responsibility.' Surely in a society where leaders are accountable to the civil society, that would have been the end of Mwinyi's political career. Not in Tanzania, where leaders are answerable only to those who appoint them; and where the populace lacks the power, thanks again to the constitution which Nyerere imposed upon the nation after he had laid exclusive claim to sovereignty.

Nyerere reacted swiftly to Mwinyi's resignation: he rewarded him with an ambassadorial post in Cairo. Only after the outage over the barbaric Kigoto murders started to fade from Tanzanians' collective memory did Nyerere recall his old crony, this time placing him right at the centre of Tanzanian politics. In 1985 Nyerere hand picked Mwinyi to succeed him.

Old habits die hard; Mwinyi was quick to show that he was no exception. On July 26, 1986, President Mwinyi's regime unleashed trigger-happy soldiers on cane-cutters at Kilombero sugar estate. The cutters had gathered peacefully at the factory's offices to demand their rightful emolument; several were shot dead and scores permanently maimed. Public calls for the perpetrators to be brought to book went unheeded. In keeping with the *CCM*'s policy of *kulindana* (protecting each other), the officials who ordered the massacre will never be brought to justice. Much to the disgust of ordinary Tanzanians, there was no outcry from the international community, as would surely have been the case had it been white-ruled South Africa.

President Mwinyi continued to sanction military campaigns against perceived troublemakers. On May 13, 1988, troops fired on peaceful demonstrators in Zanzibar, leaving two people dead from bullet wounds. Eye-witnesses claim the victims were hit from the back. Several other demonstrators were severely injured and scores more detained, allegedly for attending an illegal gathering.

Independent versions of what happened that day contradict the official account. These versions insist that Mwinyi's troops opened fire on the demonstrators after they had passed the State House quite peacefully, and not before. It was only after the demonstrators had been fired on by the troops that property was damaged by angry demonstrators; yet the government used the damage to property as a pretext for the shootings.

The scene was set for another bloodbath, this time at the main campus of the University of Dar-Es-Salaam (UDSM) during the crisis there in 1990. President Mwinyi is known to have wanted to use the Field Force Unit (FFU) to quell the disturbances; but Nyerere, then still *CCM* chairman and head of its Defence Commission, talked him out of it. However, the witch-hunt of students suspected of involvement in the disturbances continued long after the matter had been mutually resolved.

Mwinyi also used the death penalty quite liberally, in sharp contrast with Nyerere, who seemed reluctant to have condemned prisoners executed. People advocating an end to the death penalty were shocked when they learnt that since assuming office in 1985, Mwinyi had assented to the execution of more than twenty-four condemned prisoners, and that more executions could be expected in the 1990s. This is the highest number of prisoner executions in Tanzania's history.

Critics now blame Nyerere for failing to abolish the death penalty while he was still in office, although he never himself assented to prisoner executions perhaps as a public relations move for the international community. In the 1970s however, Nyerere agreed to the execution of Said Mwamwidi of Iringa who, angered by Nyerere's forced villagisation programme (discussed *infra*) shot dead Dr Wilbert Kleruu, the Regional Commissioner for Iringa. The constitution tailored by Nyerere could be ruthlessly exploited by a man such as Idi Amin, should such a person ever emerge in Tanzania; and there is no guarantee that this cannot happen, given that Tanzanians are constitutionally impotent.

Perhaps one of the best known instances of mass brutality, at least to the many thousands of peasants who suffered as a result, was the infamous *'Opareisheni Vijiji Vya Ujamaa'* i.e. operation communal villages, when Nyerere's government uprooted peasants from their ancestral homes and herded them like cattle into collectives as part of the failed *Ujamaa* experiment. Scores of unarmed peasants died during this operation as a result of unwarranted brutality by the Field Force Unit (FFU), a paramilitary unit under the Ministry of Home affairs.

In fact, many more died as a result of lack of food, water and poor sanitation in the new (*Ujamaa*) villages. It seems that those who were charged with the task of planning these villages were highly incompetent (or simply negligent) as they did not consider the great numbers of people they brought into these villages every single day.

Other villagers, of course, died in the fires when their makeshift huts accidentally caught fire. Again, planners ought to have foreseen this problem happening because most villages were located in open space. Moreover, these huts were so close to each other that whenever one of them caught fire then, fanned by the wind, the rest of the huts would also succumb to the flames. It was disastrous if this happened at night when most people were asleep. But villagers faced other perils.

Gathered completely in strange locations that lacked toilet facilities or any other vital utility, villagers had to think twice before venturing outside to relieve themselves in the wild, some distance from the huts. Failure to do this had the potential risk of people being preyed on by wild beasts that roamed the areas in which some of these villages were located. And, you can be sure, wild beasts are not that bad at detecting human scent.

However, it was those villagers who lost their lives when Nyerere's soldiers torched their dwellings; dwellings in which they had lived their entire lives that was clearly criminal.

Apparently, the torching of homes was designed to prevent the peasants from returning to them in case they were to escape from Nyerere's planned *Ujamaa* villages. So, the rationale behind this policy was that, faced with nowhere else to return, following the torching of their homes, the evacuees would have been compelled to remain into the villages where they had been forcebly taken by Nyerere's soldiers. That was the level of brutality of that infamous *'Opareisheni Vijiji vya Ujamaa.*

Sometimes ordinary criminal matters provoked horrific torture. Take the case of James Magoti, a former Dar-Es-Salaam bank manager who was detained for alleged theft together with his brother Adam in November 1979, under a presidential decree. Theft is a matter for the police to investigate and the courts to adjudicate. Magoti was severely tortured while in what was described as 'administrative detention', suffering permanent damage to important parts of his body. Since then rumours have circulated that Magoti's torture was ordered from *Ikulu* (State House) by one of two senior officials, Joseph Butiku or Issak Bhoke Mnanka, the men who were in charge of Nyerere's political police organisations. This accusation is based on claims that one of the two security leaders was in love with a woman banker working with Magoti. It is claimed that the official suspected Magoti of being in love with the same woman.

Another case that springs to mind is that of Said Seif, a prominent Bukoba businessman who was detained for several years on unspecified charges, and who later died shortly after his release, allegedly in a shoot-out with police. There is also the case of Major Kato, a member of the Tanzanian People's Defence Force (TPDF), who was detained for more than six years at Bukoba Prison without charge or trial, after the war with Uganda had ended. Sam Bakera, a Canadian-trained Ugandan engineer working at Kilembe mine in Uganda, was picked up in his own country and held for several years without trial at Lwamulumba prison camp in Bukoba, allegedly for blowing up the Kyaka Bridge during the war with Uganda.

Much of this abuse of civil liberties can be blamed on the Arusha Declaration of 1967, the blueprint for socialism in Tanzania. It provided the basis for officials to dispense justice without reference to civilised legal tenets; in short, it allowed Nyerere to ride roughshod over court decisions and the will of his own cabinet. Under Nyerere, Tanzania welcomed political refugees from all parts of Africa, mainly southern Africa. On arrival, these refugees discovered that Nyerere's government wanted them to espouse certain beliefs in exchange for a place to hide; something which is morally wrong. Many refugees who were outspokenly critical of their political movements and armed wings were locked up in Nyerere's detention camps. One of the best known instances is that of Andreas Shipanga, former Information Secretary of the South West Africa People's Organisation (SWAPO). Shipanga and Andreas Nuukwao, together with nine others were brought from Zambia in 1976 to Tanzania, where they were placed in detention. They were released some years later following a protracted campaign for their freedom by Amnesty International (AI).

South African refugees who became disillusioned with the African National Congress (ANC) and its armed wing, *Umkhonto We Sizwe* (*MK*) i.e. Spear of the Nation, were left to languish at the notorious Dakawa detention camp, near Morogoro. Some never came out alive; others who were last seen at this hell-camp are still unaccounted for. Dakawa detention camp, otherwise known as the 'Ruth First Orientation Centre', is one among several such camps in Tanzania where South African refugees were brutally tortured. In April 1990, several detainees escaped from Mazimbu detention camp to Nairobi; there they told the world of the plight of scores of detainees still incarcerated, of conditions in the camp and of compatriots who had died as a result of starvation and torture.

None of the South African refugees detained in Tanzania, many of whom were brought regularly by bus from Zambia and other Frontline States, or by the Soviet *Aeroflot* airline, were ever brought to court. All were held under the so-called Refugee Control Act, which covers virtually anything under the sun. This Act empowers the president to detain a refugee without trial for up to seven years, even for alleged political crimes committed outside Tanzania's territory. Torture and physical abuse of these detainees was further confirmed to the international media by several people freed by the ANC in August 1991. The ANC had apparently detained them because they were South African spies. Dakawa and Mazimbu camps, which Tanzania set aside for the ANC to 'rehabilitate and re-educate' so-called enemy agents, turned out to be a scandal for Tanzania, given the brutal treatment meted out to internees, with Tanzania's approval.[12]

---

12 See http://afraf.oxfordjournals.org/cgi/pdf_extract/93/371/279

Refugees from other African countries also suffered in detention in Tanzania. In 1990, Remi Gahutu, a Burundian exile and leader of *Pelipe-hutu*, a movement opposed to *Tutsi* domination of the government in Burundi, died inside Ukonga security prison in Dar-Es-Salaam. He had been held there, together with fourteen other Burundian exiles, since 1989, for allegedly participating in activities considered detrimental to Tanzania's relations with Burundi. The government insisted Gahutu died of a 'heart attack'.

However, when the United Nations High Commissioner for Refugees (UNHCR) branch office in Dar-Es-Salaam requested that Gahutu's autopsy be performed by an independent doctor, the Government Chemical Laboratory (GCL) suddenly issued a new version of the death report. It now claimed, in its post-mortem report dated November 23, 1990, that Gahutu's death had been caused by the constant inhaling of farm chemicals when he had worked as a farmer. But the US State Department, in its 1990 human rights report on Tanzania, concluded its paragraph on Remi Gahutu's death with the following statement: '...clinical information released at the end of November (1990) indicated the death may have been the result of poisoning.'

But is was only after the death of Mousa 'Lee' Membar, who had been held in the same prison cell that once housed Gahutu, that the conditions under which political detainees were being held in Tanzania came to light. Membar, leader of the underground opposition Tanzania Democratic Movement, died in Muhimbili Medical Centre in Dar-Es-Salaam on May 25, 1991, his face bloated. The government claimed he died of a 'known disease', but did not provide details.

Membar had returned to Tanzania from exile in Britain on September 14, 1990, after government agents had enticed him to return to take part in the political process. On his arrival, Membar was promptly detained without charge. The conditions in which he was being held were appalling. His solitary confinement cell was filthy and lacked adequate light and it was also poorly ventilated and infested with mosquitoes. Membar died as a result of protracted torture. The government's refusal to perform an autopsy or to hold a public inquest, not just into his death but into the treatment of detainees generally, lends weight to the claim that the state killed him. Even calls from the respected London-based human rights organisation, Amnesty International (AI), for an inquest into Member's death were ignored.

Tanzania's government has also adopted the policy of involuntary repatriation of refugees to countries where they face persecution. Yet Tanzania is a signatory to the Geneva Convention, which includes clauses related to the treatment of refugees. The United Nations High Commissioner for Refugees (UNHCR) even gave Nyerere the prestigious Nansen Award in recognition of his 'good' work for refugees. His work for refugees was not always up to standard. In 1984, Tanzania secretly returned to Kenya fifteen political exiles, including two young Kenya Air Force servicemen who had fled their country fearing for their lives after the 1982 coup attempt. It is widely believed that the two servicemen, senior private Hezekiah Rabala Ochuka and Pancras Oteyo Okumu, were hanged after being forcibly returned. Yet they had been granted refugee status by Tanzania and should therefore have been immune to extradition.

None of these abuses by Nyerere's regime sparked nationwide condemnation, unlike, for example, the Steve Biko case in South Africa. Yet Biko and, to take just one example, Tanzania's own Mousa Membar, died in similar circumstances and for much the same principles. Why no world outcry against Tanzania's abuses, you might ask? Again, it could be that in the cases I have cited, the principal actors are all black—both the victims and their persecutors. Isn't it time a black African *'Cry Freedom'* was filmed? This time the setting could be Tanzania—after all, we have the material.

In 1977, in Zanzibar, thirty-seven defendants received varying sentences in a treason trial. Thirteen others, including a prominent cabinet minister in the Union government, Abdulrahaman Mohamed Babu, were held on the mainland without formally being charged. Others were Colonel Ali Mahafoudh, Salim Saleh, Haji Othman Haji, Shaaban Salim Mbarak, Tahir Ali, Hamed Hilal, Badru Said, Abdallah Juma, Ahmed Mohammed Habib Bajabir, Amour Mohamed Dugheish and Suleiman Mohamed. The strange part of this trial drama was that the former Attorney-General of Zanzibar, Wolfgango Dourado (later High Court Judge), assumed the roles of both prosecutor and defence counsel, a legal anomaly at odds with the principles of natural justice. Apparently, this practice

Dar-Es-Salaam, August, 1982: Senior Private Hezekiah Rabala Ochuka (in a white shirt) was granted refugee status in Tanzania after his case was heard in an open court in Tanzania. Despite this, the Nyerere regime secretly returned him to Kenya, where the evidence he gave in court to support his asylum claim weighed against him back in his homeland. He was hanged there in July 1985.

201

became law during Dourado's tenure as Attorney-General under the murderous rule of Sheikh Karume. Before being appointed High Court Judge, Dourado, briefly became an outspoken Zanzibar dissident, but only after the regime he faithfully served gave him a taste of life in a Tanzanian detention centre.

In another treason trial, in 1983 on the mainland, many of the accused had in fact been granted asylum in Kenya, which should have rendered them immune from extradition. How they were repatriated to Tanzania is unclear; what is clear is that whoever was involved infringed their rights of asylum. Among the victims of this violation of international law were an airline pilot called McGhee, alias Hatib Gandhi (who died suspiciously shortly after being released from prison in January 1996), and Christopher Kadego, a charismatic officer in the Tanzania People's Defence Force (TPDF), Captains Harry Hanspope, Suleiman Kamando, Vitalis Mapunda, Zacharia Hanspope, Rodrick Roberts, Lieutenant-Colonel Protas Muchwampaka, Lieutenant Badru Rwechungura, as well as others from all walks of life.

Nyerere tolerated no opposition, or even the thought of it, as James Mapalala and Mwinijuma Othman Upindo found out in September 1984. They had called on Nyerere to repeal the 1965 law forbidding political opposition. He promptly had them locked up. Amnesty International (AI) relentlessly pressed for their release; four years later (yes, four years) Mapalala was freed from prison, but banished to the island of Mafia for a considerable period.

The all-embracing powers given Nyerere under the 1962 Preventive Detention Act (PDA) achieved their desired steadying effect, cowing the opposition and confining the finest political minds into a fortress of fear. Mass fear and docility enable regimes based on personal power to present themselves as enjoying popularity. Personality cults are built around demi-god characters like Nyerere; yet he remained a fearful figure until his death in 1999.

Articulate and eloquent, Nyerere was able to move churchmen and tycoons with his simplicity of ideas. When it came to human rights abuses, he shrewdly ducked the question by raising non-issues: if the North (richer countries) respected human rights, they should not 'squeeze' poorer countries. Then the old man would sob: 'our children are dying because we have to pay debt,' although his own children, it was noted, remained remarkably well nourished.

In making his pathetic plea, Nyerere was probably referring to the more than US$9.5 billion his government received from the West between 1970 and 1989, most of which was squandered through mismanagement, corruption and lack of accountability. For a government which for twenty years crooned 'socialism and self-reliance,' Nyerere's 'achievement' was quite the opposite: dependence on imports and foreign aid. But Nyerere operated efficient public relations machinery abroad, through which he projected himself as a respectable figure in international circles.

One glaring example was the funding by Nyerere's political police organisation of the London-based political magazine *Africa* (now defunct). As if that were not enough, the organisation even sent one of its senior operatives, Marcelino Komba, to work on the magazine as a senior writer. Komba, who until recently had remained in the United Kingdom after the demise of the magazine, had described himself as 'self-employed' and an 'economic refugee' in the UK. Since the magazine's demise there have been claims that Tanzania's political police had actually been dipping into their own slush fund to pay individuals to write letters to the magazine praising *mwalimu* and his regime. Hard-pressed Tanzanian taxpayers, who ultimately had to foot the bill, are yet to be told how much misinformation and distortion of the truth were spread as a result of this wasteful propaganda campaign.

It makes very little difference in Africa whether a ruler is educated or uneducated: active oppression of the masses, economic failure and undemocratic practises occur regardless of leaders' educational background. Sometimes, the more educated leaders are, the more often policy failures occur; many of them appear reluctant to seek advice from local technocrats, believing they are themselves sufficiently well educated. They end up formulating policy single-handedly, as Nyerere was wont to do. Nyerere would usually present an idea to his cabinet for endorsement, not for criticism or debate. When Benjamin Mkapa, a former Minister of Foreign Affairs (later president), contradicted Nyerere at a cabinet meeting, Nyerere scolded him. Mkapa was subsequently demoted and sent to Canada as ambassador, but later he pleaded for clemency from the 'father of the nation', Nyerere, and returned to Tanzania where he took up a different and peripheral cabinet post before eventually being taken back into the fold.

Nyerere introduced single-candidate presidential elections in 1970, 1975 and 1980 which were a complete sham: the electorate was only allowed to vote for or against Nyerere-the take-it-or-leave-it attitude so typical of the man. In Tanzania today, his critics contend that Nyerere surrounded himself with mediocre advisers to ensure he upheld a pliable ruling class. Others claim Nyerere did not want anyone around him who would eclipse his own political star. He would make a public issue of 'correcting' the supposed mistakes of his deputies; apparently this reinforced his political fortunes and created the impression, quite wrongly, that he was the only capable man in Tanzania. Many critics claim that Rashid Mfaume Kawawa, an unpopular politician, was used for this purpose—as a willing political pawn. Similarly, the handpicking of President Mwinyi, whom many Tanzanians regarded as unsuitable for the post, is viewed in much the same light.

But it was the ill-treatment of Chief David Kidaha Makwaia, who died on March 30, 2007, which vividly illustrates how scared Nyerere was of politicians of equal standing.

Chief Kidaha Makwaia was a highly revered East African tribal leader. His father was a *Sukuma* chief, Makwaia Mwandu, of Usiha, in the region of Shinyanga.

Chief Kidaha and Nyerere were of the same age; but, significantly, the two had been friends since they met at Makerere College in Uganda.

Apparently, Chief Kidaha succeeded his father in 1945 and was later elected paramount chief of the *Sukuma* Federation comprised of more than fifty chiefdoms. He was quite popular and, arguably, one of the most powerful chiefs in East Africa. Indeed, at one point, he was considered as a potential president.

According to the obituary published in *The Times* of London, of May 11, 2007, when Nyerere founded Tanganyika African National Union (TANU), it was Chief Kidaha, who, using his good offices and influence with the British colonial authorities, persuaded the latter to allow TANU an arena and went on to lobby subordinate chiefs in *Sukuma* land on TANU's behalf.[13]

Despite this, after independence, one of Nyerere's first

---

13 http://www.timesonline.co.uk/tol/comment/obituaries/article1774482.ece

acts was to abolish the role of chiefs. Additionally, despite their long friendship, Nyerere banished Chief Kidaha and his brother Hussein, in separate, remote districts and confined them there under Preventive Detention Ordinance.

Chief Kidaha's charisma, influence and popularity led Nyerere to believe he was potentially someone likely to eclipse his own political star and so, he had to be removed from the political scene and his power-base dismantled.

Indeed, getting rid of chiefdoms was part of Nyerere's earlier moves to concentrate power into his own hands.

Through the Organisation of African Unity (OAU) and the so-called Frontline States, Nyerere advocated the recognition of only one political movement in various countries, always a movement whose ideology corresponded with that of his own party (*CCM*). In Angola, for example, he insisted on recognition of the *Movimento Popular de Libertação de Angola* (*MPLA*) i.e. Popular Movement for the Liberation of Angola, as the only legitimate party. The result was that other political groups, including *União Nacional para a Indêpendencia Total de Angola* (*UNITA*) i.e. National Union for the Total Independence of Angola, took to the bush to fight a costly war that ravaged the country, when the issue could have been settled, as it should have been, through the ballot box. Had a celebrated African leader of Nyerere's so-called wisdom removed his single-vision monocle, and instead used his influence to encourage a diversity of opinion, Angola might have been spared the horror of the civil war that took decades to end.

As in Angola, so in Mozambique: there, Nyerere favoured *Frelimo* as the sole 'legitimate' party. The result was the same: a devastating civil war which caused enormous damage. The hard pressed Tanzanian tax payer was not excluded from the cost of Mozambique's war as Tanzania stationed troops in Mozambique for more than a decade to assist *Frelimo* in the fight against *Renamo* rebels.

The mess in which many countries find themselves is the result of the failure of democracy; a progression from repression by an alien (colonial) government to repression by one's own government (though not an elected one). The cost to the affected countries is enormous, not just in terms of life and property, but in every aspect of human existence. In the case of Mozambique and Angola in particular, these were not cheap wars: peasants, for example, had little choice but to abandon their farms when bomb craters ripped furrows through their fields; the peasants went hungry and ultimately became refugees. A whole generation of children lost its childhood: there was no room for play in a war zone. And the 'great' Nyerere was not blameless: he cared little for the politics of common sense and diverse opinions. Ultimately his myopic vision encouraged confrontation.

There was also the creation of the Frontline States, which seemed to assume the duties and responsibilities of the whole African continent. Surely a vulnerable country such as Tanzania, a key player in the Frontline, could ill-afford this new role. In addition there is the issue of sanctions against South Africa, to which Nyerere committed himself fully (with, it must be admitted, good intentions albeit without common sense). Morally justifiable as they were, sanctions struck a double blow for Tanzania: there was no spin-off from companies pulling out of South Africa, not least because our own investment climate was not conducive to private capital; and we gained little from the Good Samaritans, the *wafadhili* or donors, who had promised financial help to overcome the drawbacks of backing sanctions. Oddly, many of the very European countries which promised Tanzania financial assistance were themselves reluctant to impose economic sanctions on South African white-ruled government.

Tanzanians cannot be blamed for thinking, rightly or wrongly, that these developed nations possessed financial clout to force South Africa to dismantle apartheid. As a staunch sanctions supporter, Tanzania under Nyerere found itself way behind some of the African countries which traded with South Africa, some quite openly, and established connections in that country's lucrative markets. Tanzania was more concerned with external political matters than its own development. As it has turned out, Nyerere's ideas are largely discredited, leading to economic and social despair wherever anything similar has been tried.

Nyerere's government and *Frelimo*, which enjoyed Nyerere's whole-hearted support, have still to answer human rights violations in the pre-independence days. It is widely believed that *Frelimo* worked closely with Tanzania's secret police and that between the two they conducted several heavy-handed recruitment campaigns for *Frelimo* inside Mozambique, in the region bordering Mtwara, southern Tanzania. Sources claim that people of the *Makonde* community in Mozambique were forcibly enlisted to fight for *Frelimo*, regardless of whether they subscribed to *Frelimo*'s ideals or not. It must be noted that although every Mozambican wanted independence as much as any other African, most did not believe *Frelimo* had the exclusive right to lead after independence.

Extremely harmful allegations have been made concerning the conduct of security agents recruiting for *Frelimo*. According to these allegations, people who resisted enlistment were tortured to death. Reports of this nature were sent to Dar-Es-Salaam, but as usual the Nyerere regime declined to take any action.

Allegations of forced recruitment, with Tanzania's blessing, have been made against the now late Uganda's Milton Obote, who, with assistance from Tanzanian security agents, mounted a recruitment campaign inside Uganda in the 1970s, when Obote was exiled in Tanzania. These allegations were fuelled by the detention of Ugandan conscientious objectors by Tanzania. Those objectors were held without charge or trial; the presumption was that Tanzania wanted them to fight for Obote.

Most of these Ugandans were unemployed in their own country; recruiting agents lured them to Tanzania with promises of jobs on the TAZARA (Tanzania Zambia Railway Authority) railway line, which was then under construction. The jobless Ugandans soon found they had been lined up for work of another kind: soldiers in Obote's guerrilla army. With no means of earning a living, and under pressure from the Tanzanian government, some volunteered to join Obote's forces rather than be stranded. Those who refused were detained at various Tanzanian prisons—some for many years. Nyerere's regime never specified what crimes they were alleged to have committed; similarly, their legal status was never clarified, nor the grounds of their detention. Most Tanzanians still want to know why Nyerere approved of forced recruitment into armies of his liking and why objectors were jailed.

There also remains the question of Tanzania's military intervention in Uganda's internal affairs; a costly exercise which depleted our finances. In 1978-79, Tanzania under Julius Nyerere, fought a costly war with neighbouring Uganda, in what world opinion regarded as a legitimate act of self-defence. But was it, or was the Ugandan regime deliberately provoked into invading Tanzania?

On January 25, 1971, Apollo Milton Obote, then president of Uganda, was overthrown by his own army commander, General Idi Amin, whilst attending a Commonwealth Summit in Singapore. Obote's friend and ideological bedfellow, Nyerere, gave him a place of refuge. But Obote kept on shuttling back and forth between Tanzania and Sudan, where his band of guerrillas were based. However, due to discernable factors, Khartoum withdrew permission for Obote's guerrillas to operate from there.

Those factors, however, did not strike Nyerere as particularly significant, though perhaps the residents of Kagera, the province in northwestern Tanzania which is coterminous with Uganda, understood Khartoum's apprehension better. Nonetheless, this factor alone was not sufficient ground for dissuading a principled man from doing humanity a favour.

Consequently, Obote's rebel army was invited to Tanzania '…where Nyerere allowed them to regroup and train, and to make a series of raids across the boarder into the south of Uganda[14]'.

But it was only after Nyerere had allowed the guerrillas to make regular incursions from Tanzania into southern Uganda, via the Kagera salient, that what the residents of this region had all along dreaded became real.

Repulsed by Amin's soldiers, the rebels would retreat to their bases in Tanzania through the very same route they had used to launch those attacks.

In retaliation, the Ugandan airforce would bomb targets inside Kagera province in rapid succession, largely because of Kagera's proximity to Uganda. Despite the 'collateral damage' resulting from Amin's air bombardments inside Kagera, the rebels, with Nyerere's unstinting support, persisted in launching more raids.

Tired of these incursions, the bullfrog Ugandan dictator decided to invade the salient that provided a passage for the rebels, destroying the bridge that linked the Kagera salient with the rest of

---

14 http://www.timesonline.co.uk/tol/comment/obituaries/article1081268.ece

Tanzania. Amin, in his madness, thought he would keep the area he invaded so as to deter further incursions into Ugandan territory. He had swallowed the bait.

As it turned out, Nyerere, who calculated his moves with the astuteness of an accomplished chess player, was waiting for a valid excuse to invade Uganda and install his friend Obote back to power.

So instead of evicting Ugandan troops from the area they occupied, Nyerere, to everyone's surprise, ordered his troops to go all the way to Kampala and unseat Amin from his throne in preparation for Obote's return.

As in preceding incidents, Tanzanian troops were in this case to remain in Uganda for a couple of years—again at the expense of Tanzanian taxpayers.

On the other hand, Tanzania lacked the capacity to loan Uganda large amounts of money for its reconstruction after the war. If Tanzania had done this, there might have been a clear element of national interest.

For example, Uganda would have been compelled to buy reconstruction material from Tanzania and, perhaps, to use Tanzanian engineering companies to do the construction work. Jobless Tanzanians might have found jobs; companies on the verge of collapse would have been saved from bankruptcy; and the economy would have generally picked up.

I am not in any way suggesting these to be among the reasons why wars are fought amongst nations. Rather, what I am saying is that it is absurd, from the economic viewpoint, for a given country to fight a costly war and then let other countries which were on the sidelines do the reconstruction work, using companies and material from their own countries, whilst the country that fought the war struggles endlessly to pay for its cost.

If the countries undertaking the reconstruction in instances like this were to think of the warring leader as a godsend, that might make some sense, for Nyerere probably was a godsend for those who helped rebuild Uganda—whilst he picked up the war bill and his people suffered for it.

All told, for all the material and human cost to Tanzania, Obote went on to rule Uganda even more oppressively than his forerunner, Idi Amin. Respected human rights groups estimate that more than 300,000 people were killed during the time Nyerere's troops were stationed in Uganda; deaths which occurred under a regime over which Nyerere had enormous influence.

Not only that, but due to Nyerere's desire to ensure Obote regained his throne at any cost, it became imperative for him to remove from power the two post-Amin presidents namely, Professor Yusuf Lule and Godfrey Lukongwa Binaisa.

Currently, it is being debated that if Nyerere was truly committed to ridding Africa of brutal dictators, by whatever means, he should have looked no further than neighbouring Zanzibar, over which he had legitimate constitutional and legal powers. Sheikh Karume was a ruthless dictator whose reign of terror will never be forgotten by Zanzibaris. The argument that Nyerere's intervention would have jeopardised the Union he so much cherished cannot be entertained; principles cannot be compromised. It must be remembered that the East African Community (EAC), created by the British along European Union (EU) lines during colonial rule, was much cherished by East Africans. Yet its collapse was in part due to Nyerere's refusal to sit at the same table as the 'murderer' Amin, to discuss Community affairs.

Events in Zanzibar from 1964 followed a similar pattern to Amin's Uganda, with atrocities committed against the local people. As in Amin's Uganda, Karume's regime disrupted economic life in Zanzibar, turning what might have been the Hong Kong of Africa into a totalitarian dungeon where freedom and justice were non-existent. Nyerere had no qualms about offering military assistance to dissidents of nearby countries (Seychelles, for example) opposing democratically elected governments; yet in neighbouring Zanzibar, a tyrant embarrassed the entire black race.

In 1976/7 Nyerere offered military training to dissidents from Seychelles in order to overthrow by force the democratic administration of Sir James Mancham. Having succeeded, Nyerere then assisted a one-party regime cling to power by despatching Tanzanian troops there for a decade. Not only did Tanzania overturn the wishes of the Seychelles electorate, but Nyerere also helped root out the ideals of freedom, justice and equality—he snuffed out democracy in Seychelles. On the other hand, the retention of Tanzanian troops on the main island Mahe was a pointless burden on the shoulders of the hard-pressed Tanzanian taxpayer.

Nyerere's interference in the internal affairs of other states does not end there. In 1974/5 Tanzania trained dissidents to depose the government of Ahmed Abdallah Abderemane of the Comoros (referred to in the introduction). Tanzanians could not fathom why they had to foot the bill for installing a government of Nyerere's liking in the Comoros, at a time when our own economy was in tatters. Observers now argue that Tanzania's intervention in the internal affairs of the Comoros actually destabilised the otherwise peaceful Indian Ocean islands, and precipitated the presence of a mercenary force under the Frenchman Bob Denard, who took control shortly after Tanzanian troops pulled out.

Tanzania's involvement in the Comoros and Seychelles are testimony to Nyerere's hegemonic dreams for the region; in the end, he bled his own economy. Nyerere's Tanzania bears a direct moral responsibility for the suffering inflicted on Comorians and Seychellois, many of whom fled their countries after Nyerere-sponsored regimes forced their way to power.

Nyerere was one of the founder-fathers of the Organisation of African Unity (OAU); indeed, he stood for its ideals of pan-Africanism. Yet, he revealed a secessionist streak when he supported the breakaway of Biafra from Nigeria in 1967, and supported Biafra's secessionist leader, Lieutenant-Colonel (later General) Odumegwu Ojukwu. By recognising the breakaway state of Biafra, Nyerere countenanced the disintegration of the Federal Republic of Nigeria, a violation of the OAU Charter.

Nearer the present, Zanzibaris calling for a referendum to determine the future of their country's Union with the Tanzanian mainland were being harassed by Nyerere's secret police and continue to be systematically harassed. Many were equally jailed without charge or trial. *Maalim* Seif Sharif Hamad, a dynamic former Chief Minister of Zanzibar, was detained for a long time for calling on the mainland government to review the articles of the Union. So too were Shabaan Mloo, a veteran Tanzanian politician, Ali Haji Pandu, a former Chief Justice of Zanzibar, and others. This latter group was only released after Amnesty International's relentless efforts to get them freed. If Biafrans could be listened to, then why not Zanzibaris?

Solitary confinement had sharpened my mind, turned me into a deep thinker covering a wide range of issues, with Nyerere and

211

his regime of personal rule as central features. The more time I spent thinking in detention, the more I became convinced that Nyerere's policies, both internal and external, had had a negative impact on the lives of millions of black Africans: where his *Ujamaa* had spread, there was suffering and unwarranted hardship to be found. When historians—including many who still hold him in high esteem—reassess his role as a 'respected statesman' and 'visionary leader', many will conclude what ordinary Tanzanians already know: the man was an undemocratic tyrant, with no respect for ordinary human values (although he conned the world into believing otherwise). His contribution to the betterment of humanity was, by and large, negative and will not be readily forgotten by those who suffered under his intractable despotic rule (see also the complete open letter I wrote to President Julius Nyerere as published by *Drum*'s East Africa edition of June 1983, in the subsequent three pages).

* * * * * *

THE EXPERIMENT THAT WENT WRONG

PRESIDENT Julius Nyerere of Tanzania is cracking down on dissidents in the country who are disillusioned with his *ujamaa* policy.

Estimates of those already detained range from 1,800 to 2,000 including not only soldiers but also teachers, intellectuals and even peasants.

The arrests follow reports of recent attempts by his opponents to overthrow Nyerere. Twenty-nine opponents of the man known to his people as Mwalimu have already appeared in court facing charges of inciting people to riot. All were remanded in custody.

There are rampant shortages of all sorts of commodities which President Nyerere blames on "economic saboteurs" who smuggle goods out of the country. He has, therefore, closed all Tanzania's borders (there are eight) to prevent the smugglers leaving the country.

But some political observers believe that the closure of the borders is not only aimed at containing economic sabotage but also at preventing political dissidents from fleeing the country. It also has adverse effects on the economies of neighbouring states such as Kenya and Zambia.

What has gone wrong? For many years Tanzanians have given the world the image of a progressive and socialist country trying to be self sufficient.

The *ujamaa* blue-print as enshrined in the Arusha Declaration of 1967 envisaged the elimination of poverty by the nationalisation of means of production.

However, it appears to have failed miserably to realise the aspirations of the people.

Villagisation of people has completely failed. People cross the borders to get essential commodities. Before the closure of the borders hundreds of Tanzanians had quietly slipped out of the country fearing a crackdown.

One of the exiles, a former teacher in Kaalilo School, Bugabo division in Bukoba,

PLEASE TURN OVER

A jubilant President Nyerere explains his policies to the people.

DRUM East June 26

NYERERE POLICY 'HAS FAILED THE PEOPLE'

Mr Ludovic Mwijage has given DRUM his disillusioned picture of life in Tanzania.

'n an open letter to President Nyerere he says: "Your Excellency, no single Tanzanian today disputes the poor international economic order and ever-sky-rocketing oil prices as reasons that might have added little problems to our already economically strained country. But besides this there are other numerous major causes that add more grievous pain to the scared masses of Tanzania and more so the underprivileged.

UJAMAA: Mr President, as you must be well aware, much more than me (a mere party cadre), *ujamaa*, the so-called "poor man's stick", has, if anything, done more havoc than construction. Our vessel has finally conveyed us from miseries to more untold miseries; from freedom to virtually no freedom.

To most of us who have had to go through it all, *ujamaa* has been a terrible nightmare. The policy that is driving the country into the ditch, has completely failed to deliver and *ujamaa* is no longer a policy acceptable by the people.

The discontent among the people is obvious. It is no longer a popular policy to a common man. *Ujamaa* was aimed to alleviate distress. No one under quite normal circumstances can support the policy that has failed to improve the economic welfare of the country.

Your Utopian *ujamaa* rule has done little to bale out Tanzania's stagnating economy, though the policy has somehow managed to enrich certain people in your own ruling clique. While Tanzanians are daily going without basic commodities, factories are closing down as a result of lack of foreign exchange to import raw materials (forcing a good number of workers on indefinite unpaid leave); hospitals are

going without drugs; schools are without even chalks and there are the disgusting everendless queues everywhere in the main trading centres throughout the country. Today some Cabinet Ministers, along with other senior officials, have quietly salted away a lot of money in their foreign accounts.

The same people are holding big shares in big companies while ministers, members of the national executive committee and the central committee are everywhere in the files of the regional trading companies.

You are certainly informed, Mr President, about all this

situation though it has been going on unchecked by a "professed" committed socialist; something that makes you look a party and a partner to this.

DETENTIONS/PRISONS: Much has been said from different quarters of the country about the state of law in Tanzania. The people are held hostage by this law. Its use has been grossly abused by people in power recommending to you would-be detainees. The detention law is no longer preventive but is rather a punitive instrument you have used to silence politicians, while most of your aides use it to meet commercial ends.

(C.C.M. is not a club for big shots only but a party to serve the interests of the masses.) If C.C.M. can extend the hand of iron on her people, which party will stand to defend the oppressed? People are eager to see this law repelled and an independent body should be appointed to carry out a thorough conducted research where I believe a handful of innocent exdetainees will be turned out.

Dar-es-Salaam has one of the best legal systems in Africa if not in the world, and the general public still hold this view. I cannot see how a world reputed human rights champ-

PLEASE TURN TO PAGE 39

with KIWI you'll come out shining!

With my energetic children I need a polish that will make their shoes last longer and save me money. That's why I use Kiwi . . . of course

Kiwi gives a deep super shine. Because Kiwi Shoe Polish contains rich natural waxes that penetrate deeply into leather to make it steadily supple and soft. With Kiwi you get a super shine and *better shoe care!*

Another **KIWI** product

26 DRUM East June

214

DOUBTS GROW OVER POLICY OF UJAMAA

FROM PAGE 26

pion, a frontliner and a semi-Messiah can hold a fellow countryman behind bars for over a decade without the blessing of the law court.

Since independence from Britain in 1961, Tanzania has seen a rapid extension of prisons. History shows too that there had not been any record in our references indicating the former administrators having detained anyone without taking him to court, whether an "economic detainee or a political detainee". This clearly shows that our foreign rulers had sense and high regard for human rights. Again it should remind you to recall this and start exercising patience with your fellow politicians (though of dissident views) and stop persecuting them and throwing them in jails anyhow. The January indiscriminate arrests are a case in point.

It looks sad and shameful for the indigenous administration to institute terror and intimidation indiscriminately on the masses. You cannot, Mr President, continue to blast Pretoria over detentions of black-nationalist leaders while Tanzanians are detained and tortured (though in secrecy) in a similar way. 'Persecution and detention know no colour and on detention issue Tanzania is like South Africa, with the exception that Pretoria metes it out to blacks while in Dar, it is meted out by a black to a helpless fellow black!

May you, Mr President, consider the release of thousands of our men (Tanzanians) languishing in maximum prisons and others dying at the hands of their interrogators somewhere in Mwanza at the notorious Kigoto interrogation centre!

MILITARY ADVENTURE: Our army is already redundant, Mr President, when you consider National Service and the People's Militia to be mobilised in case of emergency like the Ugandan affair.

There is no gainful need to expand the army because we would like to satiate our weak desire to overthrow non-socialist governments or help leftist-governments to power as you have always done in three separate incidents at the expense of the falling poor tax-payers. Tanzanians are too poor to continue pouring massive aid onto these ludicrous missions.

The hope of the poor is that these military adventures should end to give you time to think of your problems back at home. It is too early for us to start spending every meagre resource on expanding the army simply because we would like to look a big power in Africa. Common people are already facing certain difficulties in the neighbouring sister states as a result of these military adventures. It is about time Dar came to its senses and lived to respect the existence of other ideologies apart from our own un-workable ujamaa. The continuous deployment of our forces in the Seychelles is in defiance of what the regime claims to stand for.

None of us has ever forgotten that senseless war in Uganda that drained our country's revenues to zero. If indeed the reasons for uprooting the dictator Idi Amin were valid as it first appeared to most of us, then what about the maintenance of our troops thereafter? It looked interesting to Tanzanians seeing convoys of lorries carrying foodstuffs to Kampala while our residents were jumping from one queue to another in search of essentials.

The government in Tanzania has remained one man's property. The constitution supposed to be under amendment as announced recently, is nothing but a mere abrogation of office to a certain longer stay in power. Worse still the chairman of the party is in over-all charge of all functions in the country. The party being "supreme" the president under so-called new constitution will be answerable to him.

In this regard, the office of the party chairman is the highest in the country and for this reason he should face the electorate directly. C.C.M. is not a vanguard party; the question of a small specific group of national executive committee members electing the leader to the top office in the country on behalf of millions of common Tanzanians should also end in Tanzania's modern politics. It is now widely felt that candidates for the chairmanship must be two from the same party to somehow bring about a sense of democracy.

Mwalimu, I conclude, by begging to point out to you there has never been political stability anywhere in the world without economic stability. Right now our independence is in jeopardy and in the short run off you will find yourself and the entire peace and law enforcing machineries at your disposal unable to control a hungry man in a Dar street. People are now in dire need of political change and economic reform. Looking forward to a better Tanzania.

A jubilant party meeting (above) shows the strength of democracy possible in a one party state but President Nyerere (below) has raised doubts.

Major Joseph Butiku (above) was Nyerere's nephew and a confidant who, together with the late Isaak Bhoke Mnanka, was directing the activities of Nyerere's six political police organisations. By virtue of this position, he is thought to have clear knowledge of what exactly happened to the scores of victims mentioned in this narrative.

Abuse of power, according to the wise, is not surprising. The picture shows Nyerere (seated left) as a man of the people. This changed after he grasped political power and abrogated the constitution to suit his own needs. This stark contrast vindicates the African saying: The language a man uses to court his wife is different to the one he uses after she marries him'.

A licence to murder? *Uhuru* (freedom) and the *Nationalist* (opposite page) newspapers both government-controlled carrying characteristic reports of murder of Tanzanian citizens.

THE NATIONALIST
FREEDOM AND UNITY

No. 1,717

Monday, October 27, 1969

Price 25 Cents

BRNO
ALL CALIBER RIFLES
Available at
TANZANIA RADIOS
AND GUNS
P.O. Box 127   Phone 20771
Nanji Stores Building
Independence Avenue
DAR ES SALAAM

EATH FOR FOUR PLOTTERS

Nine jailed 10 years

NATIONALIST STAFF REPORTER

A SPECIAL MILITARY COURT in Zanzibar has sentenced four plotters to death, nine to ten years imprisonment, and acquitted one man among fourteen people arrested recently for plotting and attempting to overthrow the Government.

The plotters were tried and sentenced under a penal decree promulgated in 1934 and which covers matters relating to treason involving attempts to overthrow the Government and incitement to mutiny.

The fourteen plotters were working in collaboration with the six people detained a fortnight ago on mainland Tanzania to subvert the Tanzania People's Defence Forces in an attempt to overthrow the People's Government of Tanzania.

The four plotters were sentenced to death by a firing squad, and a TPDF officer, Maj. Lazaro Williams, who read the names of the plotters at a mass rally yesterday said that Abdalla Kassim Hanga and Othman Shariff were the ring leaders and that all admitted before the court that they had engaged in subversive activities aimed at overthrowing the Government.

The fourteen plotters are: Abdalla Kassim Hanga, Othman Shariff, Idris Abdallah Majoro, Mohamed Punda, Idd Hassan, Yusuf Hamis Mashaka, Mohidwa Juma Hamadi, Mkata Juma Mkata, Mussa Veni Mussa, Badru Haji Makame, Abdulsalim (Handcame) Abdullah, Ali Mwibyi Zziibwe Hulua, Haji Mrango, Ngwali Ussi.

According to the announcements at the rally, Idris Abdallah Majoro, a primary school teacher was the ring leader, and he oversaw army barracks that constituted group and the Zanzibar group. He used to move to Dar es Salaam every Saturday to meet Hanga and Othman Shariff. He did so nine times and when in the capital they held secret meetings. From Dar es Salaam he took messages to the Zanzibar group.

Abdulsalim (Handcame) Abdullah, a former army officer, and Ngwali Ussi, were the people who used to transport Majoro to Kisiwandui where he caught...

(TURN TO PAGE EIGHT)

FIRST VICE-PRESIDENT SHEIKH KARUME.

DISTURBANCES IN KENYA, 5 KILLED

NAIROBI, Sunday. — A 12-HOUR curfew from six o'clock tonight was clamped on Kisumu, on Lake Victoria after five people were killed and 46 injured in disturbances during a visit by Kenya President Jomo Kenyatta.

A police report received in Nairobi from Kisumu 273 km north-west of here, indicated that in one stage the President's escort opened fire because the violent and threatening attitude of a crowd on the roadside constituted a personal threat to the President.

Kisumu provides most support for Kenya's opposition party, the Kenya People's Union (KPU).

Official sources said that the KPU leader, Mr. Oginga Odinga, who attended the ceremony at which the President opened a hospital built with Soviet aid in Kisumu, after five people were killed and 46 injured in human...

Police throughout the country have been alerted to watch for possible reprecussions in today's incidents in Kisumu. None had been reported by late tonight.

The shooting by the police escort occurred as President Kenyatta was driving out of Kisumu through threatening crowds pressing in from the sides of the road on his way to Nakuru, 144 km to the east, after opening the hospital.

The President was unharmed.

Speaking at the opening ceremony, President Kenyatta said the practice of tribalism was the biggest enemy of Kenya's development and called on the people to work together for the nation's development and progress.

He warned that the Government would not tolerate anybody who tried to interfere with the smooth running of the country.

The Kenya News Agency said the President made it clear that if Oginga Odinga, a leading Luo tribesman, had not been "an old friend" of his, he would have ordered his detention.

Expressing his thanks to the Soviet Union for their aid, President Kenyatta said Kenya was ready to accept any friend from any part of the world but warned that Kenya would not accept a friend who would like to be "Bwana Mkubwa" (Great Lord) in Kenya.

RURAL TALKS END

The African Regional Conference of Integrated Approach to Rural Development, which has been going on in Moshi for the last 12 days ended over the weekend.

The conference which was sponsored by the United Nations with participants from thirty-seven African countries, discussed common problems especially in the rural areas.

C.C. of UWT enlarged

THE UWT Central Committee has been enlarged from 10 to 20 members and two new sub-committees have been created in order to strengthen the organisation, the UWT Chairman, Mrs. Sophia Kawawa announced yesterday.

The new sub-committees which will take charge of women's rights and problems of children will fill a gap which has existed for a long time. It will also look into the recommendations made by the recent UWT conference at Mwanza concerning the operation of the Affiliate Bill for children born out of wedlock.

Mrs. Kawawa said that another new sub-committee will be in charge of all UWT buildings.

Other sub-committees in the UWT Central Committee deal with education, economic and health projects as well as publicity.

Members of the new Central Committee are Miss Lucy Lameck who is the advisor to the Chairman, Mrs. Asha Ngoma, Mama Zimbwe, Mrs. Tatu Mrea, Mrs. Mwaisekwi Ali, Mrs. R. Kuwambi, Mrs. Sayi, Mrs. Roshan Hashun, Mrs. T. Karumuna, Mrs. B. Mwambweuwa, Mrs. A. Babu, Mrs. Mhwville, Mrs. Jhavuri, Mrs. I. Lupembe, Mrs. Iuffur, Mrs. Luolinda, Mrs. Dastur, Mrs. Mandara, Mrs. M. Bubagi, Mrs. Nyirenda and Mrs. Mauwe.

The UWT Week starts today with a maximum women procession starting at the Amantesha Hall through Uhuru/ Mnazimoja Streets, Morogoro Road, the Great Lumumba ending at TANU Headquarters where the Second Vice-President Mr. Rashidi Kawawa will address them.

Kamaliza, Titi face plot trial

SIX PEOPLE announced last Saturday that Titi Mohamed, Michael Kamaliza, Major J. Hermani, Captain E. D. Lifa, Lt. K. P. Mihayo, and Lt. A. Kyaro, the six people who were detained a fortnight ago, will stand trial for plotting and attempting to overthrow the Government.

Mwalimu who was addressing a meeting of the TANU Central Committee briefed the leading Party functionaries on the activities of the six people in their attempt to overthrow the People's Government.

He said that although the people were detained to leave of this attempt, "the truth is that the pre-recognition of the six people were nonsensical and had no support."

"However, because they intended to do evil and to plunge the country into chaos, they will be tried in accordance with the law," he declared.

A Government statement said that the Central Committee was satisfied that there was no need now for anyone to worry about the security of the country and that of the Government. "By eliminating the few who have already been arrested, the whole People's Army is bold enough to its task to protect the country, and to build and defend socialism," it added.

President Nyerere also addressed Members of Parliament on the activities of the six people.

Former Uganda V.P. jailed

KAMPALA, Sunday. — Mr Wilberforce Nadiope, a former Vice-President of Uganda, was sentenced to six months imprisonment and a fine for a false defrauding an insurance company by defrauding an insurance company in a false life insurance claim.

An insurance agent, Patrick Mwase, was given a similar sentence, and four other men, including a doctor, were fined.

The magistrate, Mr. T. S. Qutidar, allowed all the men bail pending appeal.

Shs. 32,724/- were collected in Jinja Region during the month of September through sales of 1,554 hides, 489 goat skins and 71 sheep skins sold in Dar es Salaam, Iringa and Dodoma according to a report of the Regional Director of Agriculture.

Arrested on the mainland by Nyerere's political police agents, Idrissa Abdallah Majura (above) was sent to Zanzibar and was extra-judicially murdered there after the authorities accused him of being a 'courier' for the alleged plotters who belonged to Major Lazaro Williams' group. Shouldn't 'black lives matter' even where an African dictator unlawfully shoots dead his own kind, or is the meme only applicable when a person of a different race kills a black person?

Handcuffed prisoners rallied around their alleged national flag but which looks more like a bed-cover than would-be national flag.

Security forces harassing Salum Nassor, one of the alleged ringleaders of a plot to overthrow Sheikh Karume. Other alleged ringleaders are seen opposite page wearing handcuffs.

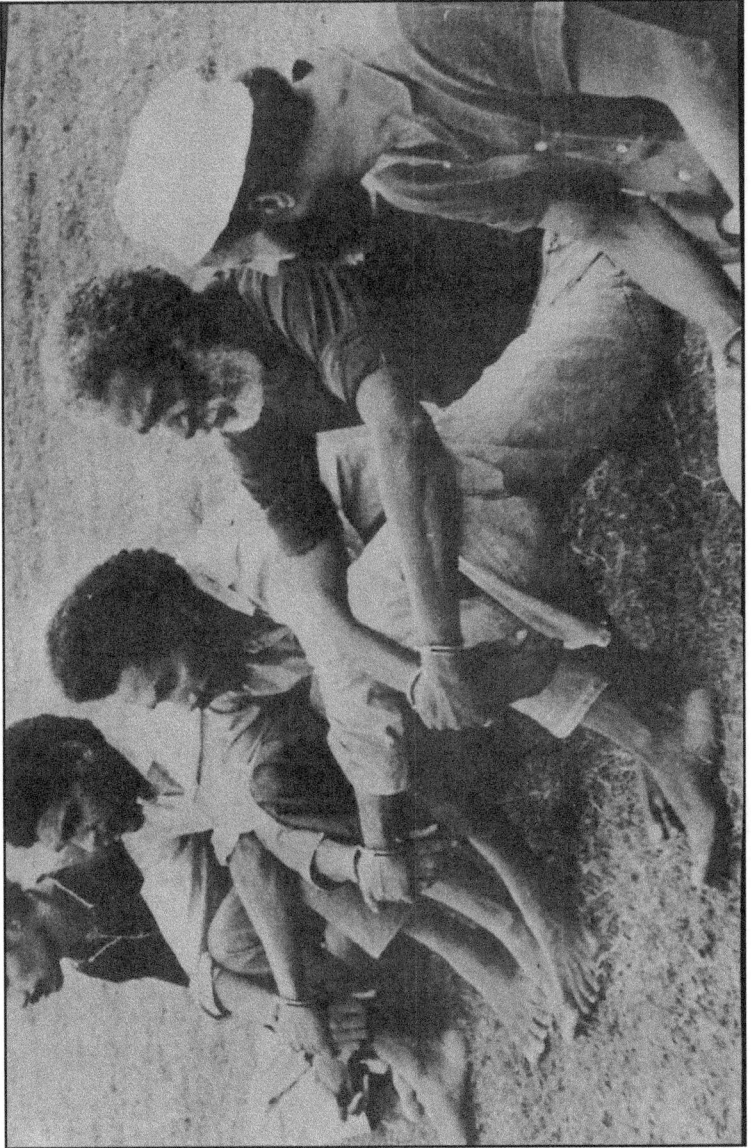

Like the majority of alleged coup plotters these two prisoners, seemed unfamiliar with firearms let alone the geographical location of countries that supposedly backed them. Indeed, Tanganyika security forces could not have taken part in this trial or other similar show-trials mentioned in this account without the approval of Nyerere as a commander-in-chief.

Soldiers from the mainland sit between alleged plotters and crowd supposedly to 'save them being molested'.

The fate of many members of Zanzibar's first (and only) freely-elected Parliament (pictured) ended tragically in the revolution that claimed 17,000 lives (see Introduction).

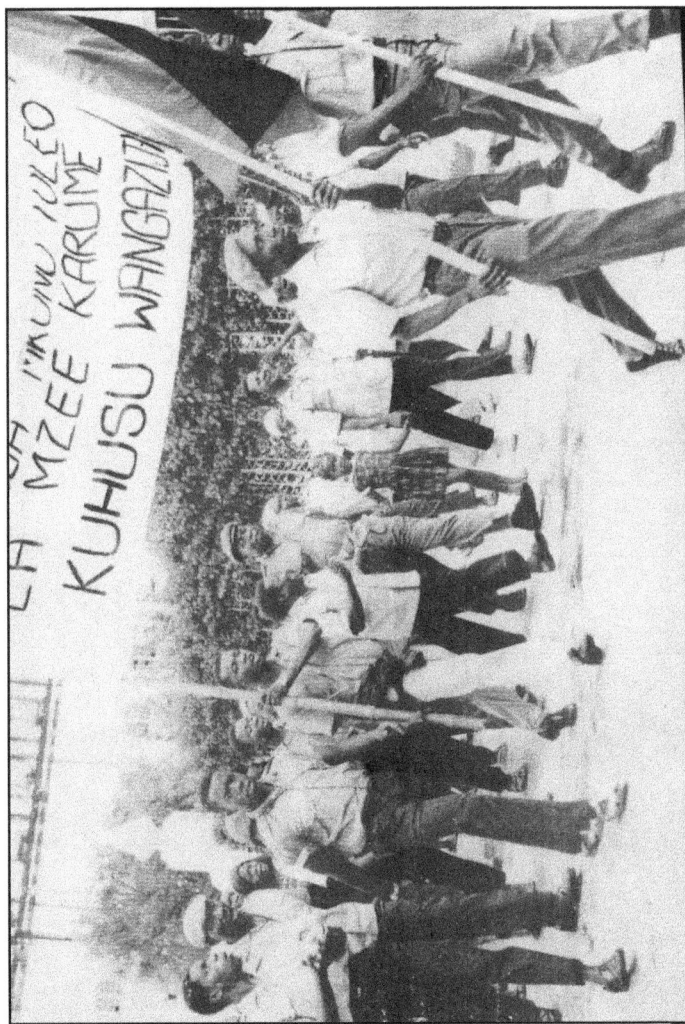

A pro-government demonstration supporting the expulsion of citizens of Comorian origin *en masse* from the islands of Zanzibar.

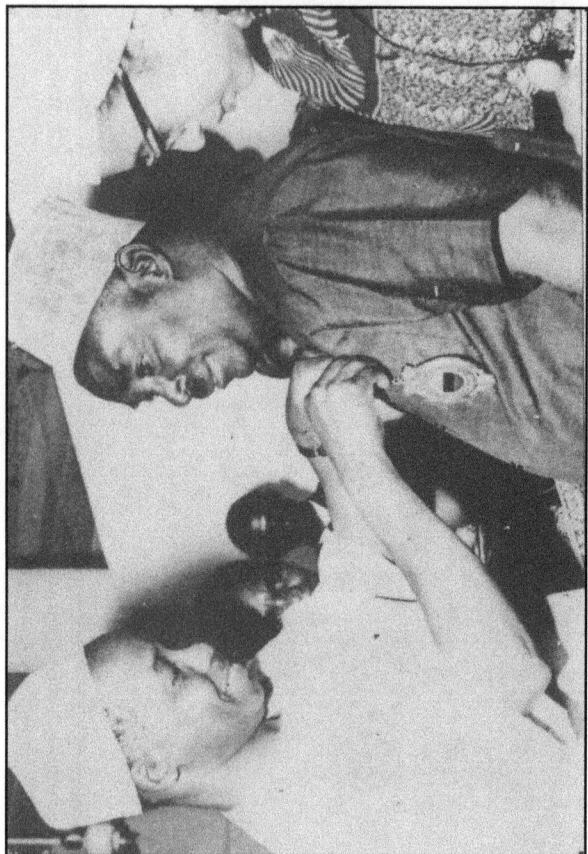

In this picture, Nyerere is seen awarding one of the country's highest medals of honour to Sheikh Karume for his 'effective leadership'. Indeed, it was the Nyerere regime that declared April 7, 'Karume Day'—that is, a public holiday to mark the date in 1972 when Karume was assassinated. Why would Nyerere do this if he truly loathed Karume's excesses as he liked to claim?

Troubled history (from above left): Sultan Jamshid (overthrown in 1964); self-styled 'Field Marshal' John G Okello (organised the revolt); rugged ex-seaman Sheikh Karume (presided over reign of terror); Salmin Amour (was involved in the forced marriages scandal); Amani Karume (demonstrated similar oppressive attributes as his father); *Maalim* Seif Sharif Hamad (the party he leads-CUF-has twice been robbed of its election victory).

The alleged perpetrators of crimes against humanity include (from top left) Abdallah Said Natepe; Seif Bakari Omar; Edington Kisasi; Hassan Nassoro Moyo; Yusuf Himid and Juma Ameir Juma.

Premier Edward Moringe Sokoine whose mysterious fatal car accident has not been resolved.

Mousa 'Lee' Membar (saluting), the regime's political police enticed him to his death at home from the United Kingdom to take part in the political process.

Remi Gahutu, leader of *Pelipe-Hutu*, a movement opposed to the *Tutsi* domination of government in Burundi. He died of poisoning while in detention in Dar-Es-Salaam.

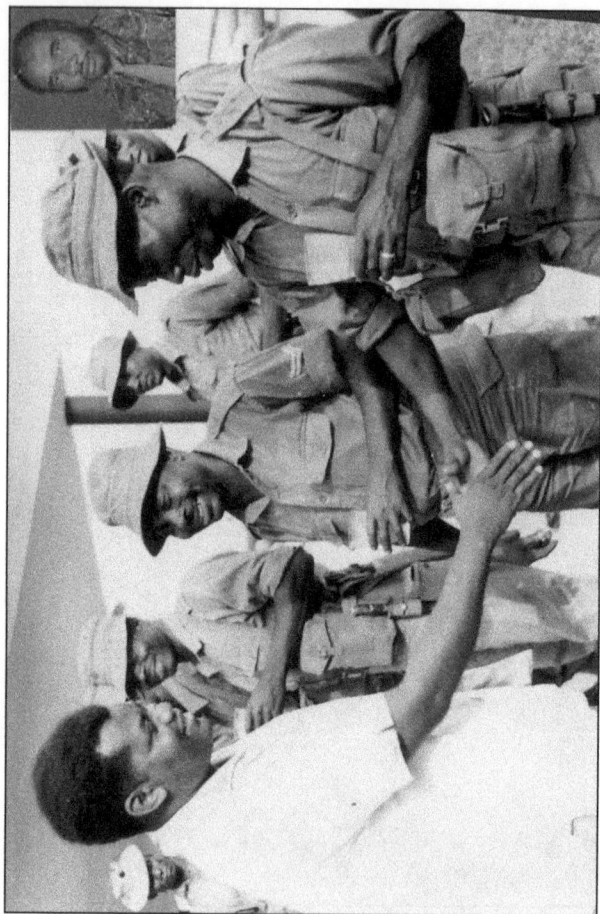

Oscar S Kambona, later stripped off his citizenship, greets Nigerian troops at the Dar-Es-Salaam airport who had come to replace the British Royal Marine Commandos March 31, 1964. Radio journalist Kabendera Shinani (insert) took his own life after the Mkapa regime deprived him of his citizenship.

DIRA YA NABWA

Nyerere si Malaika

Na Ali Nabwa

BAKURA anayeweza kukumusha kwamba Mwalimu Julius Kambarage Nyerere ni mmoja wa viongozi wakubwa duniani. Naitimia moja kubwa kwa upana wake wote.

Alikuwa kiongozi mwenye akili, maono, jasiri na fauda. Amefanya mengi kwa Tanzania, Afrika na Wafrika.

Hoyo, kumbukumbu za hivi karibuni kuadhimisha miaka mitatu tokea kufariki kwake zinaashiki. Kwani kwa kizazi Fulani, Tanzania ni Nyerere na Nyerere ni Tanzania.

Ndio. Lakini kama m hoyo, tujenize basi, Tanzania na in achi siyo na dosari? Kama siyo dosari, Mwalimu ana lawama zake katika dosari hizo.

Naamini kila aliyesoma mpaka hapa atasoma robeni mwake, "Bila ya shaka, hakuna binadamu kabila maenea yao. Saau nasi wakuwajibika kama si Kiongozi wa nchi?

Ali Hassan Mwinyi alindewa mbanga na kwa unyonge wake alikubali.

Nasema Nyerere hawezi kukwepa lawama kwa madhambi ya nchi. Naliyotokea nchi hii. Naamini wengi wa wananchi wa Tanzania walinpenda Mwalimu Nyerere, kiongozi aliyekuwa na kuhasha Lakini itafike hadi chongo kula kongozi.

Ninetangulia kusema Mwalimu Nyerere alikuwa na sifa nyingi. Z i m a n d a l i w a, zenyewe kwa njia mbili mbali, Kimu simuzungunzia zile kasoro zako ambazo nfirajisa binafsi na ambazo naona tunapaswa kuzizungumza kama ni kweli sisi ni Watanzania.

• Nayaopenda ya maelezo yanga katika sehemu one:

• Maisha ya vitisho na mateso kwa wananchi

• Kushamiri kwa umaskini na ruhusa

• Kisongoni aliyedawa na nabwa

• Mwalimu na Zanzibar Kwa leo nitanzaa na sehemu ya kwanza na inayohusu maisha ya vitisho na mateso kwa wananchi

miu akamtumbue miu aliyemfuata. Baada ya kumshukuriu, langu la chuma. Hatirangunwa, akaskeomezwa ndani, akaambiwa akae amrungumzee mwandani wake.

Fanda ya msee ilojyonu usiku umakuwa mwingi na hakurudi nyumbani, akatumwa akamfuate. Kawaida katika hii kama hiyo, watu basedi polisi na chumba cha maiti.

Alipofika *Control* na kuchora wasifu wa baba yake, kijana hayo, Abdulsamad, akapelekwa chini akamtambue. Matokeo ya msej shahuba 'solo'.

Wakati huo, watu wa Usalama walikwenda kuwakamata vijana wawili katika nyumba moja Magamoni Mapipa.

Walipofika wa walikuta alikuwa hayuope. Waliambiwa ama rafiki yake, mtu fulani ameana alikue deka hapa, mwenye deka kabila, na mwenyeye deka mwenyeye, Saib, maihu kwonohembu, mred, mpole, mwenye bishima kiasi kwamba hata kusema kwake halikuwa kwa sidi.

Tabora kushitakiwa kwa kurudwa na hati ya kundipta.

Licha ya kujitetea kwa hakuwa na haja yo hati ya kusafiria kwa sababu hakupata kusafiri, alifungwa na baadaye kupelekwa gela Ukonga kumwakia kupelekwa nani? Aliona gela zaidi ya maka mionne kabila ya kutolewa kwa "msamaba" wa Rais.

Au mfanyabishaha Seif Nasur kutoka Pemba aliahatawa kwa bucheku aliyoshika tangazo la kushtuwa Mzee Karume.

Alipouliza nani katoa habari hiyo, aliambiwa jirani zake. Kwa sodoni. Alipothibitisha kwamba yeye siku hiyo alikuwa amekwenda Morogoro kumuona michelo, aliambiwa "basi umecheka hako hako".

Ni ile hadithi ya mtoto wa mburi na mbwa wa mwitu aliyodai mburi hayo alimchafulia maji yake siku iliyopita, kwa hivyo lazima ajopwe, kwa na mwuzi alesoma shiko wewe, mama yako".

Mtu anaweza kusema pengine Rais alikuwa laryaju haya, walifanya watu wo chini. Ali Hassan Mwinyi na Abdalla Said Natepe hawalinya

yaliyotokea lakini walinwajibika kwa vile-yaliongwa na wakikakwa cin yao.

Ijatokee, kama ushahidi kwamba magereza walikuwa hawapokei maniwa (*detainee*) mpaka wapate *detention order* yaliyotokea *Offer* hiyo.

Ni Rais peke yake aliyokuwa na uwezo wa kutia saini amri hiyo ya kuwekwa mtu kizuirini.

Aboud Jumbe, akiwa Makamu wa Rais, alipofika kufanya hiyo wokati Rais Nyerere akiwa safarini.

Licha ya kuwa alikuwa amekudhiwa rasmi madraka ya kukatima, mambo yaliporkishwa Makamuni, Mahakuma ilitoa uamuzi kwamba uwozo huo hakuwa nao isipokuwa kwa Rais angetoa kwa mwandishi ajno kuhusu suala hilo.

Lakini kama maisikio menojine ambayo lazima alijua yaliyotokwa Chukua kukamatwa kwa Masheikh Dar-es-Salaam (akiwemo Muslim Mtaji tangia 1970 walipotea kwenye wanapongwa kuvunjwa kwa *East African Muslim Welfare Society* na kuanzishwa

BAKWATA.

Wajincakwa Rais Zanzibar ambako kina Sheikh Hadim Haji Abdullah na wengineo waliteswa sana.

Wenyie walifita jela akiwemo Maalim Heroun na Mzee Mboha.

Wenandaki wa maheshi haya kuribakumbu ya tukio hili. Alipata barua kutoka *All India Radio* ikanga 'offer'ya kazi.

Kwa kuwa hakuwa nayo inambukuhu 'offer' hiyo, alipata barua zanzibari kwamba Ali Jaffer, kwenda Uhabani wa India kwa mapendekezo kwaomba apewe yeye fursa hiyo.

Ubaloni ulithibahi na jomaa akaanbiwa asubiri matayansho ya safari. Lisiku uko akangia kaaka mkumbo wa Ma-"Sheikh" waliopelekwa Zanzibar. Kisu kaka pekee ni kuwa ansishi kurika jingo la *Maslam School*, Mnazi Mmoja, jijni Dar-es-Salaam wakati ule.

Na vipi habari ya Othman Sharif, aliyewachwa sikka na kwenda kufanya kazi yake ya Daktari wa wanyama Mbeya?

Aluumalitu mbali na Zanzibar, Lakini Nyerere alinakuwia na kumpeleka alikokuwa yeye na 'hadi leo khatima yake, kama ya Abdulla Kassim Hanga, haijulikuni.

Je, haya si mubimu k u z u n g u m z w a ni mapumugumzu ya Uwaraka wa Mwalimu Nyerere? Aumi mambo madogo tu?

1973: The Reverend Uria T Simango and his family.

March 15, 1975: Rev Simango (wearing a black jacket) and Paulo Gumane when they briefly appeared before Samora Machel (centre) in Nachingwea, southern Tanzania.

Rev Simango (above) reading his forced 'confession' during the Nachingwea show-trial on March 16, 1975.

Security forces (above) escorting Rev Simango to his ultimate fate
— execution — after the show-trial had ended.

Joana Simeão (pictured above) was labelled traitor and reactionary during
the Nachingwea show-trial. She too was unlawfully killed in Mozambique after suffering multiple humiliations in the form of a show-trial on
Tanzanian soil.

As this illustration shows, the government-owned *Daily News* newspaper of March 18, 1975, quoted Samora Machel, whom critics have since dubbed 'Mozambique's black Nero', as telling the prisoners he placed on forced parade that 'we won't kill you'. Whoever 'we' refers to, this was an undertaking which Machel, and by implication President Nyerere, never intended to honour.

Victims of terror (from top left): Abdallah Kassim Hanga (extra-judiciary killed); Sheikh Othman Sharrif (also extra-judiciary killed); Salehe Sadala Akida who, together with other detained colleagues, vanished from prison; Sheikh Ali Muhsin Barwani (detained for 10 years without trial); Sheikh M Shamte (detained together with Sheikh Ali); revered Chief David Kidaha Makwaia, OBE, (Nyerere banished him to a remote area).

The group of political detainees (pictured) was released after spending six years in prison without trial. They are, from right, Hashil Seif Hashil, Col. Ali Mahafoudh, Martin Ennals (an official from Amnesty International, London), Abdulrahaman Mohamed Babu, Salim Saleh, Haji Othman Haji, Shabaan Salum Mbaraka, Tahir Ali, Hamed Hilal, Badru Said, Abdullah Juma, Ahmed Mohamed Habib Bajabir, Martin Hill (also from Amnesty International, London), Amour Mohamed Dugheish and Suleiman Mohamed.

Marcelino dos Santos: attempted to philosophise the Nachingwea atrocious crimes.

September, 1992: the author (right) with Oscar Salathiel Kambona.

Nyerere (above left) hands over power to his handpicked successor, Ali Hassan Mwinyi, in 1985. Though less discussed, in his lifetime, Nyerere never quite trusted his own people to identify and choose their own leaders. Instead, in what amounted to an insult to his own people's intelligence, he chose rulers for them. The competence and performance of the rulers he chose is there for everyone to see.

Benjamin William Mkapa (pictured casting vote in 1995) was Nyerere's protégé and favoured candidate for the presidency in 1995. During his tenure, however, President Mkapa categorically refused to rescind the more than forty repressive laws (The Law Reform Commission of Tanzania: Final Report on Designated Legislation in the Nyalali Commission Report) introduced by the Nyerere regime. The commission, headed by the former chief justice Francis Lucas Nyalali, had recommended be scrapped. Observers of Tanzania's political scene doubt the incumbent president, John Pombe Magufuli (pictured opposite page retrieving a pistol from his hip), will repeal them either (Magufuli's Reformist Drive Takes an Autocratic Turn in Tanzania: Michael Jennings, WPR—Monday, October 24, 2016). The question now is whether the Tanzanian government needs such oppressive laws to protect itself from the people it purports to represent.

Widespread graft during Mkapa's tenure undermined the credibility of his successor, President Kikwete (pictured).

January 2001: Police loading seriously injured supporters of the Civic United Front (CUF), some of them unconscious, into trucks.

Kiponda, Zanzibar, September 19, 1964: Sayyid Abdulmuttalib Hashim Saleh Hussainy (pictured right, with his family) was, without provocation, gunned down by a member of the Zanzibar Revolutionary Council (ZRC), Mohamed Abdallah Ameir (Kaujore), along with five other people. But because Kaujore was '*kigogo*' (a political heavy weight), no legal action was ever taken against him.

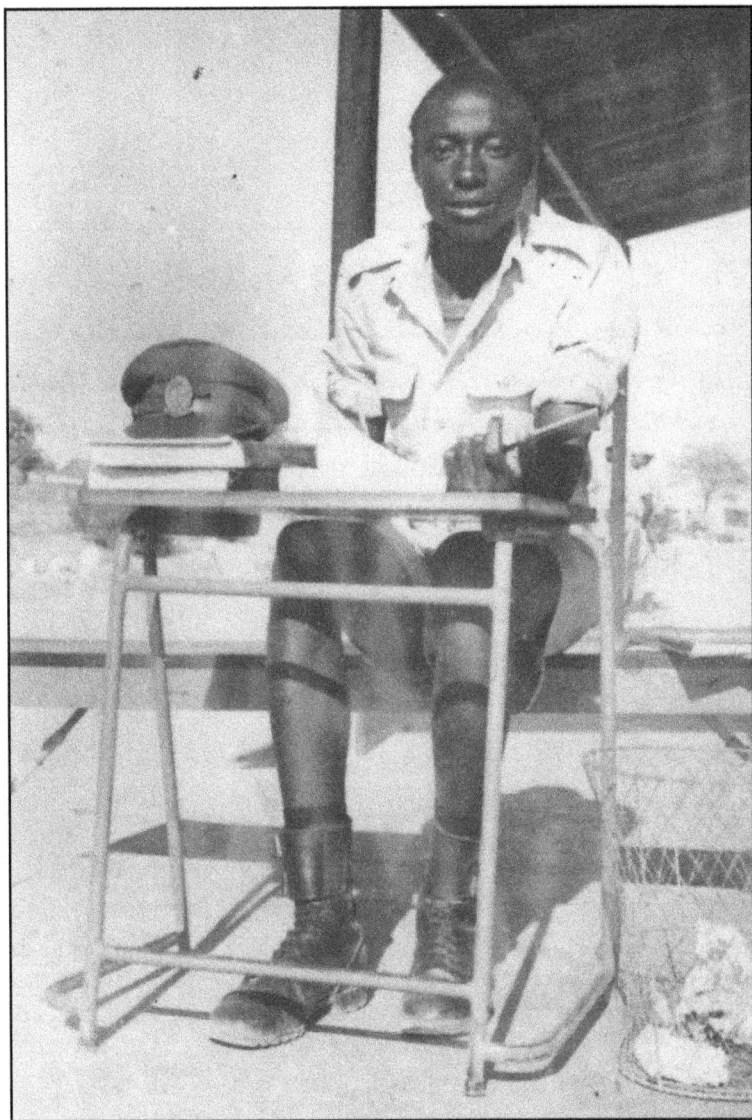

Flashback 1970: the author at quarter guard; National Service, Makuto-pora, Dodoma.

> In the Third World there is less concern and understanding about the problem of Peace and Nuclear Disarmament than in the Developed World. Similarly the Developed World has less concern and understanding about the problem of Development and Justice. I hope that your endeavour will increase understanding about both problem of Peace and Development in both "North" and "South"
>
> _____ Julius K. Nyerere .

Nyerere's handwriting (above) was similar to those of whites. But he denied others the opportunity to match his fluency in English, *Swahili* (the national language) which he spoke alongside *Kizanaki* his first language.

Sérgio Vieira (above) is alleged to have had more knowledge than most of his confederates regarding the victims of the shocking Nachingwea crimes. If that is true, then he, like Tanzania's own Major Joseph Butiku, owes the international community an explanation as to what befell the referral victims.

Sheikh Yahya Hussein (facing the microphones) ransacked the author's bag at *Jabula Inn*, in the Swazi capital, Mbabane, on behalf of *Usalama wa Taifa* (Nyerere's political police outfit). In December, 2009, Sheikh Hussein, publicly cursed with death rivals to incumbent President Jakaya Kikwete (see public reaction at http://www.jamiiforums.com/jukwaa-la-siasa/42325-sheikh-yahya-atakayempinga-kikwete-kufa.html). The Kikwete government remained non-committal.

Bibi Titi Mohamed (centre), former leader of Umoja wa Wanawake wa Tanganyika (the country's women's organisation), and Member of Parliament, who was sent to Zanzibar with other detainees to be tortured. Why would the Nyerere regime send them there, if indeed Nyerere disapproved of what was happening in Zanzibar's execrable dungeons?

1983: The author at the start of the struggle for democratic freedom and human rights.

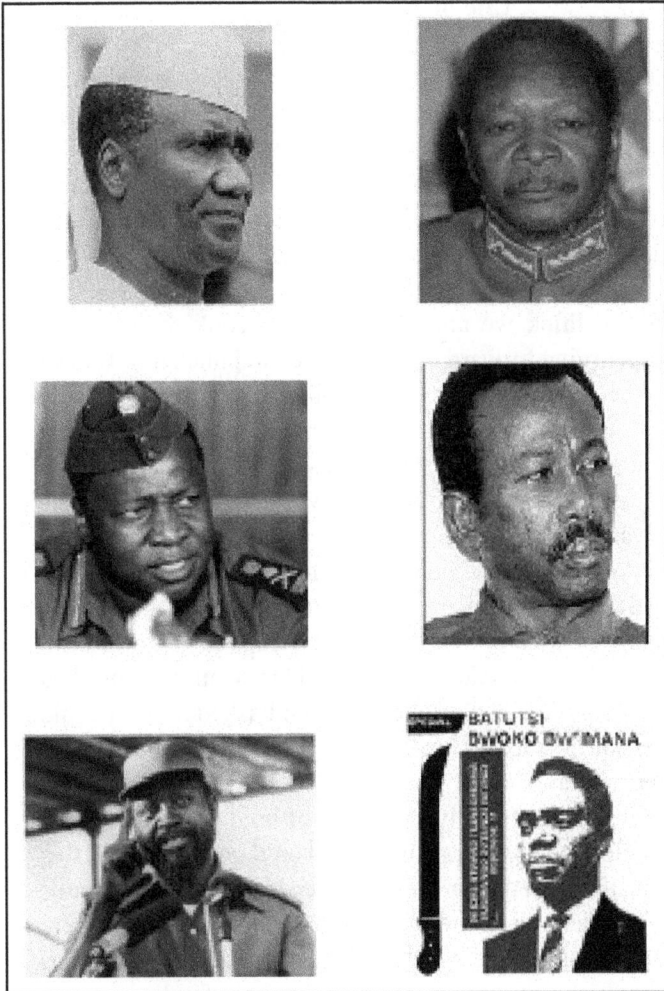

From top left: Guinea's Ahmed Sékou Touré; Central Africa's Jean-Bédel Bokassa; Uganda's Idd Amin; Ethiopia's Mengistu Haile Mariam; Mozambique's Samora Moisés Machel and Rwanda's Grégoire Kayibanda. Their tyrannical reign claimed unprecedented number of lives in the continent's political history.

Life in the Camp

Meals were terrible and the diet largely unbalanced. Breakfast consisted of tea without milk, a doughnut, scones and two boiled eggs and was routine. Normally I don't eat boiled eggs; when I suggested to one of the guards I knew as Mashaka, that I preferred scrambled eggs, he flew into a fit of anger. What I suggested, he said, was tantamount to calling the guards my 'wives.'

'Do you think we are your wives to cook for you?' he asked angrily, surging forward as if he wanted to punch me. To cool him off I flashed a smile and asked whether it was women's role in our society to cook for men. 'Naturally,' he replied, breathing easier now; it seemed his anger had subsided. He added that his wife cooked for him, not him for her, wagging his finger as he said so. He wanted it to be clear who was in control–him, not me. I wanted to drop the discussion, but before doing so I had one further suggestion: a wife as an equal partner in marriage. At this he exploded and it was too late for me to escape my punishment. From now on, Mashaka said, I was forbidden to turn on my bed without his prior permission. But even when I asked him if I could turn from one side to another he refused. He relented two days later after the intervention of his colleagues.

Evening meals usually consisted of hard porridge (*ugali*) with beans boiled in salt. Occasionally, I would get *ugali* with two pieces of meat, the most decent meal they could provide. The guards received money each week to buy food, but consumer goods were virtually unobtainable except on the black market, where prices were exorbitant; the guards made most of their food purchases there.

In Tanzania, the informal sector mushroomed and then grew stronger shortly after Nyerere enunciated his *Ujamaa* in 1967, his doctrine of bootstrap, do-it-yourself socialism. This sudden growth of the informal sector was a clear sign of the people's opposition to the system Nyerere had imposed on them.

Since the black market provided no receipts, the guards were afforded the opportunity to falsify accounts so they could pocket some of the money themselves. Indeed, it was considered a privilege, in economic terms, for a guard to be brought to the camp from other duties. Conversely, it was considered a loss of perks if one was transferred. Not surprisingly, almost every guard used the chance to buy expensive new shoes, tailored trousers and *safari* suits; the latter considered as a sign of importance in the party or government during Nyerere's rule. In Tanzania, one could tell a member of the secret police by his expensive clothing. As for internees at the camp, our monotonous, unbalanced diet was partly due to the lavish lifestyle of our guards, made affordable largely by their own wheeler-dealing. I remember, for example, that I never once received fruit or vegetables throughout my incarceration, although they were grown locally.

The guards were also involved in blackmail. They would spy on the local population for whatever purpose and many residents served long terms of imprisonment for 'undermining' Tanzania's economy. The guards also had an eye for a deal. They could, for example, place orders for bicycles using letterheads of the President's Office, under which their organisation fell. They would receive the bicycles at the official government price, and then resell them on the black market at three times the price. Apparently the money used for such shady deals was intended for the weekly purchase of detainees' food. On one occasion a row erupted at the camp after one member of the secret police had double-crossed another in a deal involving several sacks of sugar and rice. The two almost came to blows, but an outside guard saved the situation by acting as arbiter.

Spying created a vicious circle: the guards spied on the local population, sometimes even on people they had done business with, in turn, the guards were being spied upon, and, of course, they also spied on each other. A guard called Kabululu was immediately transferred after one of his colleagues reported to his superiors that he had been trying to make a small opening in the tightly sealed window of my room, to allow some fresh air in. Since Kabululu was from Bukoba, my home town, his seniors thought his alleged action might have something to do with a natural tribal bond. He never returned to the camp during the rest of my detention there.

In another incident, a guard was dismissed after it was discovered (probably by a colleague who had spied on him) that he had attempted to solicit a bribe form an elderly detainee, a Dar-Es-Salaam hotelier who had been arrested by the secret police for allegedly giving money to his son-in-law, who was an officer in the Tanzanian People's Defence Force (TPDF). The son-in-law was being held with others at Ukonga security prison on charges of 'inciting people to riot'–the official euphemism for a 1983 coup plot.

* * * * * *

Mlawa showed up at the detention camp several days after I had arrived there, dressed in his usual ill-fitting *safari* jacket. He carried a black attaché case containing papers related to my case; I was in for yet another interrogation which lasted two and a half weeks this time. Mlawa got me to sign the statement he had prepared after using his now familiar cavalier tactics; this time, though, he also subjected me to psychological torture. He would come at night, wanting me to sign the statement, which he would never allow me to read. Another detainee was being subjected to electric shock torture in the small room facing mine; he screamed continuously. Once during his screaming Mlawa opened my door and said it was my turn next. I entreated him, saying that I had been 'cooperative' and did not wish to be tortured. 'Then sign this statement,' he commanded, handing me a pen. I signed. He tossed the statement into his attaché case, closed it and left without informing me of my legal status. He did not return to see me for the next nine months.

There was nobody apart from Mlawa who could define my legal status. Detainees held at detention camps had no access to legal advice: those held in 'administrative detention', that is, in normal prisons, could expect three visits a year from a justice of the peace (a magistrate, for example); but if you were held by the secret police at one of their camps, you were not covered by this practice.

Similarly, under Nyerere's rule the names of political detainees were never published in local newspapers or the official gazette. Nyerere's government never even answered enquiries about political detainees. Detention orders signed by Nyerere were never even challenged in court, nor was there any means of challenging a presidential order, since Nyerere was the 'creator' of all institutions in the land and was above the law anyway.

Power resided exclusively in him and he exercised it alone. Indeed, as pointed out in my introduction, the system he imposed on the nation did not contain democratic checks and balances against any possible assumption of sovereign authority by a single individual. Institutions such as Parliament, the Judiciary and the Administration, under which sovereignty could have, and should have been shared and exercised, were rendered toothless. Seen in this light, democracy, which Nyerere often spoke of in his many essays and on many international platforms, never existed in Tanzania under his rule. Democracy cannot prevail where Parliament and the Judiciary do not exist as sovereign entities, but are controlled by a single-party dictator.

As the months passed and many more detainees were brought to the camp, I started to realise just how oppressive Nyerere's regime was. For Tanzanian detainees, the ordeal would begin with a knock on their door at home at about two o'clock in the morning. Members of the secret police, armed with pistols, would search for implicating, political material, while the manacled victim would suffer abuse in front of his family, presumably to demoralise him. He would then be whisked away to a waiting car and if he was in Dar-Es-Salaam, he would then be driven whilst blindfolded to the national stadium and taken to a detention centre.

As an alternative, the secret police could arrest a suspect and hand him over to the local police station, promising to collect him after midnight. Tanzania's secret police have never been answerable to anybody in the country but the President's Office: they enjoy quasi-immunity from any legal action and punishment. During the more than twenty-five years of authoritarian rule by Nyerere, thousands of Tanzanians (and other nationalities) became victims of the secret police. Since detention camp conditions were never checked, they were appalling. Nearly all freed detainees had contracted disease such as pulmonary tuberculosis, due to the lack of sufficient fresh air and a balanced diet and because of inadequate sanitation. I doubt whether detention camp conditions were anywhere near required international standards for people being held over an extended period.

* * * * * *

After two months in captivity I fell ill. The illness seemed to be exacerbated by the poor conditions in which I was being held. Yet I could not be taken to a normal hospital since I was not being held in a government prison but at a secret location. The secret police therefore had to arrange for a doctor to come and attend to me.

The doctor, a tall, heavily-built man with a thick Saddam Hussein-type moustache, seemed to take more pride in working for Tanzania's secret police than in his own profession. For several minutes he stood in the doorway, flashing his ignition key in the familiar fashion of the Third World social status show-offs, while staring at me contemptuously. He did not say a word. I was unsure if his stare was a psychological tactic to determine if I was really ill, or if it was simply a hard gaze. Finally he introduced himself: 'I am a doctor, what's the problem?' I politely inquired what sort of doctor he was: of philosophy, medicine or what? He managed a forced smile, nodding his head. 'No wonder you are here,' he muttered. He repeated his introduction and said he had been contacted to come and treat me.

I grabbed the opportunity to express my misgivings about being treated by a medical doctor associated with the political police. I told him I was unsure if he was himself a member of the secret police and if he was, what guarantee could he give that he would not harm me through injection, if he needed to inject me at all? He dismissed this, saying that if the secret police had wanted to get rid of me they could have done so without having to use such methods. He insisted he was a doctor by profession, which I already knew.

'But doctor,' I said, 'this is supposedly a secret detention camp operated exclusively by the secret police. No one else comes here except members of that organisation.' I continued, 'Your presence here could scare even the least educated person in the street that has looked upon a medical doctor just like a justice of the peace. How can anyone in my shoes reconcile the fact that a public servant of such calibre, held in such reverence, is working for the political police? It clashes with the moral authority of your profession,' I said finally. To my amazement, he was really taken in by my lecture on the ethics of his profession, which admittedly I knew very little about. At this point the doctor, absent-mindedly fingering a button on his white shirt, sat himself down, with great relief, on my wooden bed. He seemed disorientated and his face continually changed expression whilst he kept drumming his fingers on his thigh. I now stared at him, sort of returning his earlier stare. He struggled for something to say.

'Look,' he said, 'I don't work for the secret police. No way!' Continuing to defend himself, he said he had been 'borrowed from Muhimbili Medical Centre' in Dar-Es-Salaam to treat internees. He insisted that his appointment was purely on a professional basis and again said he did not work for the secret police. I believed him, if only because of his spontaneous disorientation after my accusation. But the question remained: why was he considered suitable for the job ahead of his colleagues? Did it not prick his conscience treating badly bruised detainees when he knew they had sustained the injuries as a result of physical torture? I decided against following this line of questioning. After all, I had already taken away much of his authority by having him explain he had no links with the secret police. I thought it better that I left him with some authority, rather than to continue to humiliate him with a barrage of questions. After that, we became friendly and he would drop by to pass greetings whenever he was required to treat other detainees at the camp.

* * * * * *

Sometime in late February 1984 a guard nicknamed Wasiwasi came to remove my handcuffs because of Mlawa's 'compassionate consideration'. On the orders of Mlawa, I had been in handcuffs ever since being transferred from Mtwara; it was part of my punishment. Wasiwasi could not tell me why Mlawa had not shown 'compassion' at Mtwara when my left hand had become infected or at Oysterbay immediately after my arrival. Wasiwasi would only say he was obeying orders—but he was withholding something.

The next day a sympathetic guard gave me a clue as to what had happened. He told me the British news agency *Reuters* had filed a report about my abduction from Swaziland. Apparently Tanzania's local news agency, *Shihata*, had followed up the story and called on the Principal Secretary to the Ministry of Home Affairs, A. Malamia, to clarify the report. Of course, Malamia denied any knowledge of my abduction and referred *Shihata* to the Ministry of Foreign Affairs, which declined comment. No doubt Mlawa's sudden show of 'compassion' had been prompted by the *Reuters* report.

Generally, I was now being treated better, although occasionally a guard would accuse me of being a 'capitalist lackey', acting on my master's orders and out to wreck the 'advances' made by Tanzania. I was now allowed an hour daily to exercise in my room; minor restrictions, such as not being allowed to sit up on my bed when I was tired of lying, were lifted; the guards, including the particularly nasty ones, started to care a little more, even asking me what I needed to eat. I realised that coverage of my abduction by an international news agency, and its later circulation to a wider audience, had eased my plight.

Around June 1984 I developed insomnia. The exercises I was permitted to perform were not heavy enough to enable the body to sweat and get tired; they were light exercises, such as walking back and forth for an hour. At this stage a benign guard, Edward Kalibete, at great risk to himself, volunteered to smuggle in some sleeping pills for me. This was well beyond the call of his duty, but I supposed his humanity got the better of him. I soon realised that reliance on sleeping pills was not a viable option: first, there was the danger of developing a perpetual reliance on them, which I did not want; and second, I would regularly need to increase the dosage to induce sleep. I feared I might become immune to the tablets.

But before I could tell Kalibete that I no longer needed the sleeping tablets, he was unceremoniously fired, allegedly for trying to obtain a bribe from an elderly Dar-Es-Salaam hotelier held at the camp. Kalibete's arrival at the camp, which was about the time of the *Reuters*' report, had brought improvements in my own treatment. Kalibete was at pains to preach to other guards not to mistreat detainees who did not resist their authority. He told me that orders to torture detainees came directly from Brigadier Kombe, the then Director of Intelligence (DI), or, from Mlawa. Now that he had been fired, I could no longer get my sleeping pills.

Oyster Bay now suddenly experienced an influx of detainees. Several reasons accounted for this; the first being the deliberate torching by unknown persons of the Bank of Tanzania (BoT). Several bank employees were regularly being brought at midnight for interrogation; some were tortured in order to extract confessions. I wondered why on earth the political police needed to become involved in an arson case, which should have been the responsibility of the normal police department or criminal investigation division. Were the police so incompetent that their work had to be handed over to the torture specialists? Of course, the political police never had to prove anything: once a suspect admitted, usually under duress and after torture, that he had been party to a certain criminal act; he was consigned straight to Ukonga security prison. There he could serve an indefinite sentence under presidential decree. Those thought to be innocent would be freed after spending two to three months at the camp.

At about the same time, calls for a referendum on Zanzibar's future in the Union were gathering momentum. Dar-Es-Salaam responded in its usual manner—repressively—cracking down harshly on supposed agitators and enemies of the Union. Many of them were brought to Oyster Bay, where they endured extensive questioning about their activities; many were physically abused.

Whilst the Zanzibar debate ensued, its impact brought about some changes on the mainland and in its prisons. Members of Zanzibar's secret police started being posted to the mainland; one of them, a short man who looked to be in his late forties or early fifties, landed up at Oyster Bay. A staunch Muslim and likeable man, he offered to buy me a rosary for praying; something that even fellow Christian guards had refused to do.

My Zanzibari guard lost no time in falling in love with the wife of one of the outside guards who were subordinate to the inside guards, at least in this case. The woman, tiny and with a small, beautiful voice, was clearly half her lover's age. She often came inside with her new boyfriend and since my door was now always open, I could get a glimpse of her. Soon she had started to cook food for her new boyfriend; when my Zanzibari guard explained my plight to her and asked if she could include some food for me, she was happy to do so. That man was a godsend, though I did not approve of his affair with the junior colleague's wife. Not only was he risking his career, he was risking detention if his colleagues even got wind of what he was up to. During the first days of this romance, I was able to get hold of old newspapers, often from other empty rooms inside the camp. I read absolutely everything that was printed, including advertisements for Sheikh Yahya Hussein, the so-called astrologer who had nicked items from my bag in Swaziland and given them to Tanzanian intelligence.

* * * * * *

By February 1985, after more than one year at Oyster Bay, I started to become despondent. I began to lose hope that I would ever come out alive; as if to reinforce those fears, I developed a dry cough (coughing without producing sputum), which the camp doctor treated but failed to establish the cause. Having spent a whole year in a poorly ventilated environment, without having seen the sun at all, I was not surprised I had developed that cough. By mid-March my health began to worsen and my legs started swelling as a result of poor circulation. The guards telephoned Mlawa to inform him of my failing health, but he seemed unconcerned and did not show up. The guards summoned their doctor, but his locum came. The doctor I was used to was in the regions, visiting other detention camps. His assistant, a short, thin man, prescribed some chloroquine pills, assuming that I was afflicted with malaria. Two weeks later, on March 24, 1985, I started to vomit blood. Then I lost consciousness.

* * * * * *

Release from Solitary Confinement

Early in the morning of March 26, 1985, I regained consciousness and realised I was being fed intravenously. I was in a small room with the curtains of the only window fully drawn; two armed secret police guards, both familiar faces, sat against the only door, which was shut, facing me. My bed was small and had a reddish rubber cover, almost like an operating bed. A beautiful nurse sat on the floor next to the guards, fixing me with her gaze. It was the first time I had seen a woman since my abduction in 1983. My face lit up; she smiled and told me in English that I was 'off danger.' From her distinguishable accent I could tell she was a *Chagga* from Kilimanjaro. She had a light complexion and a natural smile, enough to melt the heart of any young bachelor. She was very intelligent but I could not work out how she was connected to the secret police. Nevertheless, her mere presence in the room made me feel relieved; her smile soothed much of my pain and dejection and she addressed me with great nobility.

I soon found out that I was being held at a special clinic where political policemen and their families received treatment. The next day the doctor in charge, the one with whom I was familiar, recommended I go on a special diet which included bananas–my tribal staple food and the nurse offered to prepare them. Mlawa arrived that day, accompanied by three of his senior colleagues, carrying a roast chicken wrapped in old newspapers. I could hardly believe it. My chief interrogator and torturer of yesterday; the man who had forced me to implicate innocent people, was now offering me an olive branch—a roast chicken.

How strange humans can be, I thought. Mlawa looked so different that day from the person I had known during my interrogation. I would have eaten Mlawa's chicken, if only in observance of my Christian faith: when someone slaps you on the left cheek, turn the right cheek to receive the same. Unfortunately, I could not eat Mlawa's chicken as it was no longer warm.

My illness turned out to be a blessing in disguise. Fearing that I might die in police custody, the government set me free conditionally. The decision was first communicated to me by the doctor in charge on March 26, 1985, and later confirmed to me by Mlawa at about midnight on March 27, 1985, when I was blindfolded and taken from the hospital back to the camp. I was to be released the following day.

Things now started to move faster. Mlawa, claiming that the Tanzanian government was 'very kind', gave me underwear (mine was already worn out), an ill-fitting pair of trousers, a T-shirt and a pair of carpet slippers. Mlawa issued several verbal threats to dissuade me from telling anyone about my experiences at one of their secret detention camps. If I dared to talk, he told me, they would not hold me in 'luxury' next time, but would send me to Sumbawanga or Kigoto. Both places are well known in Tanzania as the 'killing fields.' I told Mlawa I would not be talking at all.

At about 10 am on March 28, 1985, I heard Mlawa's car, an old Saab with a defective exhaust pipe, pull up outside the camp. I was blindfolded again and led to his car by two armed members of the secret police. We zigzagged several times as we drove from the camp, then Mlawa drove straight on before suddenly braking and stopping. The blindfold was removed; it was time for another lecture on the code of silence.

'You don't have to say what happened to you to anyone,' Mlawa said, 'not even to the police.'

'Do you expect me to see the police?' I asked, and he replied that that was where we were going. 'Then I am not free,' I said.

'You will never be free as long as you remain a political nuisance,' he snapped back as the car pulled away again.

I was unable to adjust myself to the outside environment. I couldn't face the sun; I reacted to it with the sensitivity of an albino. On the way I noticed police stopping people everywhere, demanding to see proof of their having paid 'development tax'; many people were being loaded into police vans. It was hot as usual in Dar-Es-Salaam when Mlawa finally pulled up outside the Central Police Station, which also houses the offices of the Regional Police Commander (RPC).

* * * * * *

Minutes later I was at the counter handing in the few belongings I had. A nervous police officer, who looked like a probationary sub-inspector, judging from his shoulder pips, instructed a desk sergeant to lock me up in the cells. When the sergeant asked what charge he should indicate in the charge book, the officer replied nervously that he should write it was on Swai's (his name) instructions. That done, I was led down to the underground cells and pushed into a cell with common criminals. The cells were overcrowded, filthy and stinking; some of the internees urinated in their cells. There were three juveniles in my cell who had been locked up for nearly two weeks on suspicion of having stolen an outboard engine from the Dar-Es-Salaam harbour. They claimed they had been held for so long because they didn't have the money to buy their freedom. The cell also contained two elderly citizens: one had been held for more than three days for violating a traffic law and the other had been held for a week on unspecified charges. They claimed some people being held for serious crimes had been released but they had no money to bribe their way to freedom and had been forgotten. I suggested to them that Tanzania should provide an alternative to custody for elderly people, juveniles and minor offenders, in order to avoid congestion in the police cells. One replied that this would not be possible because people were being arrested simply so that police could extract bribes from them. 'Police here, my son,' he said, 'arrest people to make money.'

He was soon proved right. As the underground cells received more occupants, the police above would go through the wallets deposited with them by the unfortunate offenders and one by one those with thick wallets would be called upstairs. Soon the cells would be half-empty, only to be filled again in minutes with new faces; and so it would go on. This seemed to be a common practice at the Central Police Station in Dar-Es-Salaam.

Meals were provided once a day at about three o'clock in the afternoon. The usual menu was semi-cooked maize porridge with boiled beans, which contained weevils.

* * * * * *

After I had been in the cell for several hours, a police officer called out my name. I identified myself as he opened the cell; he asked me to accompany him upstairs. He led me into a large office. There, a fat man in full police regalia sat at a large table cluttered with piles of files; flanking him were four junior colleagues, all in uniform. From his epaulettes, I guessed he was a senior superintendent or a similar rank. He lifted his eyes from the file he was reading and looked straight at me; his face showed kindness and sympathy. He asked if I was Mwijage, and I replied that I was.

'I am John,' he said, 'the officer commanding the station here.' He said he had called his colleagues so that he could advise me of my legal and constitutional rights in their presence. It was the first time since my abduction that someone, a Tanzanian policeman at that, had said anything of legal and constitutional rights. I was amazed. He said I had no police record and, as far as the police were concerned, they therefore had nothing against me. I listened attentively, like a student attending a talk by a visiting lecturer. 'Then why am I here, sir?' I asked politely. He replied that I was being held at his station in 'protective custody' on instructions from the President's Office and that they would hold me until further instructions were received from the same office.

John and his colleagues looked genuinely surprised when I told them that I had been held by the secret police for more than a year at Oyster Bay detention camp. I had, of course, breached Mlawa's warning, but I didn't care in the least. John nodded his head; he was puzzled. The other four police officers, in the presence of their commander John said *'pole'* to me—a *Swahili* word for sorry. I was then taken back to the underground cells.

As we sweltered at night, detainees would exchange stories about how they had come to be locked up. Some criminals had been caught red-handed trying to pick-pocket passengers on an up-country train; others described how easy it was to rob women passengers who had small children with them; some were simply locked up because they did not have train tickets; others again told of how they had stolen office stationery, and then sold it on the streets. It seemed petty crime was the leading functional sector of Tanzania's economy; so many people, out of a need to survive, were involved one way or another. I thought it sad that our citizens were being forced into crime as a result of the failed *'Ujamaa'* policies being followed by Nyerere. I wondered that if the state saw it fit to punish the children of its own failed policies, then what sort of punishment would be appropriate for the parent, the creator of such policies that had driven its children to despair.

Every morning John and his entourage would do their

rounds of the underground cells, counting the inmates one by one. He would listen to everybody's complaints but did nothing about them, or lacked the means to do anything. Some inmates complained of being held for more than two weeks without being charged; others moaned about poor sanitation and bad food. Some even spoke of being victimised by the officers who had arrested them or by members of the people's militia (*mgambo*).

Two days later a police corporal, who introduced himself as Anthony, came to see me. Anthony, a short, brown man who appeared to be in his forties, said he had come to see me because he had been told he would be escorting me to my home in Bukoba the next day. He was very excited and asked if I was Tanzania's ambassador to Swaziland. I did not thank him for that compliment but laughed instead. I wondered aloud if I looked more like an ambassador than a prisoner. Anthony said not but added that he had asked because he was normally assigned to duties at the High Court. He had usually escorted judges; now he had been assigned to escort a prisoner. 'I always escort big people,' he said confidently, almost as if working at the High Court was the pinnacle of his career.

I told Anthony I was a detainee, not an ambassador. Besides, I said, Tanzania did not even have a resident ambassador in Swaziland but was represented in the kingdom by its Mozambique ambassador. His geography was poor: he spoke of Swaziland and Lesotho as if they were millions of miles away. Yet Anthony was very friendly and when he left we shook hands, promising to see each other the next day.

* * * * * *

Corporal Anthony and I took our seats in an overcrowded third-class compartment in the up-country train. Anthony, kit bag under his feet, nursed his semi-automatic rifle throughout the journey. Surprisingly, he bought no meals throughout the trip. I thought that maybe he had not been given sufficient funds or that he was simply exercising frugality. Two men in plain clothes, probably members of the secret police, followed us wherever we went, even when I went to the toilet.

The train derailed often, creating fear among passengers

that an accident was likely. The railway line between Dar-Es-Salaam and Mwanza, a major link, was constructed during the time of German East Africa. Since independence from the British in 1961, the line had never had any major repair work done on it and consequently it has claimed the lives of many passengers as a result of accidents and derailments. Maintenance is very poor; certainly not anything like it was during colonial times. The big shots in State House seemed not to care in the least; instead, Nyerere's government pursued wasteful policies, allocating vast sums to projects which turned out to be white elephants. The transfer of the capital from Dar-Es-Salaam to Dodoma springs to mind and the construction of Dar-Es-Salaam International Airport is another. Nyerere himself was wont to waste: in 1984 he used US$88 million of French aid funds to refurbish his large private jet. Critics thought the money should have been used to improve the country's railway system, in order to reduce the number of accidents. As it turned out, the jet of the 'father of the nation' became a financial burden to the poor Tanzanian tax-payer.

Unfortunately, the habit of wasteful spending seems to have been passed on to Nyerere's political heirs. Not so long ago, in October, 2004, the government of President Mkapa received a new aircraft it had ordered from Gulf Stream Aerospace of America, so as to expand what has become known as Tanzania Government Flight (TGF) agency.

It did this at a time when, for example, passengers travelling between Dar-Es-Salaam and Kagera region could not do so by road, as the roads were in an appalling condition with poor surfaces and potholes, rendering them extremely dangerous. Also, boats ferrying passengers between Kagera and Mwanza region were very old and often overcrowded sometimes resulting in accidents that claimed many lives. In addition, it was not unheard of for armed bandits to waylay buses on long journeys and relieve passengers of their possessions.

Due to these factors, passengers had to make a circuitous journey through Kenya and Uganda respectively, before finally making it to Kagera region.

One might think that these problems should have been addressed prior to the purchase of the aircraft. However, as noted earlier, this was not to be the case. Indeed, Frederick Sumaye, the former prime minister seemed to know better.

He was quoted by the *IPP Media* on October 16, 2004, as saying that the aircraft was purchased '…for the safety our leaders'. This would seem to imply that in developed countries that give aid to Tanzania; as the national leaders have no such jets, they are not as 'secure' as the leaders of Tanzania.

Sumaye went on to 'educate' Tanzanians that 'This (plane) is a working tool, like a motor vehicle and such other machines. It is not a luxurious property as some people believe'. This is certainly open to conjecture.

However, Mark Mwandosya, the then Minister of Transport and Communications was more candid. 'This' he said 'is a unique aircraft, modern, and the first of its kind across Africa, south of the Sahara'. He called on Tanzanians '…to be proud of it'. Proud of it! A mendicant nation, with almost half of its national budget paid out of its foreign aid feeling 'proud' of buying a 'unique' jet that no country in sub-Saharan Africa has. Mphw!

After a tiresome two-day journey we arrived in Mwanza, where we caught an evening boat to Bukoba, arriving the next morning. Corporal Anthony, in the presence of the two plain-clothes men who had been trailing us throughout the trip, handed me over to the Bukoba police. Unfortunately, the regional police commander (RPC), a gentleman called Mgema, had gone to Rusumo, the region's border post with Rwanda, on a 'goodwill mission.' His deputy refused to open and read the letter delivered to him by Anthony. The officer deputising for Mgema said he had not been given the power to open letters from the President's Office. I understood only too well; since my ordeal began, I noticed that the mere mention of the President's Office frightened people. The officer in charge said he had no alternative but to place me in 'protective custody', pending the return of Mgema.

Bukoba police station's cells were not underground. They had adequate ventilation but the toilet was flooded badly with human excrement floating around. Meals were served once a day; it was the usual *'ugali'* (hard porridge) with beans containing weevils. It seemed the police had only one supplier of beans for the whole country. Friends and relatives who could have brought me food were scared; orders from the office of Nsa Kaisi, Kagera's regional commissioner and a former member of the secret police, were that people bringing me anything should have their names and addresses taken.

I slept on a hard, bare floor in an overcrowded cell with ordinary criminals for two days and thereafter I was transferred to a less crowded cell known as the 'VIP cell'. It had only two inmates: the principal of Gera Rural Development College in Bukoba and his bursar. The two were being held on charges of fraud and theft. It was claimed they had siphoned off several million Shillings of the college's funds; a charge they both denied. The police treated them like dignified people, providing them with everything they required—it is probable they had bought off the police. They received meals from one of Bukoba's best hotels, the *Mbuni Hotel*, and a police courier regularly brought them beers and whisky; the men also had their own bedding. 'Money speaks in Tanzania,' one repeatedly said one night when he got drunk.

By contrast, petty criminals had it rough. The cell next to ours held a middle-aged man who had been caught brewing the illicit drink *gongo*, a locally brewed gin, at his home, in order to generate income. The people's militia, *mgambo* and the notorious traditional defence group, *sungusungu*, had caught him and then beat him badly before handing him over to the police who beat him yet again. I heard him scream and beg the police for mercy, but to no avail.

Another victim of police brutality was a man called Mutunzi, a rural intellectual from Ibwera, Kianja, Bukoba district. Police allegedly caught him selling a stolen cow to a man in the neighbouring village; he was tied with a sisal rope and so badly beaten that his body was swollen. Another case involved an elderly man from Bukoba rural district who had been arrested and severely beaten by police, allegedly for possessing a cow hide which police claimed was from a beast that had earlier been reportedly stolen. The cow hide had in fact been found buried in the old man's banana groves. Like Mutunzi, the old man faced more than eight years in prison if found guilty.

Another young suspect, who was allegedly found in possession of some ampicillin capsules, anti-malaria pills and two vials for a syringe, was also badly beaten while in police custody. His case was regarded as particularly serious as it fell under the so-called Economic and Organised Crime Control Act; his case was to be heard by the *Mahakama Maalum* (Special Court). He faced up to fifteen years imprisonment if convicted, for 'undermining' Tanzania's economy.

Ironically, the men who had allegedly emptied the coffers of an educational institute did not have even a scratch on their bodies; in fact, they seemed to be highly respected by the police, who even allowed them to drink in their 'VIP cell'. I wouldn't be surprised if they were actually later acquitted, for their wealth would have worked in their favour before Tanzania's courts.

When Mgema returned from his 'goodwill mission' he proved equally unhelpful. He said there was little he could do about my case unless he received new orders from higher authorities. In my third week at Bukoba Police Station Nsa Kaisi sent some of his men down to interrogate me. Nine people from the party's regional office, as they described themselves, paraded me for yet another spell of interrogation. I was tired of being interrogated and simply told them what Mlawa had instructed me: that I had strict orders not to talk to anyone about my case. I told them I would not budge unless they could produce proof that this presidential order had been revoked. In addressing them, I made it sound as if the president was akin to God the Creator. The strategy worked. They did not know what to do next. Finally, they resorted to pursuing a routine line of questioning—my age, interests and to my surprise, where I had travelled prior to my abduction.

Nyerere's secret police had failed to find out anything about my travels; I did not want them to and was able to keep them away from that line of questioning. But I had travelled, and my travels had been precipitated by my resignation from the post of head teacher at a school in Masai steppe, Arusha. I had resigned to protest victimisation and injustice; but as I was later to find out, my resignation was not accepted.

The perpetrator of this victimisation was a school inspector from Monduli district, a bachelor aged about thirty-eight at the time. He had an insatiable sexual lust and used his status to have sexual intercourse with women teachers, whom he would promise a good report. One day he asked me if I could arrange for him to have sex with any of the Arab women in my district. I personally knew most of these women; they were the wives and daughters of men who had shops in the area. When I inquired why he was so keen on Arab women or women of mixed race, he smiled and said this was because he had never had intercourse with one before. He said he had confidence in me and had therefore assigned me this task.

It is hard to describe how I felt after that. First, the office in Monduli had not appointed me head teacher because I had the ability to find women for my superiors: my appointment was based on merit; on my ability to teach. I felt affronted. Moreover, his insistence on women of other races (Arab and coloured women in this case) debased him. I could not believe that an educator, and my own boss at that, could be so afflicted with an inferiority complex. Nevertheless, I told him that matters of sex should be mutually resolved between the parties involved and should not involve third parties. In order to have me change my position, he attempted to blackmail me: he claimed I was in love with one of my ex-students and that I had impregnated her. The girl he was referring to had completed school years earlier, long before I had been transferred to the area. He restated his demand that I should do my utmost to get him an Arab woman. Again I reiterated my unwavering position.

A week later he returned with the same demand and I restated my position and told him bluntly that I thought he was abusing public trust and his own office. He stormed off and showed up the following morning at my school in the company of the adult education coordinator of the area. He demanded to inspect my school, without having given prior warning; it was clear he had decided to get back at me for not organising an Arab woman for him. Thereafter, he wrote a terrible report on my school, refusing to acknowledge even the visible achievements made during my time. I had, for example, persuaded Masai elders to build their *manyatas* (huts made of dry cow dung) near the school in order to contain truancy among Masai pupils. I had gone to the school on my promotion in order to revive it after my predecessor fled to Kenya after being involved in a bribery scandal together with the ward party secretary.

I was deeply angered at being victimised in this manner and resolved that I would continue to fight for the truth and justice. I decided it was time I gave up teaching, albeit temporarily, and made up my mind to visit other countries to see how their societies were managed. I always believed education through personal experience was invaluable, perhaps equal to the knowledge gained from books and institutions. To ensure that Tanzania's political police were kept off my trail, I fooled them into thinking I was ill and had gone on sick leave. Oddly enough, they accepted the story and did not take any further action. I quietly slipped out of the country for Mozambique, where I worked for some time immediately after independence. Later I worked in the Seychelles and managed during this time to visit Japan, Belgium and what was then, West Germany.

When I returned to Tanzania I found that the education office in Monduli had rejected my resignation, which I mailed to them together with one month's salary; the latter in lieu of three months notice. I had purposely mailed my resignation because I did not want my superiors trying to talk me out of it. Subsequently, the office refunded the one month's salary and treated my long absence as leave-without-pay. I was then transferred to Bukoba, my home town, at my own request. In Bukoba, the struggle to campaign for a more open society had lately been gathering momentum.

So when Kaisi's men tried to find out about my travels when they visited me at Bukoba Police Station, I was quite firm in my response: I was never to talk about my case without written consent from the President's Office. Kaisi's men did not press me any further on my travels—I am not sure they even knew that I had travelled. They simply back-pedalled and ordered me to return to my cell.

The next morning four plain-clothes officers escorted me to my mother's home at Kyaka. To my surprise, the men had no transport of their own and had to rely on public transport. On the way to Kyaka one of the men insisted that I give him money for transport; otherwise, he threatened to return me to the police cell. I was apprehensive, but then thought it better to give him the money he demanded. I discovered later that he had deliberately played this card because he had seen friends in Bukoba giving me money.

* * * * * *

275

Banishment Order

We congregated in the tiny, dusty office of the officer commanding Bukoba rural district, a man of impeccable character called Mwakatume who originated from Mbeya region. Detective Senior Superintendent Mwakatume was flanked by his immediate lieutenant, a young, balding sub-inspector in uniform. The ten-house cell leader (a government watchdog for every ten houses) of our area, my mother and her friend were summoned to Mwakatume's office; also present were the four officials who had brought me home and the government security officer of our area a certain Hokololo. Mwakatume wasted no time in reading to me the banishment order from the President's Office, which had been sent to the Kagera regional police commander, Mgema, who in turn passed on details of the order to Detective Senior Superintendent, Mwakatume.

The banishment order was clear: I was not allowed to leave my village without first obtaining permission from Mwakatume's office. 'But I will have to leave my village in coming to ask for permission,' I pointed out—the police station was in fact not in my village but in Kyaka township. Mwakatume replied that I would have to seek permission to leave the village from the ten-cell leader. Permission to travel to Bukoba, he said, would have to be obtained from the President's Office, through his office. An application to travel to Bukoba would have to be lodged three weeks before the intended departure date. The police would also visit me often, as part of the banishment order.

After being detained without trial for nearly two years, I was now forbidden to travel freely in my own country, to engage in gainful employment or to indulge in any income-generating activity. Worse still, I was not allowed to resume teaching, my profession. So I was not free and there was no guarantee I would not be returned to detention once I had recovered and the authorities thought it fit to lock me up again. I resolved that I had to walk to freedom, just as soon as the possibilities allowed me to.

* * * * * *

Escape to Freedom

From Kyaka I could have easily made it to Uganda; but there was a war going on in Uganda between government troops and Yoweri Museveni's fighters. Besides, there were still some Tanzanian military and intelligence personnel in Uganda and I could never be sure that they would not recognise me. I was not prepared to take any chances this time; I had learnt from bitter experience; if I had any doubts, I would simply not take the chance. An alternative escape route was via Ngara to Rwanda, although this would mean going through Bukoba district. I opted for this route.

A woman friend working in a 'socialist shop' at Kyaka gave me some money, enough to cover my basic requirements for the journey. As luck had it, a Catholic priest, who was on his way to deliver the holy sacrament to a patient, unwittingly assisted in my escape. Since there was no transport, he volunteered to drop me beyond the place where he was going. I considered the place where he dropped me to be safe. Once there, I flagged down a lorry and climbed in the back, heading for Biharamulo. From there I hired a young man with a bicycle who took me halfway to Ngara. I could have asked him to take me straight to Ngara, but that would have been risky. I walked the rest of the way to Ngara, using footpaths wherever possible to avoid the main road; just one more security precaution.

It was dark when I reached Ngara. Going to the guest house was out of the question as I had no party membership card, which was essential to carry when travelling. Nor did I have the letter from my ten-cell leader authorising me to travel which was a government requirement then for all *bona fide* travellers. I didn't have any form of identity at all. Still, I could not be walking at night through an area teeming with wild animals.

As I sat under a huge tree contemplating my next move, a young man pushing a bicycle with a flat tyre recognised me and approached me. I did not recognise him; there was no way I could, as my memory took time to recollect faces after my detention. The young man introduced himself by his first name and I politely asked him to remind me where we had met. He replied that it was at the regional educational offices in Bukoba. I did not ask him what he was doing there; in my own interest, I wanted the issue of introductions to be over quickly.

I did mention to him that I was going to Rusumo border post to buy some essentials, adding that I had missed my transport. Without hesitation the fellow invited me to spend the night at his home. His parent's home was a well-built, modern house, and I sensed they must be middle-class people. Renewed fear built up that I might be recognised and identified.

The young man used his spare key to open the front door and his father emerged from an inner room to greet the visitor. There was a rude shock awaiting me. The father was in fact Twalib Songoro, a former party chairman in Kagera region and a staunch Nyerere supporter. I was briefly disorientated while the young man introduced me to his father; I even had difficulty remembering my false name I had given to his son. I could not tell if they noticed anything odd.

I was shown to a seat close to a bundle of newspapers written in *Arabic* or *Farsi*—I couldn't distinguish which. There were also some copies of *Uhuru* (Freedom), the party newspaper and in front of me hung a picture of Nyerere displaying his sharpened teeth in a broad smile. After staring at the portrait for a while, I realised that Nyerere and Hitler had similar moustaches.

I was offered a cup of coffee, and then thought it wise if I tried to remove any suspicion from my host's mind. I praised the 'advances' the Kagera region had made under his leadership and under the guidance of 'our beloved party of peasants and workers'. As I rambled on, I wondered if the old man believed me, since we both knew in our hearts that the opposite was true. Bukoba was on the brink of social and economic ruin: the government seemed to deliberately neglect the region, perhaps because it felt most of the people there had not fully supported *'Ujamaa,'* in the belief that it would never work. And *'Ujamaa'* did not work. The Kagera region contributed to foreign exchange earnings through its cash crop, coffee, but the region's infrastructure was in a shambles. The road network was appalling, potholed and battered, and the telephone system had for years been very poor. The once prosperous Bukoba cooperative union (BCU), which was established long before Tanzania gained independence, had been disbanded by the government in a deliberate attempt to reduce its financial clout and to punish the people for opposing government policy. Nyerere never offered a senior cabinet post to any politician from the region, because of their 'anti-*Ujamaa*' tendencies. Students from Bukoba with *Kihaya* (Bukoba's main tribal language) surnames had been compelled to change them in order to be selected for higher education. Those who did not risked not being selected. So, if, for example, a student was Anthony Lwegelela, he had to drop Lwegelela, and perhaps call himself Peter or Ahmed in lieu of Lwegelela. This is how bad things had become. Nyerere then sent Nsa Kaisi to take over as regional commissioner; his job was to 'discipline' the local people and to revive the fortunes of the party. The former army lieutenant-colonel went about his job with enthusiasm, locking up people and arbitrarily confiscating their property.

On the other hand, Musoma, Nyerere's region, enjoyed prosperity unmatched by any other region, not even those which are major producers of cash crops. Peasants in Musoma received payment for their crops in one or other form; in other regions crops were left rotting because poor roads rendered it difficult to reach remote areas. Now look at the road between Mwanza and Musoma: it is the best maintained in the whole country. Compare that to Dar-Es-Salaam's then pot-holed roads which used to claim lives almost every day. Tanzanians from the northern parts, from the shores of Lake Victoria, became successful business people. These 'true northerners,' as they were sometimes known, dominated government institutions, the security agencies and the army–and continue to do so today. When the deprived people of the rest of Tanzania complained, Nyerere accused them of 'tribalism;' thereafter, they preferred to remain silent.

To obtain financial support from the developed nations, Nyerere's government pumped money into a selected few *'Ujamaa'* villages, including, of course, his own Butiama village. Butiama is the only village in Tanzania where peasants enjoy life insurance, which is especially desirable in the Tanzania of today. Several villages received preferential treatment, so they could be held up to potential donors as models of success.

The former regional party chairman, Songoro, in whose house I now sat, knew all this as much as I did. He likened Nyerere to former United States President John F Kennedy, and described him as a 'gift to Tanzania from God.' It is perfectly possible that Songoro was laying the praise on thick for his visitor, whom he did not know. He had to play it safe.

Songoro, his son and I had the evening meal and the son then showed me to the guest's room. I did not see Songoro's wife at all, if indeed he was still married. Songoro, perhaps in recognition of the praise I had for Nyerere, instructed his son to take me early the next morning to a truck driver in the next village who travelled every day to Rusumo border post. I noted that he used his former title, chairman, when he gave instructions to his son about what to tell the driver. He used the words *'mgeni wa mwenyekiti'*—the chairman's visitor—whom the driver was to give a ride to Rusumo. I appreciated his kindness.

The next morning, after their five o'clock prayers, the son took me to the truck owner. By about 10am I was at the border post. Before crossing the border, you have to go through customs as there is only one bridge linking the two sides. If I was to get past customs, I would have to perform well; moreover, I hoped nobody would recognise me.

I surprised myself with my composure and self-confidence. The truck driver had introduced me to the immigration officials as the 'chairman's visitor,' which automatically cleared me of any suspicion and enhanced my credentials. After exchanging greetings with the officials I asked if there was a restaurant on the Tanzanian side where I could have breakfast—I knew there was none.

'Oh no, we don't have any restaurants here,' a senior official replied. He advised that I cross the bridge to the Rwandan side, where there were plenty of restaurants. I did not waste any time. I descended the hill across the bridge and entered Rwanda. I was not in the least concerned about what happened behind me. I was well on my way to freedom.

* * * * * *

It was on May 12, 1985, that I finally managed to reach international agencies in Kigali, the capital. The delegation of the United Nations High Commissioner for Refugees (UNHCR) took extraordinary, urgent measures to protect me. They accommodated me at various places—I cannot name them since these facilities may still be used to protect refugees—during my three-month stay in Kigali. In this time, the UNHCR looked for a country of resettlement for me. As for me, I had no identification, no national passport and no baggage. I had simply left Tanzania the way I was dressed on that day.

Because Rwanda is so close to Tanzania, and because relations between the two countries were warm, I feared I would become a political football and end up back in detention in Dar-Es-Salaam. Fortunately, that did not happen, thanks largely to the UNHCR in Kigali and particularly to Anthony Verwe, the resident representative, and Phillip Hesser, the UNHCR protection officer at that time, who on a number of occasions physically protected me. Indeed, at one point I had to take refuge in his residence when I felt my security threatened.

By the beginning of August 1985 my Red Cross passport had arrived from Geneva (see pages 282 to 285). On August 5, 1985, Phillip Hesser saw me off at Kanombe Airport, on my way to Lisbon, Portugal, where I had been accepted as an invited refugee.

* * * * * *

No. 316148

Lieu ⎫
Place ⎬ Genève
Lugar ⎭

Date ⎫
Date ⎬ 15 juillet 1985
Fecha ⎭

Ce document a été établi à la demande du porteur et en raison du fait qu'il déclare ne posséder aucun passeport, ni définitif, ni provisoire, et qu'il est dans l'impossibilité de s'en procurer un. Ce document ne préjuge pas de la nationalité du porteur et demeure sans effet sur celle-ci.

Le délégué soussigné du Comité International de la Croix-Rouge déclare avoir fourni ce document au porteur pour lui permettre de justifier sa présence à son lieu de résidence actuel et pour lui faciliter le retour immédiat ou ultérieur dans son pays d'origine, ou son émigration; il certifie avoir reçu de celui-ci les déclarations suivantes concernant son identité:

The present document has been established at the request of the bearer and because he has stated that he does not possess any passport, whether regular or provisional, and that he is unable to procure one. This document is no proof of the bearer's nationality and has no effect on the latter.

The undersigned delegate of the International Committee of the Red Cross declares having issued this document to the bearer to enable him to justify his presence at his present place of residence and to facilitate his immediate or subsequent return to his country of origin, or his emigration. He certifies having recorded the bearer's statements concerning his identity, as follows:

Se expide este documento a petición del portador, el cual declara no poseer pasaporte alguno, permanente o provisional, y hallarse imposibilitado para procurárselo. Este documento no prejuzga la nacionalidad del portador ni puede afectarla de ningún modo.

El delegado abajo firmante del Comité Internacional de la Cruz Roja declara haber facilitado este documento al portador para permitirle justificar su presencia en el lugar de su actual residencia y procurarle el regreso inmediato o ulterior a su país de origen, o su emigración; certifica, además, haber recibido del interesado las declaraciones siguientes relativas a su identidad:

Nom de famille ⎫
Family name ⎬ MWIJAGE
Apellidos ⎭

Prénom(s) ⎫
First name(s) ⎬ Ludovick
Nombre(s) ⎭

Date de naissance ⎫
Date of birth ⎬ 8.6.1951
Fecha de nacimiento ⎭

Lieu de naissance ⎫
Place of birth ⎬ Kishanje, Tanzanie
Lugar de nacimiento ⎭

Nom et prénom(s) du père ⎫
Family name and firstname(s) of father ⎬ Mwijage Kaigwa
Apellidos y nombre(s) del padre ⎭

Nom et prénom(s) de la mère ⎫
Family name and firstname(s) of mother ⎬ Mwijage Ana-Marie
Apellidos y nombre(s) de la madre ⎭

Nationalité ⎫
Nationality ⎬ tanzanien
Nacionalidad ⎭

Pays d'origine des ascendants:
—parents
—grands-parents
Country of origin of:
—parents ⎬ Tanzanie
—grand-parents
País de origen de los antepasados:
—padres
—abuelos

Profession ⎫
Occupation ⎬ teacher
Profesión ⎭

3

Accompagné de
Accompanied by
Acompañado por } enfants au-dessous de 16 ans
children under 16:
hijos menores de 16 años:

Nom   Prénom(s)   Date et lieu de naissance
Name   First name(s)   Date and place of birth
Apellidos   Nombre(s)   Fecha y lugar de nacimiento

_____

_____

_____

_____

_____

Adresse actuelle: c/o UNHCR
Present address: P.O.Box 867, KIGALI
Dirección actual:

Depuis
Since   12.5.85
Desde

SIGNALEMENT   DESCRIPTION   SEÑAS PERSONALES

Cheveux   Yeux
Hair   } black   Eyes } brown
Cabello   Ojos

          Nez
          Nose
          Nariz

Signes particuliers   } scare on left knuckle of first
Distinguishing marks   finger
Señales particulares

4

Témoignages fournis à l'appui de ces déclarations:
Evidence furnished in support of above statements:
Testimonios en apoyo de estas declaraciones:

_____

_____

_____

_____

Pays de destination
Country of destination } Portugal
País de destino

Le présent titre ne pourra être prolongé lorsque le porteur aura atteint le pays de destination qu'il y figure.

Le porteur s'engage à retourner le présent document au Comité international de la Croix-Rouge, 17, avenue de la Paix, Genève, Suisse, dès son arrivée dans le pays de destination.

The present document may not be renewed either after its bearer has reached the country marked on it as the place of destination.

The bearer of the present document undertakes to return it International Committee of the Red Cross, 17, avenue de la Geneva, Switzerland, immediately on his arrival in the country of destination.

Este documento no podrá prolongarse cuando su portador haya llegado al país de destino que en él figura.

El portador se compromete a devolver este documento al Comité Internacional de la Cruz Roja, 17, avenue de la Paix, Ginebra, Suiza, inmediatamente después de su llegada al país de destino.

Signature du titulaire
Signature of the bearer
Firma del interesado

5

Validité du document
Validity of the present document 〕 15-10-85
Validez del documento

Signature du délégué
Signature of delegate
Firma del delegado

Ch. van ~~~~~ (signature)

Cachet de la Délégation
Delegation stamp
Sello de la Delegación

[Stamp: COMITÉ INTERNATIONAL DE LA CROIX-ROUGE · GENÈVE]

Empreintes digitales (obligatoires)
Finger-prints (compulsory)
Huellas digitales (obligatorias)

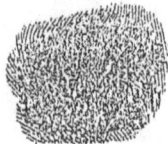

Photographie (facultative)
Photograph (optional)
Fotografía (facultativa)

6

N° 680/85

VISAS
VISA

de transit / voor transit / for transit

Valable pour ....
Geldig voor Benelux
Valid for ....
Délivré le / Afgegeven op / Issued on 0 2 AUG 1985

Ce visa est valable pour .... journey/transit(s)
Dit visum is geldig voor één .... reis(zen)
This visa is valid for one ....
avec arrêt de 7 jours .... Sept jours
met oponthoud van 7 dagen,
broken for 7 days,

à effectuer avant 10.08.85
te volbrengen vóór
to be completed before

ATTENTION ! ....
OPGELET ! ....
ATTENTION ! ....

[Stamp: AMBASSADE DE BELGIQUE · BELGISCHE AMBASSADE · A KIGALI · TE KIGALI]

(signature)

D VERWAERDE
Attaché affaires consulaires

[Stamp: BELGIQUE / BELGIE / GRATIS]

COMITÉ INTERNATIONAL
DE LA CROIX-ROUGE
GENÈVE

7

COMITÉ INTERNATIONAL DE LA CROIX-ROUGE · GENÈVE

Ce document est intransmissible et ne constitue
pas une pièce d'identité; il est délivré à titre gratuit.

The present document is not transmissible and is
not an identification paper; it is issued free of charge.

Este documento, personal e intransferible, no es un
documento de identidad y se expide gratuitamente.

REPUBLIQUE RWANDAISE
IMMIGRATION
05 AOÛT
AEROPORT — KANOMBE
ENTREE · SORTIE · TRANSIT

GUARDA FISCAL
AEROPORTO LISBOA

VISTO ... TRANSITO ...

CONCEDIDO A. ...

PASSAPORTE N° ...

ENTRADA
06. AGO. 1915
LISBOA
GUARDA FISCAL

PORTUGAL

Leaving Portugal

I had to leave Portugal several months later after failing to achieve means of self-support.You see, Life has meaning when the individual assumes responsibility for himself. I was no longer in charge of my life, other forces were. Sadly, when one is not in control of one's life, those in charge take on the status of mini-gods who can dispense favour or withhold it as they wish. I considered it imperative that I assumed responsibility for my own life. As the adage goes, 'It is better to die on your feet than to live on your knees.'

After roaming around central Europe in search of gainful employment I landed a job as a *Swahili* teacher in Bad Honnef, at the German Foundation for International Development (DSE), and later on at the Cologne-based Association for Development Cooperation (AGEH), the volunteer service of the Catholic Church in Germany. But I had to terminate full time teaching several months later because the German immigration authorities could not grant me a residence and work permit. I had been allowed to teach while the authorities at the institute filled in the application for my work permit, apparently with no guarantee that it would be successful.

After termination of full time teaching, the former institute (DSE), permitted me to give the occasional one-hour lecture on political topics such as 'East Africa: Thirty Years of Political Independence,' or the collapse of the East Africa Community (EAC) and its impact on the ordinary people of the region. Since some of these were well publicised and Tanzania was therefore able to send some of its people to hear what I said, I strictly confined myself to the general failures of the East Africa Community without specifically singling out Tanzania. Most of the participants were going either to Tanzania or East Africa as experts of some sort. I didn't doubt that they would be able to see for themselves how the high priest of 'African socialism,' Nyerere, had 'succeeded' in 'developing'(impoverishing) his country through his much celebrated *'Azimio la Arusha'* (Arusha Declaration) now dubbed *'Angamizo la Arusha'* (meaning the Arusha Declaration of 1967, which devastated the lives of many Tanzanians).

One significant aspect was the way black African

participants felt about their continent's woes. Once, during one of these discussions, one African participant blurted out ruefully, his Rastafarian plaits flowing wildly, 'These colonialists should be punished for what they have done to us.' He did not say who should punish them. But he thought every problem facing black Africa today—starvation, corruption, economic mismanagement and so on—all stemmed from the white man's 'imperialism'. Sadly, many African rulers (even the most enlightened) perpetuated this view, today held by many Africans, that the blame for our own problems should be placed elsewhere. Everything is blamed on the white colonisers: clan and brutal tribal wars, economic stagnation, the lot. True, whites have committed grave injustices against blacks—from slavery to colonialism—but it is this very 'victim' attitude that enslaves black Africans more than anything else.

Most black Africans seem to be prisoners of their imagined past. In this regard they are not unlike their black counterparts in the United States who suffer from the malaise known as 'plantationism.' Some American blacks often say they are not doing well because their forefathers were slaves on the cotton plantations. By contrast, African leaders seem eager to evoke memories of their own people's imagined past hardship by constantly referring to unseen 'enemies.' To suggest that the new generation of Europeans should be held to account for the doings of their forebears is unrealistic. Black Africa can do its best to attract the interest of the developed nations for financial and other support, but to suppose that Europe can solve all Africa's problems, as this participant did, is pure fantasy. Enslavement of blacks is something whites would prefer to forget as much as black African leaders like to forget how they bungled their new-found independence.

* * * * * *

I went to Iceland because I thought chances of being granted a work permit looked brighter than in Europe. Efforts by both institutes in Germany to obtain a work permit so that I could continue teaching had proved futile. At one point the Association for Development Cooperation (AGEH) had appointed a senior staff member to accompany me to the immigration authorities in Siegburg to fill in a new application for a work permit and permission to stay in Germany. But the senior immigration official we spoke to was doubtful I would be granted one.

However, it was on our way back from Siegburg to Cologne that I realised the efficiency of Nyerere's public relations machinery overseas. On the *autobahn*, the staff member who had accompanied me broke the silence by eulogising Nyerere, the 'revered' leader whose victim I was. The official thought Nyerere was a fine Christian gentleman who could not harm a fly, let alone a human being. He believed Nyerere was a successful 'democratic leader' who had united Tanzania, which he considered to be the most peaceful country south of the Sahara. The official had apparently read some of the books Nyerere had written and believed he was one of the greatest thinkers of our time—but a 'democratic leader?' I wondered what the official would think if a one-party system was imposed on his country. Would the German people accept that as a 'democratic' system of government? If it was unacceptable to the Germans, why then should Tanzanians accept it? I told the official that I recognised some of Nyerere's achievements, such as moulding national unity, adding that the inability to give credit for someone's achievements made it difficult to spot that person's failures. Still, I personally had no doubt that Nyerere's failures outweighed his successes.

As the official rambled on about Nyerere, I interjected to remind him that Nyerere was, after all, not the German chancellor but the Tanzanian president. 'It is the wearer of the shoes who knows where they pinch,' I said looking directly at him. As of Nyerere's 'great' ideas, I reminded the official of the old saying that 'The end justifies the means.' If in the end, Tanzania went down the drain because of Nyerere's ideas, few people would then remain convinced that the ideas were so 'great' after all. The official dropped the subject until we left the *autobahn* and stopped, when we shook hands and I thanked him for his encouragement.

******

We became more politically active during the following years and we had been responsible for publishing pamphlets regarding Tanzania. The purpose of the pamphlets was to inform the world of the extent of the violation of human rights in Tanzania, to press for political and economic reform and to mobilise supportive Tanzanians to propagate and promote principles of human rights and democracy.[15] For their part, the Zanzibaris in exile in Britain were publishing a newsletter known as '*Free Zanzibar Voice*' which started in 1964, edited by a Zanzibari dissident, Ahmed Seif Kharusi of the Zanzibar Organisation. When Kharusi died in 1985, the editorship passed on to another staunch dissident who previously had spent three years in Zanzibar jails, Suleiman Sultan Malik. He later transformed *Free Zanzibar Voice* into the *Zanzibar Newsletter*. Encouraging events occurred on the world scene in 1990: communism collapsed in Eastern Europe, as did Tanzania's ideological bedfellow, Romania's Nicolae Ceausescu, followed by the fall of the Berlin Wall. Around this period our group NUNA (National Union of Nationalist Activists), an underground group calling for political change, had launched a newspaper, *Tanzania Argus*, in its campaign for democratic freedom. I was the group's Publicity Secretary and one of its founder-members, and the brain behind the publishing of *The Argus*. *Tanzania Argus* began to appear on newspaper stands in Europe and Africa; even at a time when press freedom in Tanzania was severely restricted. The group's honorary chairman was Joseph Kasella-Bantu, a former Member of Parliament and the first Publicity Secretary of TANU (Tanganyika African National Union), the party which had successfully campaigned for Tanganyika's independence from Britain, leading to independence in 1961. Kasella-Bantu's penchant for collective leadership and democracy had apparently upset Nyerere's autocratic rule. As a result, Kasella-Bantu was placed under lock and key, without any charge for more than eight years, by courtesy of the state. He was essentially a non-violent person, the sort who was ready to die for a cause but never, as others wrongly do, kill for one.

It brings to mind the saying that a brave man is ready to die in a war, but he should not start a fight simply to show his bravery. That saying was most appropriate regarding Kasella-Bantu. Unfortunately, and not unexpectedly, detention had left its mark on his health, and he was prone to repeat himself or sometimes completely forget what he had said earlier. Despite that,

---

15See The Mail, page 4, *Newsweek*, July 27, 1987

he remained wholly committed to political change and economic reform, and he made a positive contribution to that end.

I remember how we used to sign clandestine letters and mail our underground publications to senior government officials and Members of Parliament, appealing to them to take the interests of their constituents to heart and to end one-party rule. Although most of our publications were confiscated by the Tanzanian secret police, Kasella-Bantu persisted with the exercise. Abroad meanwhile, as our campaign for political freedom and human rights shifted to top gear, Dar-Es-Salaam reacted by complaining to some African governments where *The Argus* was widely read that we were using their countries as a 'launching pad' to 'attack' the *CCM* regime. Some countries which bothered, such as Swaziland, issued an official order in 1991, signed by the then Minister for Home Affairs, Senzenjani Tshabalala, that due to my political activities I was barred to enter the Kingdom of Swaziland. Well, I thought, that was part of the struggle. You know, a struggle is not cricket, snooker or African reed dance. Ironically, Tanzania feels it has the exclusive, legitimate right to welcome and protect opposition forces from all over Africa—including Swaziland—but those it perceives as its opponents should not enjoy this right in other African countries. Ah, yes—do unto others what you would hate them to do unto you!

* * * * * *

In April 1991, I left Iceland briefly, to participate in an interview on a *Swahili* programme broadcast by *Radio Deutsch Welle*, and later to be interviewed on an English language programme on *Third World Voice* in Denmark. By now, we had changed the formation of our newspaper to that of a magazine. Again I needed to approach subscribers to see if they could offer financial support for our magazine, which we planned to produce every month.

Unfortunately my Convention Travel Document (CTD) was about to expire and I had appointments with potential subscribers after the expiry date. Although I had moved to Iceland, I was still holding a CTD issued by the Portuguese authorities and I was required to return to Portugal every two years to have it extended.

Consequently, I approached the Portuguese Embassy whilst in Copenhagen to ask if it was possible for the embassy to send my CTD to Lisbon for extension. I was assured by an embassy official, Ms Sylvia Hinnerfeldt, that this was possible.

However, she directed me to send my CTD to Mr. Thor Thorsteins, of the Portuguese consulate in Iceland, and she said that Mr. Thorsteins would then forward my CTD to Portugal for extension. She stated that as I was on a business trip to Denmark I would have to receive my extended CTD through her embassy in Copenhagen. On July 11, 1991, I sent my CTD to Mr. Thorsteins by special delivery, as instructed by Ms. Hinnerfeltd. I kept in contact with Ms. Hinnerfeldt regarding these arrangements.

However, despite all solid assurances from the Portuguese embassy in Copenhagen, on August 6, 1991, I received a letter from the same embassy in Copenhagen informing me that I no longer had asylum rights in Portugal, as I had taken up permanent residence in another country. However, at this time, I did not have 'permanent' residence anywhere other than Portugal.

If the Portuguese authorities had merely assumed that as I had been granted the right to work in Iceland that I had 'permanent' residence there, then at the time they confiscated my Convention Travel Document (CTD), I was not in Iceland, but abroad, for reasons stated earlier.

Bewildered, I decided again to visit the Portuguese Embassy in Copenhagen to get some answers to these puzzling questions. There I got in touch with the diplomat with whom I had seen earlier, Sylvia Hinnerfeldt. However, she did not tell me why she had not given me the true facts of the case at our previous meeting. This despite the fact that I trusted and relied on her for the truth.

Indeed, she could not explain why when I was in Lisbon in 1987, to seek extension of my CTD, the Portuguese authorities had not informed me that I risked losing my asylum rights in Portugal if I took employment in another country. Her only explanation was that this was due to bureaucracy. Bureaucracy! A familiar word I thought. The religion of bureaucracy seems to have its own perculiar manner of functioning, not usually fathomable to ordinary minds. Perhaps bureaucracy is a thorn in the side of any large administration; even successful governments have it; and administrations such as Portugal's limp from the abyss of active dictatorship, would probably be lost without it. I often think that the wheels of bureaucracy become jammed with sand, and if they were to roll, they would take a considerable time to do so. This situation could explain Portugal's recent experiences of dictatorship; when a dictator leaves, like Salazar (António de Oliveira) it does not mean the end of dictatorial traits in the country.

For more than six months I remained marooned (stranded would be an understatement), in Copenhagen, without documentation, and technically without legal protection. This despite the latter being promised by the Portuguese authorities through the United Nations High Commissioner for Refugees (UNHCR). All my projects collapsed, leaving me heavily indebted; debts which to this day I have struggled endlessly and without success to settle, with creditors pressing for payments.

Significantly, the Portuguese government ignored my many requests for redress over several years; redress which I felt I was entitled, since it was the Portuguese government's decision to confiscate my travel document, resulting in my financial ruin.

Even so, despite being ignored, and the many years that have elapsed since the confiscation of my travel document, I still remained determined to press the Portuguese government for redress.

Indeed, on July 23, 2005, I wrote to the Portuguese president, then Jorge Sempaio, appealing for his help and for him to intercede in order to achieve this. On August 16, 2005, I received a letter from President Sempaio's office, which promised that the matter would be brought to the attention of the Portuguese premier, José Sócrates.

On September 16, 2005, the prime minister's office wrote to me, saying that the matter would be referred to the Home Office for action. Despite the hope raised by this response, I heard nothing from my putative protectors, despite having written to them as recently as January 22, 2009, to inform them that I had not heard from the Home Office.

At this juncture, I reasonably believed that I had exhausted everything within my power to obtain redress from the Portuguese authorities without success.

On the other hand, I firmly believed that in terms of the European Convention on Human Rights, my fundamental human rights had been infringed by the Portuguese authorities. Despite this, I rejected the idea of initiating a process, as foreseen in the Convention, which would have resulted in lodging an application with the European Court of Human Rights.

Firstly, I considered that taking such a course of action would make me appear confrontational, not withstanding that my fundamental rights had been violated.

Secondly, I felt that if I had any energy to expend, it would be better spent on the forces that precipitated my departure from my homeland.

That notwithstanding, I probably will keep trying to find answers as to why the Portuguese authorities decided to deprive me of my livelihood, without even giving me a hearing and offering no plausible explanation.

Indeed, I feel inclined to do this, not only for the record but also for the sake of many European friends who had wholeheartedly supported me following that unprecedented decision. I am sure they too would like answers as to why that happened.

Throughout this narrative, one must have observed the kind of price one must pay for cherished beliefs and values. For this, I accept full responsibility without reservation.

Notwithstanding, whether the Portuguese had any moral ground to justify reneging on the responsibility which they had voluntarily accepted, will, in the course of time, remain completely open to question.

Finally, the demise of *The Argus*, resulting from that decision, must have inspired the anti-democratic factions in Dar-Es-Salaam, of whom *The Argus* was critical, to uncork the champagne in celebration.

It was not until one afternoon towards the end of November, 1991, that I received a phone call from the Icelandic Red Cross. The Red Cross official, a woman, informed me that the Icelandic government had decided to grant me residential rights and to issue me with a new CTD to enable me to leave Denmark. It was one of the best pieces of news I had received since my abduction in 1983, and I thanked the official profoundly. 'Thank you, thank you very much indeed,' I repeated into the telephone.

Misfortune has its positive side and my experience was no exception. I had faced severe hardship and uncertainty for many years, most of it in Portugal, but now I had no reason to return to Portugal as that country had nothing more to do with my refugee status. Looking back, I am amazed that I managed to persevere for so long in the face of so much difficulty. I never lost hope, even when it seemed there was no cause for hope. People live by hope: the hope that things will improve; the belief that no matter what happens, something good will come of any situation in the end. Hope sustains one, and it certainly did that for me.

As I re-gathered my composure and reflected on my new future with its remarkable turn for the better, my mind turned, as always to Tanzania. Concerted pressure from donor countries had dragged Tanzania, squirming as ever in the face of the slightest criticism, down the road to multi-party democracy. But Nyerere's *CCM*-ruled country moved grudgingly, howling, kicking and squealing down the track. *CCM*—the 'mother party,' the sole party, the everything in Tanzania—decided, on its own, as usual, that it should be referee in the multi-party game and that it would set out the conditions for the eventual multi-party poll. Not surprisingly, these conditions are restrictive and have been identified as such by many Tanzanians. There is little doubt that with such restrictive rules, Tanzania's *CCM* rulers wished to have a tame opposition.

One of the most restrictive rules remains unchanged in the statute book from the days when Nyerere's ever-present Intelligence Service had unlimited powers to lock up even the mildest critics: the 1962 Preventive Detention Act (PDA), under which myself and many other Tanzanians were detained for advocating political change and economic reform. The retention of this dreadful law could prove detrimental to opposition parties in the future. I say this because I know that the forces of democracy in Tanzania, and perhaps in most of Africa, have been talking democracy to undemocratic rulers, who will not hesitate to seize the slightest opportunity to revert to their old authoritarian ways. If democracy is to succeed, then the people implementing it should have faith in it and believe in it. Already we have heard of black African leaders complaining they were 'blackmailed' by 'external forces' (those vague, overworked expressions that African despots so often hide behind). Others are saying that multi-partyism is un-African, thus implying that dictatorship is African. African leaders seem to be insinuating that to be an African is to be evil, and the people they rule will just have to stomach that. Again, it is said that some African leaders complain that 'You can't import democracy to Africa from America like Coca-cola,' and that the whole thing is a 'Western concept'. Oddly enough these leaders never mention what is wrong with this 'Western concept'; and if multi-partyism is indeed a 'Western concept', why can it not be accepted with grace? After all, we all borrow knowledge from each other—East from West, Africa from Europe, reader from writer, and teacher from pupil and so on—in order to develop. Many Africans have been schooled in Western communities under Western systems, using books written by Western scholars; and today black Africans cannot do away with such education just because it is 'Western'. In fact, African leaders usually make sure their children get a Western-type education, usually in a Western country. Black Africans are part of a global village and are affected by global changes. Being African is an identity, and one that we should like to be proud of one day, but it doesn't mean we should want to live in medieval times and revert to primitive ways just because 'we are African.' We have to move with the times. Some of the pronouncements of African rulers on multi-party democracy seem to show that many are reluctant participants in the move towards democracy. Indeed, one needs to look at the level of electoral fraud throughout most of Africa; plus the (alarming) tendency by some African rulers to align themselves with criminal syndicates so as to milk the public coffers dry, in their quest to perpetuate themselves in power under the guise of democracy. The examples of fraud highlighted in the introduction of this book support that contention. Recently, both President Mwai Kibaki of Kenya and Zimbabwe's Robert Mugabe refused to relinquish power despite having lost the elections. It is the same old story: in mid 1993 Nigeria's General Ibrahim Badamasi Babangida (IBB) reversed the wishes of the Nigerian people by annulling the election results as he precariously clung to power. In Burundi (late 1993) a bloody military coup deposed the three months old, democratically elected government of assassinated President Melchior Ndadaye. And, apart from countries such as Benin, Botswana, Cape Verde, Ghana, Lesotho, Mali, Namibia, Senegal and South Africa, which are considered to be truly democratic and free, the rest of the countries in sub-Saharan Africa are either quasi-free or under active dictatorship.

The West and supporting nations can do more to prevent African nations, who are now moving towards democracy, from relapsing into one-party rule or military dictatorship at a later date. Supporting nations which started the wheels of democracy moving in Africa should have used their financial muscle to ensure that the ruling regime handed over power, say, at least for 120 days prior to elections, to a transitional/custodian administration. Such an administration should have been headed by the country's Chief Justice (CJ), for example, and the interim administration, made up of technocrats appointed by the Chief Justice, should not have been allowed to join the race for political office. During this transitional period, the ruling party should have campaigned on equal terms with other parties and should not have enjoyed any advantages that would have enabled it to engage in intimidation and subterfuge, or rig the process in its favour. The interim administration should have laid down conditions that would have ensured all contending parties had equal access to the media, facilities for public meetings and so on. A neutral, transitional administration was imperative for African countries emerging from active dictatorship to democratic rule. To allow the ruling parties, which for decades showed no liking for democratic rule, to dictate the conditions under which multi-party politics should operate, was like placing the rights of a goat in the hands of a lion. However, there is another concerning issue.

Unless Africans refuse to be swayed, the recent arrival to the continent of a new emerging power, China, may potentially undermine the gains that Africa has made in the area of human rights and democracy.

This follows China's declared policy of 'non-interference' in Africa's internal affairs. Without doubt, this policy is actuated by China's own abysmal record on human rights and democracy. However, it could also be a cavalier manouevre, on the part of the Chinese, to gain advantage over those they accuse of 'meddling' into Africa's internal affairs.

Seen in this context, there is every reason to believe that African rulers, who reluctantly embraced multi-partyism, may see China as a congenial political bedfellow because of its policy. Such partnership could result in the erosion of gains made recently in those areas.

The latter could even prove worse if, in an attempt to fend off the prospect of losing their influence in Africa to China, the West choose to look the other way as those gains are being eroded. If this were to happen, then Africans again would have been left to the whims of their dictators if it were not for institutions like the International Criminal Court (ICC) or, in a much broader sense, the international community, which, as part of the function imposed on it by international law, would have to try reign in a dictator's actions. But qualms amongst reform-minded Africans prevail nonetheless.

Lately, an influential section of pan-African media which, ironically, is based in the West and mostly managed by Africans, has been hailing China's arrival to the continent in extraordinarily positive terms. It contends that China is the best 'alternative' to the Western presence in Africa and that 'China never colonised Africa'. Well, yes.

But, the fact that it did not colonise Africa does not mean that it cannot do so today, or even in the future. Indeed, when it decided to occupy Tibet (since 1951) it did so with decidedly clear intent and maximum resolve. Those Tibetans today that feel China should leave them alone to manage their own affairs have not, for sure, been treated very kindly by their Chinese occupiers.

And, although unlike China, some Western countries did colonise Africa, there is evidence to show that not all countries in Africa were under colonisation. On the contrary, some countries were even established with active help of the Westerners themselves. Reasons for this may, or may not vary, but it does not negate that fact.

For example, between 1821 and 1847, the citizens of the United States of America developed Liberia. It declared itself independent in 1847. Sierra Leone was established in 1787 by the British as 'Province of the Freedom'. On the Horn of Africa, Ethiopia is arguably Africa's oldest independent country. Apart from that, other African countries (including Tanzania) were under trusteeship (protectorates), and not colonised as such.

Furthermore, it can be contended that the Chinese are not in Africa to perform the role reminiscent to that of Mother Teresa. On the contrary, they are there to actually extract Africa's vast mineral resources in order to satiate growing domestic demand for such resources, and also to find new markets for Chinese goods.

Equally, their 'win-win' policy which is seen by some Africans as a solution to their endemic economic woes, should be treated with equal circumspection until we see tangible results.

From the beginning of this narrative, I have highlighted factors which, to a large extent, resulted in Africa's current mire of misery; factors which 'win-win' policy alone cannot resolve without a comprehensive solution to these factors.

More importantly, if China's 'non-interference' policy is not carefully planned, it may further erode transparency and the rule of law, which could take the countries concerned back to regimentation.

In any case, there are Africans who are questioning the wisdom of changing horses in mid-stream.

This, in essence, is what is concerning some reform-minded Africans. As you have seen in this narration, scores of African lives have been lost to achieve whatever little Africans have achieved in that sphere.

Otherwise, outside those concerns, one sees no reason why the Chinese should not trade with Africans, as other countries do.

Nonetheless, Africa remains as unstable as ever: Angola, Burundi, the Comoros, Central Africa Republic (CAR), the Democratic Republic of Congo (DRC), Côte d'Ivoire, Eritrea, Ethiopia, Guinea Bissau, Libya, Madagascar, Mali, Somalia and South Sudan provide some examples and even in Tanzania, one of the most peaceful countries on the continent, religious tension is rising high and threatening stability. Simultaneously, in South Africa, despite majority rule, black-on-black violence continued for several years unabated, threatening to plunge the country into civil war. Black South Africans blamed the so-called 'third force'— unruly white elements in the South Africa security service—for instigating carnage, but did not blame themselves for that unbridled slaughter. Such a situation provoked serious doubts. If the people who were now masters of their own destiny were susceptible to manipulation by the forces that previously dominated them, then what will happen in the future? After all, the whites and other forces will still be there to manipulate them. Isn't the victim's mind the cardinal tool in the hands of the victimiser? Surely, serious African thinkers must at some point have wondered that if black-on-black violence continued on this scale, then the whites could have become the majority race in South Africa by the start of the 21st century. And how does the ANC explain the litany of corruption scandals that has characterised its government since it assumed power in 1994? Has the so-called 'black empowerment' benefited most underprivileged South Africans or a tiny group of senior ANC cadres? How could black South African leaders so brazenly enrich themselves in a manner unseen during white minority rule? Is this what the 'armed struggle,' to which Tanzania committed its meagre resources, was all about? The incompetent handling of the independence of African states following the retreat of colonialism raises far more serious questions than answers. Indeed, the formation of so-called African banana states has taken place entirely due to avarice and the seizing of power by incompetent, undemocratic rulers and the complacency of the African people. The day is not far off when the international community, through the United Nations, may be compelled to place some African nations under trusteeship, if only for as long as it takes to end the carnage and restore order. Perhaps the United Nations should only remove its presence once such nations show they can govern themselves in accordance with internationally acceptable standards. No doubt this notion of United Nations trusteeship over African countries in perennial turmoil will sound ridiculous to many, as it is easily mistaken for colonialism. However, the fact remains that when a neighbour's house is on fire, one's own house also feels the heat; and if the wind blows in your direction, your house could also catch fire. One may only need to look at one potential factor to understand the metaphor of fire and the wind that I mention: the prospect of failed African states such as Somalia, for example, becoming a haven for terrorists which might undermine global security. Bringing a semblance of order in such countries would be in the interests of the entire world community. The task of defining Africa's new democracies is more a daunting one than the simple demand for the introduction of democracy. The task of building a better, just, democratic, and prosperous Africa has only now begun.

I stared out of the window at the road in Copenhagen, thinking of Africa and the phone call I had just received from Reykjavik. It had been a good day. I gathered my thoughts, shook myself out of my daydream and retreated from the window to a sofa next to the telephone which had brought me the good news of my CTD. I curled up and for the first time since my abduction and subsequent release and exile, I enjoyed really peaceful, uninterrupted nap.

* * * * * *

The First Multi-Party Election of October 1995

It was supposed to be 'free and fair.' However, the supposedly retired ex-president, Julius Nyerere, seemed intent on influencing the election results. Armed with his familiar black ceremonial baton and dark glasses, he embarked on a nation-wide helicopter tour campaigning for the ruling *Chama Cha Mapinduzi* (*CCM*) presidential candidate (best described as 'his' preferential candidate), Benjamin William Mkapa. The majority of Tanzanians were left wondering whether this was the role befitting the 'father of the nation,' the title Nyerere so dearly relished, although he was no more than the 'father of the *CCM*,' *his* party.

For this election the benevolent international donor community gave the government 21 million American Dollars. For its part, the government appointed an Electoral Commission, headed by Judge Lewis Makame, refusing categorically to include any member of the opposition. Judge Makame was empowered by the government to do anything he pleased concerning the election. He could, for instance, disqualify candidates, appoint election supervisors, order ballot papers sent to a particular polling station and decide how many could be sent. He could also declare the election in one region null and void, whilst in other regions polling continued as usual. As the chairman of the Electoral Commission, Judge Makame could, without taking into consideration the impact of the overall election results, order a certain part of the country to go to the poll one week ahead of another part, provided this was in the best interests of the incumbent party, which appointed him commissioner.

Indeed, Zanzibar held its first multi-party election on October 20, 1995, while the mainland held its own election on October 29, 1995. What followed, according to many neutral observers, was 'deliberately organised chaos'. Indeed, the Commonwealth and many donor countries, including Denmark, Belgium, Ireland, Sweden and the Netherlands, amongst others, did conclude that the election result in Zanzibar did not reflect the true wishes of the electorate.

However, Dr Salmin Amour, the *CCM* presidential candidate for Zanzibar, who claimed to have won by a disputed narrow margin of 0.4% after four days of counting the 333,899 votes cast in the islands of Zanzibar and Pemba, became more dictatorial than he ever was before the introduction of multi-partyism, since being hastily sworn in as president.

Innocent people were routinely harassed and physically abused for being perceived as sympathisers of the rival party, Civic United Front (CUF) which many observers believe was robbed of its election victory. People from Pemba island, where not a single seat was won by the ruling *Chama Cha Mapinduzi*, were discriminated against at the instigation of Dr Salmin Amour's government. People were dismissed from their jobs, on suspicion that they sympathise with the opposition.

In early 1996, *Majira*, a mainland based, popular newspaper, was banned in Zanzibar for reporting the truth about the ongoing violation of human rights.

Dr Salmin Amour refused to form a Government of National Unity (GNU) with the main political rival CUF, if only to mould the unity of Zanzibar and that way avert the imminent split of the two islands.

The mainland election, which took place nine days after the Zanzibar election, was equally marred by massive irregularities and vote rigging, thereby prompting the Electoral Commission to nullify the election results in Dar-Es-Salaam, which was the opposition's strong base. The election in the capital was repeated several days later. Many polling stations did not have ballot papers for the presidential candidate and voters were asked to return later to vote for president. Many voters, feeling a sense of frustration and anger, never came back.

It was terrifyingly disturbing that so many irregularities could occur in such a well-funded election and with so many foreign observers. If this could occur in the city where so many of the observers were based, then what about the rural areas where vigilance was less stringent? Then there is the crucial factor of *'nyumba kumi'* (ten-households), a political system reminiscent of the now defunct Soviet style of collectivisation i.e. one person (party cadre) speaking for ten-households (not very democratic); through which the single party exercised its notorious suppressive powers over the rural peasantry, for thirty years.

Once the *CCM* candidate, Benjamin William Mkapa, had been declared winner and sworn into office, it was not long before

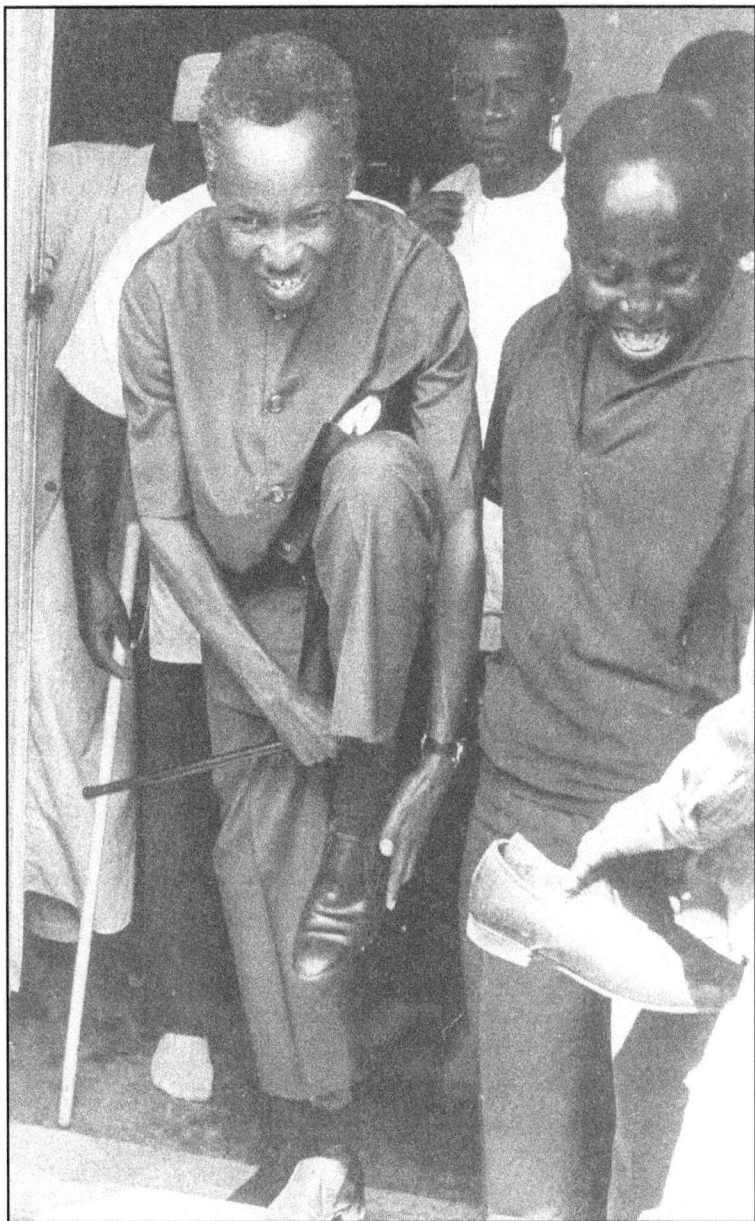

The 'father-of-the nation' (seen here adjusting his shoes), after claiming to have walked out of political life. However, events preceding the first multi-party election in thirty years presented a radically different picture.

Lawrence Gama, whose office vowed to 'deal accordingly', with Tanzanians who supported the opposition during the first multi-party elections of October 1995.

the office of the *CCM* Secretary-General, then Lawrence Gama, himself a former director of Nyerere's political police organisation, issued a letter directing all *CCM* officials country-wide to begin 'dealing accordingly' with Tanzanians who manifested support for *CCM*'s 'foes' (contending opposition parties which participated in the election).

Not surprisingly, Nyerere, having openly campaigned for the *CCM*, failed to even add his voice of disapproval to what happened during the election and after. Instead, the 'teacher' who used his valuable talent to teach his nation to beg, vowed he would never let *his* country go 'to the dogs,' i.e. members of the opposition.

* * * * * *

Epilogue

Throughout the chapters of this book, I have made critical observations on matters such as human rights, democracy and other issues ultimately affecting the future and well-being of our society.

My objectives were, and are, to increase the awareness of Tanzanians and general Africans of the true meaning of human rights and democratic freedom and to realise that with self-analysis and self-criticism the methods of achieving these essentials of society are within our grasp. This is providing we accept that the responsibility for our lives, our society and specifically our government is our own and we must begin now to help ourselves.

This self-recognition and acceptance of responsibility is essential if we are to rationalise and fulfil our aspirations for social and economic progress and also to foster new and trusting links with developed nations and attract local and international investment.

The current practice of most African nations to seek growth solely through foreign aid and investments is a short-term measure with no future guarantees. The onus is on us, the Africans and our governments, to drag ourselves out of the poverty trap and improve our quality of life by immediate and long term planning to exploit our vast natural resources.

How we can expect the Danish Minister of Finance, or for that matter, the British Chancellor of the Exchequer to spend sleepless nights in their offices, over endless cups of coffee, initiating plans for the development of irrigation schemes, agricultural expansion and economic growth for Tanzania and other African nations when the leaders of those nations are apathetic, is beyond belief. Sub-Saharan Africa is not in the sorry state it is today because its people are incompetent and lazy. On the contrary, black Africans are industrious, intelligent, versatile and receptive to new ideas. A Belgian missionary, who was running a parish next to my village organised the villagers to build three classrooms and a teacher's house. Bricks were made by the local people and the houses were finished within the wink of an eye. They are still standing, although they have not received a lick of paint since the minister returned home. Lazy people would never have achieved such a feat. However, what is disturbing is that the African people who built these brick houses under the supervision of a Belgian minister were themselves living in squalid mud huts. How can such a paradox occur? Is it lack of enterprise and ability or bad leadership and organisation? Even within the black 'diaspora' from North America to Haiti, few seem to manage to sustain a useful, satisfying and progressive existence compared with their paler neighbours. Whilst their past and current plight could be attributed to racial prejudice and economic deprivation, the question of their future remains—who will release them from their poverty trap? Will they expect those whom they believe responsible for their plight to originate the escape; or will they decide that the solution will be realised through their own efforts? Regarding African nations: have over sympathetic Europeans worsened and prolonged our plight by diminishing our self-reliance?

These issues might seem sensitive ones to many, but they must be addressed by we black Africans ourselves, with complete self-awareness and honesty; as inevitably we must reverse this miserable situation immediately and for our lasting future. We must examine our perpetual reliance on foreign aid and the effect of this on our ability to survive unaided and on our international status.

Few African leaders have accepted the fact and responsibility that the vast natural resources of our continent; fertile soil, an enormous water supply, rich mineral resources and a labour force for all levels of employment; if managed skilfully could produce a high degree of independence within a decade.

It must be difficult for those outside Africa to understand how a continent with such potential can fail with such a basic need as feeding its people—the responsibility of each individual country.

Africans should decide what type of aid is required, whether projects are conducive to the country's needs and whether the donor nations' motive is to help the people or the current government. Governments come and go, but the people, the land and their mutual needs, remain. How is it possible to best assist the indigent rural peasantry, which comprises over ninety percent of the entire African populace? How can they be led into deciding and organising their future, and by whom?

It is clear that the younger generation of politicians was marginalized by their older predecessors who had failed to provide vision and hope for Tanzania's youth and future. The challenge is now with this younger generation of politicians, whose education and knowledge of the past should have prepared them for it. Theirs are the new needs, the new aspirations and the new responsibility.

Those who have accepted trust and leadership must take up the challenge to ensure the future prosperity and progress of their country and their people.

* * * * * *

Postscript

Why Nyerere Should Not be Proclaimed Saint

Throughout this narrative I have demonstrated to the reader the nature and scope of criminal abuse of public governmental power by Julius Nyerere's regime of personal rule. Similarly, I have demonstrated how the Nyerere regime supported violent liberation movements and tyrannical regimes in the region. In addition, I also show the reader how Nyerere cared little for the families of innocent victims murdered by regimes that enjoyed his unstinting support.

Likewise, within Tanzania itself, I have furnished the reader with evidential facts about the enforced disappearance of political prisoners from administrative detention, as well as extra-judicial killings, most of which occurred after the staging of public show-trials. As I show in this narration, all these incidents took place with Nyerere's full knowledge and approval.

One of the core values of Catholicism is the sanctity of life. Indeed, it is on the basis of this value, amongst other things, that the Catholic Church precludes its faithful from the use of contraception, claiming that contraception inhibits creation. This is despite its tangible benefits in relation to reproductive health, family planning and the right of women (especially in Africa, where they still lack the power) to have control over their own bodies. Those favouring the use of contraception contend that these benefits far outweigh any other considerations, including those built around religious beliefs.

So then, if the Catholic Church can so firmly speak for life which has not been created, why then ignore the life which was already created but then taken away violently and unlawfully by the ruler it now seeks to canonise? Unless the Holy See can show that the life of Julius Kambarage Nyerere has greater value than those of his victims, the international community should, as a matter of principle, vehemently oppose Nyerere's canonisation.

As I show in this narrative, Nyerere was a dictator who abhorred democracy to the point of persecuting its proponents. Indeed, none of the few African post-independence democratic leaders such as Sir Seretse Khama of Botswana or Léopold Sédar

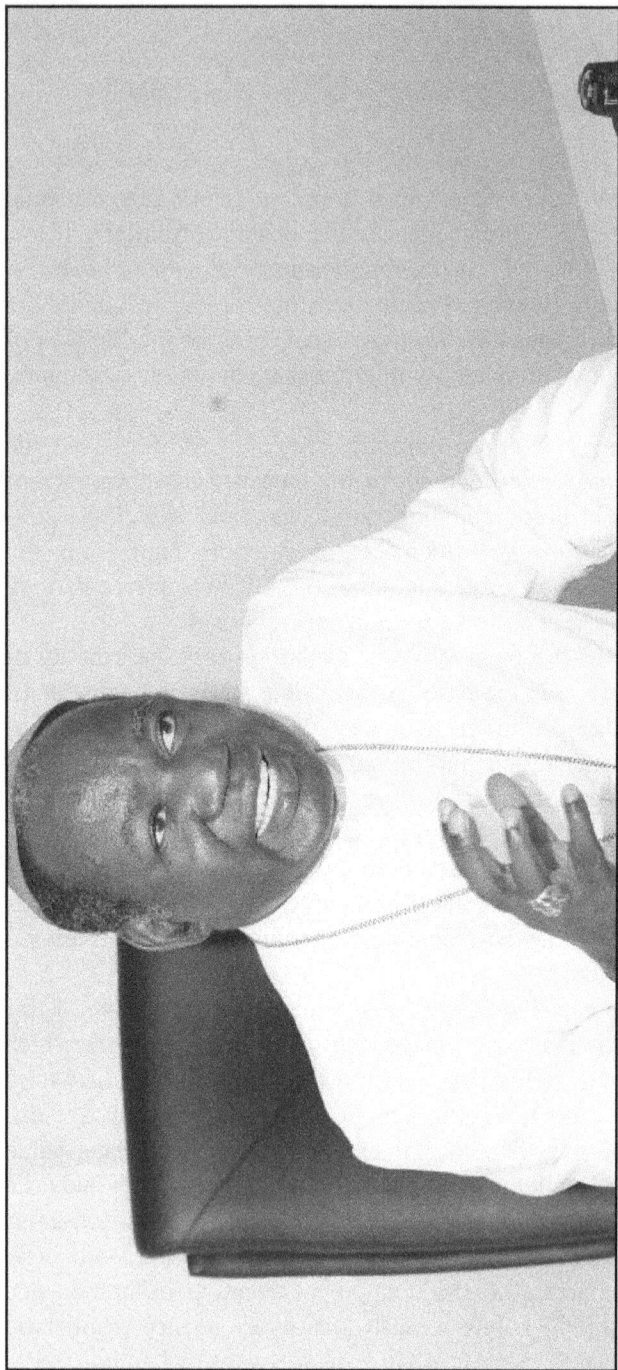

His Eminence Polycarp Cardinal Pengo (pictured) argued that the Catholic Church in Tanzania presented Julius Nyerere's cause 'based on his life as a Christian and how his faith had influenced his entire political career'. But people who disagree with the cardinal say horrendous human rights abuses which occurred under Nyerere's regime of personal rule had nothing to do with Christian values.

In the end, the decision to canonise the first post-independence ruler of Tanzania will be made by His Holiness Pope Francis (pictured above). One hopes he will carefully consider the evidence presented in this account prior to declaring Julius Kambarage Nyerere a saint.

Senghor of Senegal has a street in Tanzania named after them. Instead, it is dictators such as Sheikh Abeid Amani Karume, Samora Moisés Machel and Ahmed Sékou Touré, amongst other dictators, whose names are given to streets and landmarks in Tanzania.

Nations, including those which are already considered developed, attained what they have because they are built on the basis of certain permanent values; values which reflect the intellectual and social aspirations of the nation's people. It is therefore absurd to suppose that the Tanzanian populace would, out of their own will, embrace despotism as a core value that would form the basis on which to construct their developing nation.

Dictatorship, regardless of its classification, is not a value which humanity can freely embrace. It is an abhorrent political system which is often imposed on the people by the dictator himself and is maintained through fear and deprivation.

Indeed, in an unstable world, sanctifying dictatorship of any form would inevitably set a wrong precedent for posterity, much as it would undermine secular values and, by implication, community cohesion in non-theocratic societies. It is this salient value that we all share which should concern the international community more than the canonisation of a Third World potentate totally undeserving of such an honour.

•Author

******

www.ingramcontent.com/pod-product-compliance
Lightning Source LLC
Chambersburg PA
CBHW021535260326
41914CB00001B/21